The Art of Military Coercion

The Art of Military Coercion

Why the West's Military Superiority Scarcely Matters

Updated and Completely Revised Second Edition

Rob de Wijk

Amsterdam University Press

Cover design: Coördesign, Leiden
Typesetting: Crius Group, Hulshout

Amsterdam University Press English-language titles are distributed in the US and Canada by the University of Chicago Press.

ISBN 978 90 8964 674 3
e-ISBN 978 90 4851 941 5 (pdf)
e-ISBN 978 90 4851 942 2 (ePub)
NUR 754

Printed and bound by CPI Group (UK) Ltd, Croydon, CR0 4YY

Contents

Part 2 Strategic Culture: How the West Coerces

like the WEU, NATO was to militarily restrain Germany. Finally, the new alliance would ensure a continuing commitment to European security. Lord Ismay, NATO's first Secretary General, summarized its goal as follows: "to keep the Russians out, the Germans down and the Americans in."

The signatories of the North Atlantic Treaty of April 4, 1949, pledged the determination to "safeguard the freedom, common heritage and civilization of their peoples, founded on the principles of democracy, individual liberty, and the rule of law." Since its foundation, the member states have always considered the Alliance as a "community of values." Some former Communist countries wished to join NATO because of its collective defense guarantee, but they also stated publicly their desire to join the Western "club." President Vaclav Havel, the first head of state of a former Communist country ever to visit the NATO headquarters, described NATO as a "thoroughly democratic defensive community" and as "a tool of protection of its freedom and of the values of Western civilization."[30] The former minister for foreign affairs of Hungary, Geza Jeszenszky, wrote in 1992 that "today, in Eastern Europe all swear by freedom of conscience, civil liberties, a free economy, the observance of human rights, and self-determination."[31] Consequently, the former Communist countries need "a mental framework, which has long characterized most societies in the West."

Only countries that considered themselves as belonging to "Western civilization" wholeheartedly applied for NATO membership: Hungary, Poland, the Czech Republic, Slovenia, and the Baltic States. There was considerable controversy over NATO membership in those countries that only partly belonged to "Western civilization," such as Ukraine, Bulgaria, and Romania. For European countries belonging to other civilizations, such as those in the Caspian Sea region, NATO membership was not even an option, although they had every reason to join a collective defense organization.

The *Council of Europe* is the embodiment of many characteristics of Western political culture. The statute was signed in May 1949. Its preamble was dedicated to "a closer unity between all like-minded countries of Europe." Membership is open to all countries accepting the principles of the rule of law, fundamental freedoms, and human rights. A separate protocol obliges the signatories to hold free elections at reasonable intervals and by secret ballot. In 1950, the member states of the Council of Europe finalized the

30 President Havel's address to the NATO Council, 23 March 1991. Reprinted in *NATO Review*, April 1991, pp. 31-35.

31 G. Jeszenszky, "Nothing Quiet on the Eastern Front", in *NATO Review*, June 1992, pp. 7-9.

European Convention for the Protection of Human Rights and Fundamental Freedoms and subsequently created a Court of Human Rights. This court not only contributed to the strengthening of human rights, it also contributed to the development of general principles of international law.

A clash between divergent views occurred during the Helsinki Process. This process began as a series of meetings in Helsinki in 1975 under the title of the *Conference on Security and Cooperation in Europe* (CSCE) and in 1994 transformed into an organization (the Organization for Security and Cooperation in Europe, or OSCE). The Final Act was signed in August 1975. Follow-up meetings took place, as well as conferences devoted to specific topics. The genesis of the idea behind the Helsinki Process can be traced back to the 1950s, a time when Soviet foreign minister Molotov was alarmed by the prospect of Germany joining NATO. Consequently, at a foreign ministers' meeting of the four great powers in Berlin in early 1954, he presented the idea of a conference on European security.

In the decades to come the idea surfaced time and again. The Soviet Union had keen interests in such a conference because it could thereby gain influence in Western Europe through a security structure outside NATO and its Warsaw Pact. Moreover, the Soviet Union also wanted to legitimize the status quo in Europe so that interventions in its sphere of influence would become more difficult. Finally, Moscow sought ways to constrain the process over ever-increasing contacts between its satellite countries and West European countries. The United States was interested in the process because it could support mutual force reductions in Europe and US-Soviet strategic arms reductions. In general, the Americans saw the process as an instrument for "Russia management."

Most West European politicians had a more idealistic objective, namely to eliminate the division of Europe. This sentiment was especially strong in the Federal Republic of Germany, which recognized the importance of free movement of people, ideas, and information. The negotiations of the Final Act lasted two years. The scope ranged from principles on sovereignty and the peaceful settlement of disputes, to the promotion of tourism. The first "basket" of the Final Act listed ten generally accepted principles of state behavior drawn from the United Nations Charter. Apart from items intended to reassure the Soviets – such as non-intervention in internal affairs – it included principles such as sovereign equality, refraining from the threat or use of force, and fulfillment in good faith of obligation under international law. Principle VII – respect for human rights and fundamental freedoms, including the freedom of thought, conscience, religion, or belief – caused the most problems. James Ring Adams observed that the "theory of human rights embedded in the Final Act is primarily that of the Western liberal tradition."[32] Indeed, the issue of human rights caused much acrimony throughout the Helsinki Process. Suppression of national minorities, dissidents, Jews, and religious activists was common practice in the Soviet Union. A major obstacle was a difference in perception of the concept of human rights between the Soviets and the Americans. The Soviet delegation viewed the concept in economic, social, and cultural terms and maintained that employment, housing, and social justice should also be included. The Americans tend to think of human rights in political and civil terms. This caused bitter East-West arguments during the negotiations. The American delegation accused the Soviets of abusing the concept, because they repressed civil and political rights. Moreover, in parallel with the debate on human rights, the Western countries reviewed East European human rights. They concluded that abuses of freedom of expression, religious liberties, and discrimination against national minorities was in conflict with the Western concept of human rights.[33] The OSCE has developed a comprehensive *corpus* of norms and standards as part of the Helsinki process. These include conduct between nations, the development of democracy, the social market economy, human rights, minority rights, and political-military rules of conduct. Observation of these is closely linked with stability and the prevention of conflicts.

Western institutions are also committed to free trade or market economy, which is another characteristic of Western civilization. The devastation wrought by the Second World War resulted in initiatives aimed at economic and social recovery and peaceful relations among the European nations. Political leaders agreed that this could be best done through closer union. In 1946, Winston Churchill appealed for "a kind of United States of Europe."[34] On May 7-10, 1948, he chaired the privately organized Congress of Europe on European unity in The Hague.

The Schuman Plan of May 1950 proposed economic, military, and political institutions. The first step was the creation of the *European Coal and Steel Community* (ECSC) by Belgium, Luxembourg, the Netherlands, the United Kingdom, and France. The integrative process was strengthened by the *Eu-*

32 J.R. Adams, "From Helsinki to Madrid", in M.F. Plattner (ed.) *Human Rights in Our Time, Essays in Memory of Victor Baras* (Boulder and London: Westview, 1984), p. 118.

33 J. Fry, *The Helsinki Process: Negotiating, Security and Cooperation in Europe* (Washington: USGPO, 1993), p. 99.

34 Winston Churchill, speaking in Zurich, Switzerland, on 19 September 1946,

ropean Atomic Energy Commission (EURATOM) and the *European Economic Community* (EEC). The principle of free trade was most visible in the EEC, which established a custom union. Also, the World Bank, the International Monetary Fund, and the World Trade Organization operate on the premises that Western models of market economy and democracy are mutually reinforcing. These organizations have designated democratic reform as a condition for loans and development assistance. Today's *European Union* (EU) is firmly based on typical Western values such as "democracy and the rule of law (...), respect for human rights and fundamental freedoms." According to the Amsterdam Treaty of 1997, one of the objectives of the EU's common foreign and security policy is: "to safeguard the common values."[35]

The debate about Europe's Christian heritage intensified during the EU's enlargement debate. Both the German Chancellor Helmuth Kohl and former French president and chairman of the EU's Convention, Valery Giscard d'Estaing, argued that Turkey, as a Muslim state, did not fit in "Europe." Giscard d'Estaing was more explicit. He argued that Turkey with its Muslim population and high birthrate had "a different culture, a different approach, and a different way of life." Consequently, Turkey should not be allowed to join the EU. His view was supported by other Europeans, mostly Christian Democrats, who felt that the influx of non-Westerners, especially Muslims, could form a threat to Europe's Christian identity.

In 2003, during the drafting of the convention texts, a furious debate took place over whether God and Europe's roots should be mentioned explicitly in the EU's draft Constitution. The result was codified in the final version, which was signed in Rome by the Heads of State and Government on October 29, 2004. The Constitution states that "The Union is founded on the values of respect for human dignity, liberty, democracy, equality, the rule of law, and respect for human rights" (Part I, Article 2).

Although the Constitution was rejected by referenda in France and the Netherlands in 2005, the preamble of its successor, the Lisbon Treaty, which entered into force on December 1, 2009, mentioned "the cultural, religious and humanist inheritance of Europe, from which have developed the universal values of the inviolable and inalienable rights of the human person, freedom, democracy, equality and the rule of law."[36]

35 Treaty of Amsterdam, Title V, article J11.

36 European Union, *Consolidated Treaties* (Brussels: march 2010), p. 15.

Transatlantic differences in political culture

As a direct consequence of the far-reaching geo-strategic developments of the 1990s and reinforced by the neo-conservatism of the George W. Bush Administration, the differences between the European and American variants of Western civilization became clearly visible.

While Europeans emphasize *liberties,* Americans emphasize *freedom.* The latter stresses individual freedom more strongly. In the 2002 National Security Strategy, President Bush explained that "Freedom is *the* non-negotiable demand of human dignity."

In contrast to Europe, *religion* plays a fundamental role in American politics. Protestantism in America involves a belief in the fundamental opposition of good and evil, right and wrong. In the eyes of many Europeans, American politicians use these simple notions to solve complicated foreign policy questions.

Crucially, as has been argued before, Americans have a sense of mission to promote values; Europeans do not. American political values are embodied in "the American Creed" defined by Gunnar Myrdal as "the essential dignity of the individual human being, of the fundamental equality of men, and of certain inalienable rights to freedom, justice, and fair opportunity."[37] The Creed is viewed as the crucial defining element of American identity and the product of the distinct Anglo-Protestant culture of the founding settlers. Key elements of that culture include freedom, democracy, civil rights, Christianity and religious commitment, dissenting Protestant values of individualism, the work ethic, laissez-faire, and equality of opportunity. Throughout history, Americans have tried to realize the values embodied in the Creed. In the 17th and 18th centuries, Americans defended this mission in biblical terms. They were the chosen people and the New World was the promised land. Many Americans still believe their values are universal and should be spread across the world. Samuel Huntington wrote that the creedal definition allows Americans to believe that theirs "is an 'exceptional' country because, unlike other nations, its identity is defined by principle rather than ascription, and at the same time, to claim that America is a 'universal' nation because its principles are applicable to all human societies."[38] The 2002 National Security Strategy is a clear expression of this. It promised a "single sustainable model for national success: freedom,

37 G. Myrdal, *An American Dilemma* (New York: Harper, 1944). S.P. Huntington, *Who Are We: The Challenges to America's National Identity* (New York: Simon and Schuster, 2004), pp. 47-48.
38 S.P. Huntington, *Who Are We,* pp. 47-48.

democracy, and free enterprise." The promotion of this model became an important inspiration for America's foreign policy during the first decade of the 21st century. In November 2003, President Bush stressed that other peoples looked to the United States as a beacon of light, "a bright and hopeful land where freedom was valued and secure."[39]

Nothing like the Creed created Europe. Over half a century, the Europeans created a postmodern system that comes very close to Kant's pacific union (see chapter 2). The British diplomat and strategist Robert Cooper observed that this system, embodied in the EU, has some fundamental characteristics:

- Mutual interference in each other's domestic affairs. As a result, the distinction between domestic and foreign affairs became blurred, borders became irrelevant, and the concept of sovereignty weakened.
- The obsolescence of force as an instrument for resolving disputes. Self-imposed rules of behavior were codified and monitored.
- Security had become based on transparency, mutual openness, interdependency, and mutual vulnerability.[40]

The postmodern system was created after initiatives taken by the United States. After the Second World War, the European Recovery Program – also called the Marshall Plan, after the US Secretary of State George C. Marshall whose address at Harvard University on June 5, 1947, contained the original idea – forced the European states to work together economically. Bilateral aid to European states was not very effective, and existing international institutions such as the International Bank for Reconstruction and Development were not well-suited for the task. Consequently, Marshall proposed a multinational regional initiative. The European states should consult together to assess their needs and provide the US government with detailed requests. For the purpose of consultation, the Organization for European Economic Cooperation was formed in 1948. This started the process of ever-increasing economic and political cooperation and unification.

The ongoing process of European unification and the establishment of a postmodern system is nothing less than a revolution, which could have a significant effect on shaping the future world order. The European Commission's President, Romano Prodi, argued that: "Europe needs to project its model of society into the wider world. We are not simply here to defend our interests: we have a unique historic experience to offer. The experience

39 G.W. Bush, Address at the National Endowment of Democracy, November 6, 2003.

40 R. Cooper, "The new liberal imperialism", *The Observer,* April 7, 2002.

of liberating people from poverty, war, oppression, and intolerance. We have forged a model of development and continental integration based on the principles of democracy, freedom, and solidarity, and it is a model that works. A model of a consensual pooling of sovereignty in which every one of us accepts belonging to a minority."[41]

The development of this system clearly distinguishes Europe from other regions and states, including the United States. It is neither a state nor a federation. It is a distinct entity with some of the characteristics of both a state and a federation. Some of its policies are supranational. Within the World Trade Organization, the EU negotiates on behalf of all member states, and agricultural policies are decided upon in Brussels. Security and defense policies, however, are developed strictly on a national basis, but can be harmonized in common positions and joint actions.

The obsolescence of the use of force within this system explains the reluctance of most EU member states to use force outside the system (Chapter 4); growing interdependency explains the preference of the multinational approach. Nevertheless, due to the ongoing European integration process and the need to protect common values and interests, the subject of the actual use of force is attracting more attention.

The emphasis on multilateralism and loss of sovereignty go hand in hand. As a result of European integration, Europeans have been steadily surrendering powers to Brussels. This has led to the development of common European foreign, security, and defense policies. In contrast, Americans do not see any source of democratic legitimacy higher than the constitutional nation-state.

The United States does not fit into this postmodern system. Due to its superpower position, its leaders are neither willing nor capable of accepting the fundamental characteristics of the postmodern world. The United States has developed into a new kind of empire, one that will not defend its interests by enlarging its sphere of influence through conquest, but by imposing its rules and values on other states. For that reason, the United States is reluctant to accept international organizations, such as the International Criminal Court, which is a typical example of a postmodern construct.

In summary, Europeans favor cooperative security, based on multilateralism and the rejection of great power conflict as the dominant security problem. Cooperative security requires giving international organizations domestic and international legitimacy. Americans are instrumental multilateralists because they use international organizations to win international

41 R. Prodi, *2000-2005: Shaping the New Europe*, European Parliament (Strasbourg), February 15, 2000.

support, but if support is not gained, Americans end up going it alone to support their grand strategy of primacy.

The latter strategy rejects the subordination of American interests to international bodies or international law. Primacy advocates are unilateralists, promoting the creation of large armed forces to be sized and shaped to defend the nation's interests.

The emergence of the postmodern system supports the ideas of scholars belonging to the Functionalist school, which is closely related to Liberalism. They assert that institutions are an important cause of international peace and stability. They argue that there is a strong connection between institutions and economic cooperation. Functionalism, or liberal institutionalism, focuses on explaining cooperation in cases where state interests do not conflict and where states have incentives both to cooperate and not to cooperate because they have mixed interests. Functionalism claims to accept some of the assumptions of the Realist school of thought, while arguing that cooperation is easier than most Realists recognize. Cooperation under anarchy is possible, because states act as rational egoists; they have much to gain from cooperation. Economic cooperation is essential in a world of economic interdependence. Cooperation in one field could spill over into others. This happened to the member states of the EU, where economic cooperation has led to ever-increasing political cooperation in the field of law and external and internal security.

Shared interests create a demand for new international arrangements as well.[42] These arrangements or "international regimes" contain norms, rules, principles, and decision-making procedures. Realists argue that the early postwar regimes rested under the political hegemony of the United States. After the mid-1960s, US dominance was challenged by the increasing rapid economic growth of Europe and Japan. Yet economic interdependence and cooperation continued to grow. Here, the viewpoint of Functionalists and Realists diverges. Functionalists believe that interdependence increases the need for policy coordination and more cooperation, while from a Realist perspective, the diffusion of power undermines the ability of anyone to create order. In *After Hegemony*, Robert O. Keohane explained that cooperation can, under certain conditions, develop the basis of complementary interests, and that institutions, broadly defined, affect patterns of cooperation that emerge.[43]

42 D. Mitrany, *The Functional Theory of Politics* (London: St. Martin's Press for the London School of Economics and Political Science, 1975).

43 R.O. Keohane, *After Hegemony: Cooperation and Discord in the World Political Economy* (Princeton: Princeton University Press, 1984).

Conclusion

Interventions can only be understood in the context of Western political culture, which, in turn, is based on Latin Christianity. Liberal democracies use force to defend interests and to promote non-materialistic issues, such as ideology and values. The former can be explained by the Realist school of thought; the latter by the Liberal or Idealist school of thought.

Nevertheless, Western governments frequently put forward normative "universal" principles such as humanity and democracy as reasons for intervention. The idea that values should be defended, together with worldwide materialistic interests, helps in explaining the activist nature of liberal democracies' foreign policy.

Non-Western states have always been confused by the seeming inconsistency of Western policies. The friction between self-interest and ideology, including democracy and human rights, has led to contradictory policies and double standards. Democracy is promoted, but not if it gives power to non-Christian religious fundamentalists; Western governments declared genocide in Bosnia sufficient grounds for intervention, but largely ignored genocide in Rwanda, Burundi, and Sudan; non-proliferation is considered important for Iran, Iraq, Pakistan, and India, but not for Israel; Saddam Hussein's annexation of Kuwait was not tolerated, but the Turkish partition of Cyprus, the Indian takeover of Goa and the Indonesian seizure of East Timor were; China's human rights policies were criticized, but human rights abuses by allies in the Gulf region, such as Egypt and Saudi Arabia, were tolerated. These examples demonstrate that Western governments are usually more forgiving to friendly states with a similar cultural background, or undemocratically governed countries that are important to Western interests.

The universal pretense of Western thinking constitutes a threat in the eyes of many non-Western countries, if this goes together with the setting aside of cornerstones of international law. On some occasions, the friction between self-interests and ideology has led to divergent views within the Western world itself. In 1997, Denmark presented a draft resolution that was submitted to the Human Rights Commission of the United Nations. The text criticized Chinese violations of human rights. At the Noordwijk meeting of the EU Council meeting in 1997, France, Germany, Spain, and Italy did not support the resolution but favored a "critical dialogue" on this issue with Beijing. The reason for this approach seemed to be economic self-interest, which prevailed over moral values and political principles.

On the whole, contradictory policies are a fundamental characteristic of Western political culture. Regarding the United States, Henry Kissinger observed in *Diplomacy*: "In the 20th century no country has influenced international relations as decisively and at the same time as ambivalently as the United States. No society has more firmly insisted on the inadmissibility of intervention in the domestic affairs of other states, or more passionately asserted that its own values were universally applicable. No nation has been more pragmatic in the day-to-day conduct of its diplomacy or more ideological in the pursuit of its historical convictions. No country has been more reluctant to engage itself abroad even while undertaking alliances and commitments of unprecedented reach and scope."[44]

There is confusion as well. The Commission on America's National Interests observed that, in the wake of the Cold War, the American public's interest in foreign policy has declined sharply and that political leaders have been forced to attend to immediate domestic politics. Confusion has become the defining feature of American engagement. According to the Commission, the explanation for this is that expansionist Communism as a fixed point disappeared.[45]

Especially military interventions have led to fundamental debates, both inside and outside the Western world. The international legal order is largely a Western construct, but if interests are at stake, liberal democracies ignore or demonstrate unwillingness to obey the rules they created themselves, and the values they stand for. In 1994, US President Clinton refused to call the mass murders in Rwanda and Burundi genocide, because this would require military action. The disastrous experience of Somalia a few years earlier made the Clinton Administration reluctant to carry out another humanitarian intervention.

44 H. Kissinger, *Diplomacy* (New York: Simon and Schuster, 1994), pp. 16-17.

45 Commission on National Interests, *America's National Interests*, p. 1.

2 Liberal Democracies and Interventions

Consider the following hypothetical example. After decades of civil war, it has become clear that the United Kingdom cannot cope with the situation in Northern Ireland. The international community wonders how many more innocent Catholic and Protestant civilians must die. After many failed attempts to put pressure on the British government to find a solution, China takes the initiative for a humanitarian intervention. The Chinese leadership tries to seek support within the Security Council, but efforts to obtain a mandate are vetoed. However, all members, except for the US and of course the United Kingdom, agree that the atrocities must stop. Subsequently, China, supported by some allies, carries out a humanitarian intervention. Despite heavy protests, other countries have no other choice but to accept China's actions, because it is now the world's leading power.

This example seems far-fetched, because liberal democracies simply cannot imagine a situation where other, non-Western, states intervene in their domestic affairs. At the same time, however, liberal democracies show little restraints in interfering in the domestic affairs of others. This, of course, leads to accusations of the use of double standards by the West.

The attitude of liberal democracies not only points to measuring with different standards, it also demonstrates ignorance of how others see the West. On the one hand, the citizens of liberal democracies consider themselves as peace-loving people, seeking to promote stability and values and to defend their interests peacefully. On the other hand, although they do not fight each other, for ideological reasons and self-interest, Western liberal democracies have intervened frequently. This chapter provides a closer look at how liberal democracies use intervention to achieve their foreign policy objectives.

Democracy and the justification of interventions

For Western leaders, normative reasons have always been important to explain or justify interventions. In recent history, all American presidents have used democracy to justify interventions. US President Richard Nixon argued that "at times it will be necessary to use American power and influence to defend and extend freedom in places thousands of miles away if we are to preserve it at home."[1]

1 R.M. Nixon, *Beyond Peace* (New York: Random House, 1994), p. 38.

President Ronald Reagan justified the 1983 intervention in Lebanon by arguing that "if America were to walk away from Lebanon, what chance would there be for a negotiated settlement producing a unified, democratic Lebanon?" Similarly, Reagan argued that the invasion of Grenada was "a military operation to restore order and democracy." In 1989, the United States unilaterally intervened in Panama to remove President Manuel Noriega from power. President George H.W. Bush Sr. defended this invasion by arguing that "the goals of the United States have been to defend democracy in Panama."

In his September 1993 *Bottom-up Review* of the armed forces and his 1994 *National Security Strategy of Engagement and Enlargement,* President Bill Clinton observed that "when a people attempts to hold free elections and establish a constitutional democracy, the United States and the international community should not only assist but should also 'guarantee' the result."[2] For that reason, Clinton defended the US involvement in the crisis in 1994 in Haiti as an attempt to restore democracy. The Security Council authorized the US to carry out Operation Uphold Democracy in an effort to restore the government of Jean-Bertrand Aristide.

President George W. Bush argued that the principal reasons for Operation Iraqi Freedom were to destroy Saddam Hussein's weapons of mass destruction, to prevent him from supporting international terrorism, and to bring freedom and democracy to the Iraqi people. On March 17, 2003, he argued that in a free and democratic Iraq "there will be no more wars of aggression against your neighbors, no more poison factories, no more executions of dissidents, no more torture chambers and rape rooms."[3]

In 2011 President Obama justified the use of military force in Libya where US "safety is not directly threatened, but [where] our interests and values are."[4] The President argued that the United States had no choice: "Qaddafi declared he would show 'no mercy' to his own people. He compared them to rats, and threatened to go door-to-door to inflict punishment. In the past, we have seen him hang civilians in the streets, and kill over a thousand people in a single day. Now we saw regime forces on the outskirts of the city. We knew that if we waited – if we waited one more day, Benghazi, a city nearly the size of Charlotte, could suffer a massacre that would have reverberated across the region and stained the conscience of the world (...). It was not in our national interest to let that happen." Consequently, the

2 M.H. Halperin, "Guaranteeing Democracy", in *Foreign Policy*, Summer 1993, p. 105.

3 D.E. Sanger, "Bush's doctrine for war", *The New York Times*, March 18, 2003.

4 President Obama, Address to the Nation on Libya, March 28, 2011.

President assigned the forces "to protect the Libyan people from immediate danger, and to establish a no-fly zone."

There are several reasons why leaders of liberal democracies use the concept of democracy to justify interventions. First, democracy is the key characteristic of Western society and considered to be universally applicable. Consequently, an intervention to promote values such as democracy and freedom can be sold more easily to the public than an intervention to promote interests. Second, there is supposed to be a close link between democracy and peace. George Marshall once argued that governments which systematically disregard the right of their own people are not likely to respect the rights of other nations and people, and are likely to seek their foreign policy objectives by force and coercion.[5] The connection between democracy and peace seems to be universally accepted. In 1990, the Conference on Security and Co-operation in Europe declared that "the development of societies based on pluralistic democracy and the rule of law are prerequisites for progress in setting up the lasting order of peace, security, justice, and cooperation."[6] Furthermore, in 1996, the United Nation's Secretary General Boutros Boutros-Ghali argued in his *Agenda for Democratization* that democracy was one of the pillars on which a more peaceful, more equitable, and more secure world could be built.[7] The United Nations Security Council also adopted a resolution that strongly supported Western democratic principles, by declaring that periodic and genuine elections are the crucial factor in the effective enjoyment of a wide range of other human rights.[8]

In 2005, the UN established a Democracy Fund with the intention of "strengthening countries' capacity to implement the principles and practices of democracy." The World Summit reaffirmed "that democracy is a universal value based on the freely expressed will of people to determine their own political, economic, social and cultural systems and their full participation in all aspects of their lives" (...) and "that while democracies share common features, there is no single model of democracy, that it does not belong to any country or region, and reaffirm the necessity of due respect for sovereignty and the right of self-determination."[9]

5 *Department of State Bulletin*, October 3, 1948, p. 432.
6 Copenhagen meeting of the Conference of the Human Dimension, June 29, 1990.
7 B. Boutros-Ghali, *An Agenda for Democracy* (New York: United Nations Publications, 1996).
8 UN Assembly Resolution 46/137 of December 17, 1991.
9 United Nations, *World Summit Outcome Document*, October 24, 2005, para. 135.

Throughout modern history, liberal democracies have abstained from war against each other. According to some scholars, "the absence of war between democracies comes as close as anything we have to an empirical law in international relations."[10] Others have argued that this democratic peace thesis is "gaining the status of a 'paradigm,' as a growing number of observers regard it as the most compelling way of looking at international security."[11] In testing the democratic peace proposition statistically, it was found that liberal regimes were peace loving.[12]

According to the liberal school of thought, the combination of democracy and market capitalism provides a successful method of gaining economic prosperity and security. Democratic values promote respect for the rule of law and provide the basis for a moral and political consensus amongst states that adhere to them. An additional explanation is that liberal democracies believe they have developed useful instruments for conflict resolution.

The idea that democratic states do not fight wars against each other is not particularly new.[13] Immanuel Kant's (1724-1804) essay *Zum ewigen Frieden* (*Perpetual Peace*), written in 1795, is considered to be the most important contribution.[14] He received direct inspiration from the events of the French revolutionary wars. Kant described how perpetual peace could be brought about. Three elements are necessary: the establishment of constitutional law, international law, and cosmopolitan law. Law guarantees the internal working of the state in a democratic manner. He understood democracy to include representative government, the legal equality of citizens before the law, and the absence of arbitrary authority. International law regulates the interaction among states. Liberal democratic states will establish a zone of peace between them. Kant wrote that the spread of democracy would

10 Jack Levy, "Domestic Politics and War", in: Robert I. Rotberg and Theodore K. Rabb (eds.), *The Origin and Prevention of Major War* (Cambridge: Cambridge University Press, 1988), p. 88.

11 Charles Kegley and Margaret Hermann, "A Peace Dividend? Democracies; Military Interventions and Their External Political Consequences", *Cooperation and Conflict,* vol. 32, no. 4 (1997), pp. 339-368.

12 Dean Babst, "Elective Government: A Force for Peace", *The Wisconsin Sociologist,* vol. 3, no. I (1964), pp. 9-14.

13 Doyle, "Liberalism and World Politics", p. 1156. Even with differing definitions, it is found time and again that democracies do not wage war against each other. See for example: Bruce Russett, *Grasping the Democratic Peace, Principles for a Post-Cold War World* (Princeton, NJ: Princeton University Press, 1993), p. 10. Rudolph J. Rummel, *Power Kills: Democracy as a Method of Nonviolence* (New Brunswick, NJ: Transaction, 1997), p. 44.

14 James Bohman and Matthias Lutz-Bachmann, *Perpetual Peace; Essays on Kant's Cosmopolitan Ideal* (Cambridge, MA: MIT Press, 1997).

lead to an ever-expanding "pacific union." The modern European Union reflects these Kantian ideas.

International law and a pacific union will come about through an understanding between states themselves, instead of through the building of institutions. Cosmopolitan law will operate together with international law. Cosmopolitan law, of which Kant emphasized the right to hospitality, is extended to all states. Hospitality will pave the way for increasing contacts and trade. It is worth remembering that in those days only three democracies existed, as Kant understood them: the United States of America, France, and Switzerland.

Claude-Henry Comte de Saint-Simon (1760-1825), Auguste Comte (1798-1857), Herbert Spencer (1820-1903), and Emile Durkheim (1858-1917) have also contributed to the theory of democratic peace. For example, Spencer maintained that industrial society is inherently pacific, depending on peaceful cooperation rather than antagonism between entities. With the expansion of industrial activities "in place of a uniform belief imperatively enforced, there come multiform beliefs voluntarily accepted (...) military conformity coercively maintained gives place to a varied nonconformity maintained by a willing union."[15]

Since the end of the Cold War, the idea of an ever-expanding zone of democratic peace has enjoyed renewed interest. Modern thinkers, such as Michael Doyle, have argued that the basic claim of liberal international theory holds that states have the right to be free from foreign intervention: "Since morally autonomous citizens hold rights to liberty, the states that democratically represent them have the right to exercise political independence."[16] Mutual respect for these rights then becomes the touchstone of international liberal theory. Zeev Maoz and Bruce Russett have also argued that the use of democratic norms explains the peaceful relationship between democratic states.[17]

If democracy brings peace and stability, the replacement of autocratic governments by democratic ones should be an important foreign policy goal. Encouraging pluralism, free and fair elections, the development of market economies, and socializing military and security forces to respect

15 T.H. Spencer, *The Evolution of Society,* in R.L. Corneiro (ed.) (Chicago: The University of Chicago Press, 1967), p. 61.

16 M.W. Doyle, "Kant, Liberal Legacies, and Foreign Affairs", *Philosophy and Public Affairs,* 12/3 (1983).

17 Z. Maoz and B. Russett, "Normative and Structural Causes of Democratic Peace 1946-1986", *American Political Science Review,* vol. 87, No. 3, September, pp. 624-638.

democratic norms are considered to be crucial for bringing peace and democracy. Others argue that foreign aid should be used to punish or reward states for their human rights record and to promote democracy.

Extending the "zone of peace" became an important foreign policy objective for the Clinton Administration.[18] In his 1994 *National Security Strategy* the President wrote that the active promotion of democratization as one of the pillars of post-Cold War US foreign policy would strengthen the "community of democratic states." For that reason, the Clinton administration took the initiative to enlarge NATO in 1998.

Under the administration of George W. Bush, intervention became a prominent tool for the promotion of democracy. This was based on the belief that democratic states are inherently peaceful and stable. In the Western conception of democracy, the people have political rights, such as the right of free and fair election of executives and legislatures, and the right to establish political parties. Another prerequisite for democracy is that the people also enjoy civil liberties such as the freedom of speech, the freedom of assembly, freedom from media censorship, freedom of religion, and the freedom to establish trade unions. Some even argued that the potential for failure in the process of democratization must be seen as a grave danger to international stability.[19]

In his 2004 *State of the Union Address,* President Bush argued that "America is a nation with a mission, and that mission comes from our most basic beliefs. We have no desire to dominate, no ambitions of empire. Our aim is a democratic peace – a peace founded upon the dignity and the rights of every man and woman."[20]

In reaction to President Bush's interventionism and unilateralism, his successor, Barrack Obama, embarked on a different course. The new president focused more on negotiation and collaboration. Obama terminated Bush's wars in Afghanistan and Iraq, and was reluctant to involve the United States in new wars, including the intervention in Libya in 2011. In 2008, the term "Obama Doctrine" was used to describe Obama's foreign policy.[21] Then-Senator Obama mentioned five pillars of his foreign policy, should he

18 Max Singer and Aaron Wildavsky, *The Real World Order, Zones of Peace/Zones of Turmoil* (Chatham, NJ: Chatham House Publishers, 1993).

19 G.S. Sullivan, *America's Army into the Twenty-First Century,* National Security Paper 14, Institute for Foreign Policy Analysis (Washington 1995), p. 5.

20 G.W. Bush, *State of the Union Address* (Washington, D.C., 20 January 2004).

21 Lynn Sweet (July 16, 2008), "The war over the war", *Chicago Sun-Times.* See: http://www.suntimes.com/news/sweet/1058012,CST-NWS-sweet16.article.

be elected: "ending the war in Iraq; finishing the fight against al-Qaeda and the Taliban; securing all nuclear weapons and materials from terrorists and rogue states; achieving true energy security; and rebuilding our alliances to meet the challenges of the 21st century." There is, however, a clear correlation between Obama's soft approach, weakened American power caused by the financial crises that started in 2008, and the rise of countries like China that are causing a fundamental geopolitical shift.

Contemporary ideas of an ever-expanding zone of peace and stability of liberal democracies are closely linked to the fear that global instability is a threat to interests and humanity. Global stability is considered a prerequisite for the economic development of industrialized states. The idea is that regional conflicts weaken global stability and place the security of all states at risk. For most industrialized liberal democracies, global stability is believed to be a national security concern. A healthy economy is dependent on a well-functioning international market. Former Secretary of Defense Dick Cheney once argued: "the worldwide market that we're part of cannot thrive where regional violence, instability, and aggression put it at peril. Our economic well-being and security depend on a stable world."[22] Indeed, global stability has become a powerful justification for intervention as well.

If there is a clear link between democracy, peace, and stability, then global stability will increase if the number of democratic states is greatly expanded. This is supported by the findings of the watchdog Freedom House. Freedom House ranked 88 countries as "free" in 2013. But for the eight subsequent year, the democracy index has shown more declines than gains worldwide. In 2013, 54 countries showed significant declines, compared with 40 that showed notable gains.[23]

The conclusion that liberal democracies constitute a zone of peace cannot solely be explained by the emergence of a pacific union. On the one hand, war *among* highly developed, industrialized states is unlikely because the costs outweigh the benefits. Since liberal democracies fall into this category, they are vulnerable to instability and destruction. War threatens the very social and political fabric of the state, with trade virtually coming to a halt. The result is economic collapse and political and social chaos. More chaos is created by the destructive power of industrialized democracies' military machinery. War will lead to the destruction of much that has been achieved.

22 D. Cheney, "The Military We Need in the Future", *Vital Speeches of the Day* (Washington, October 15, 1992).

23 http://www.freedomhouse.org/report/freedom-world/freedom-world-2014.

As a consequence, liberal democracies have few incentives to declare war on each other.

On the other hand, democracies are relatively immune to being a target of interventions. One explanation was given by Charles W. Kegley and Margaret G. Hermann.[24] They argue that the adversaries' image of a country and its likely strategies for dealing with conflict may be critical determinants of whether force is used. This assumption is based on the idea that liberal democracies' leaders are restrained by the population. In addition, if a democracy is attacked, the whole population will be mobilized. The mass public in a democracy becomes the actor the aggressor will have to face. This explanation, however, is not supported by the fact that democracies are the most frequent interveners.

A better explanation is that war against liberal democracies makes little sense. The military power of liberal democracies reflects their economic power and technological advancement. Liberal democracies are simply militarily too powerful to wage wars against. Moreover, after the Second World War, most liberal democracies became members of mighty military alliances, while the nuclear capabilities of France, the United Kingdom, and the United States also contributed to the deterrence of aggression. After the Cold War, it was clear that no single country could pose a meaningful risk to this powerful alliance. Despite dramatic reductions in strength, NATO still had about four million armed men and women at its disposal. In addition, reservists numbered almost 5.7 million. In comparison, Russia had 1.5 million active troops, with 2.4 million more in reserve. On the eve of the 2003 Gulf War, Iraq's active forces numbered 382,000, with 650,000 reservists. These are impressive numbers, but the armed forces of both countries are no match for NATO.

In conclusion, the enormous military power based on innovative technological thinking and nuclear deterrence greatly contributed to the absence of aggression against liberal democracies. Consequently, there are few, if any, examples of deliberate military aggression with regular forces against liberal democracies. Since the Second World War, deliberate aggression has only taken place against colonies or overseas territories, such as the Falklands. For example, there are only three cases of direct aggression by Arabic states against liberal democracies. In 1978, Egypt carried out a raid on Larnaca Airport in Cyprus; in 1985 it carried out a raid on Luqa Airport in Malta. Both were attempts to rescue countrymen being held hostage on

24 Hermann and Kegley, "Ballots, a Barrier against the Use of Bullets and Bombs: Democratization and Military Intervention", *Journal of Conflict Resolution,* vol. 40, no. 3 (1996), pp. 436-460.

a plane. In 1986, Libya fired a missile at Lampedusa, an uninhabited Italian island. Until September 11, 2001, this was the only direct attack on NATO territory since the Alliance was created.

Democratization and war

We must not forget that the democratic peace thesis applies only to mature democracies. There is evidence that in the transitional phase of democratization, countries become more aggressive and war prone. Edward Mansfield and Jack Snyder observed that states that make the major leap from total autocracy to extensive mass democracy are about twice as likely to wage wars in the first decade after democratization as are states that remain autocracies.[25] The former Yugoslavia and the former Soviet republics of Armenia and Azerbaijan have found themselves at war while experimenting with varying degrees of electoral democracy.

There is a striking connection between democratization, nationalism, and war. Democratization creates new politically significant groups, usually with diverse and incompatible interests. During the process of democratization, for example, when the international community demands "free and fair" elections, these groups may compete for popular support. One way of mobilizing mass support is through ideology, especially nationalism and ethnicity. An effective strategy to gain the support of particular groups is to make clear that other groups are an economic or physical threat, which can only be neutralized if a vote is given to certain politicians. Therefore, rising nationalism and focus on ethnicity go hand in hand with rising democracy. A striking example is the Balkans. In Serbia, the political and military elite of the old regime, facing enormous pressure to instigate democratization, created a new basis for legitimacy through nationalist propaganda and military action. They won elections by exploiting the ethnic differences within the country.

Nationalist propaganda is an effective instrument for gaining mass support, but once mobilized, the mass is difficult to control: "Governing a society that is democratizing is like driving a car while throwing away the steering wheel, stepping on the gas, and fighting over which passenger will be in the driver's seat. The result, often, is war."[26] The problem is worsened by

25 E.D. Mansfield and J. Snyder, "Democratization and War", *Foreign Affairs,* May-June 1995 pp. 79-97.

26 Mansfield and Snyder, "Democratization and War", p. 89.

the weakening of the state's authority during the transition from autocracy to democracy.

New groups may also undermine the power base of the old political elites, which need to gain mass allies to defend their weakened positions. The old elites, threatened by social and political change often take inflexible views of their interests, and could be challenged to defend their positions with the use of force. The old elite could also shore up its prestige at home by embarking on risky foreign policy adventures. Consequently, if one state liberates another state and brings democracy, a stabilization force is needed for a lengthy transformation phase.

As elections are an attractive exit strategy for peacekeepers after a conflict has ended, the international community could contribute to the failure of the democratization process. Paul Collier explained that "although the risk of violence falls in the year before an election, it rises in the year after". His explanation is the power struggle in the run-up to balloting. After the vote the winner no longer feels the pressure to take the interests of the defeated into account, whilst the loser accuses the winner of fraud.[27]

Finally, it is unclear if the peoples of other civilizations are willing to accept the universality of Western democratic principles. For example, the Islamic resurgence is anti-Western.[28] For many centuries, fundamentalists felt humiliated by the West or by Christian civilization. They see themselves as the sole custodians of God's truth, commanded by him to bring it to the infidels. But at the same time they find themselves dominated by these infidels. In addition, they feel humiliated and frustrated by various remedies, most of them imported from the West. Humiliation and frustration were complemented by a new confidence and a sense of power, which arose from the oil boom of the 1970s. This new sense of confidence and power was reinforced by contempt. Fundamentalist Islam sees the Western world as morally degenerate and consequently weak. This comes as no surprise because fundamentalists, in their rejection of modernity, favor a return to the sacred past of pure Islam. Consequently, it is unlikely that they will adopt Western principles, such as democracy, which also emphasize a strict separation of religion and state.

27 P. Collier, "Five myths about the beauty of the ballot box", *The Washington Post*, November 08, 2009. http://articles.washingtonpost.com/2009-11-08/opinions/36907523_1_free-elections-democratic-election-political-violence.

28 For example: B. Lewis, *The Crisis of Islam* (London: The Orion Publishing Group, 2003).

Democracies and interventions: the Cold War period

During the Cold War, Western powers undertook multiple interventions within their spheres of influence in order to counter Soviet-Communist influences. Other Western powers often intervened in their (former) colonies to protect, amongst others, their nationals, and to support friendly regimes. Countries outside their own sphere of influence were seldom coerced by Western powers, because this could lead to a confrontation with the other superpower. The United Nations did not play a significant role during this period. Members of the Security Council did not accept interference within their respective spheres of influence and could usually not agree on any given form of coercive measures. The Security Council provided mandates for the initiation of military force on few occasions such as the conflicts in the Congo (1960-1964) and Cyprus (1963-1964). The same applied to the use of sanctions. The declaration of sanctions against Rhodesia (1966) and South Africa (1977) by the Security Council were exceptions. Almost all other sanctions were imposed by the Western powers unilaterally or together with allies.

Undoubtedly, the self-image of peace-loving liberal democracies originates from the fact that liberal democracies constitute a zone of peace in a turbulent world. But there is little statistical evidence for the peace-loving nature of liberal democracies in general. In relations with non-democratic states, liberal democracies are as aggressive and war prone as any other form of government or society.[29] Indeed, there is evidence that democratic states have been involved, proportionately, in more wars than non-democratic states.[30] According to Kegley and Hermann, 20% of those states initiating interventions between 1974 and 1979 were democracies. This figure rose to 50% in the 1986-1991 period. Democratic states have also used covert intervention as an alternative to other means of influencing the policies of another democratic state.[31] Finally, the democratic peace proposition

29 M. Doyle, "Kant, Liberal, Legacies and Foreign Affairs", *Philosophy and Public Affairs,* vol. 12, no. 3 (1983), pp. 205-235, p. 225.

30 C.W. Kegley, Jr. and M.G. Hermann, "Military Intervention and the Democratic Peace", *International Interactions,* vol. 21, no. 1 (1995), pp. 1-21, p. 9. The same conclusion is reached by: A.E. Levite, B.W. Jentleson and L. Berman, *Foreign Military Intervention, The Dynamics of Protracted Conflict* (New York: Columbia University Press, 1992), p. 14. See also: C.W. Kegley, Jr. and M.G. Hermann, "Ballots, a Barrier against the Use of Bullets and Bombs".

31 C.W. Kegley Jr. and M.G. Hermann, "How Democracies Use Intervention: A Neglected Dimension in Studies of the Democratic Peace", *Journal of Peace Research,* vol. 33, no. 3 (1996), pp. 309-322.

cannot account for civil war in democratic states, because civil war is not absent in democracies.[32] Even though quantified research proposes that "in general, the more democratic a nation, the less likely it will have domestic collective violence," it is not completely ruled out.[33] The United Kingdom, for example, has been fighting a civil war in Northern Ireland for decades.

The United Kingdom, the United States, and France – three long-term democracies – rank high on the scale of warring states in their own right. They are among the most frequent interveners and rank higher than "expansionist powers" such as the former Soviet Union. This could explain the perception in other parts of the world that Western states have neo-colonial or imperialist foreign policy objectives and are not peaceful at all.

Table 2.1 Most frequent interveners during the Cold War period[34]

Actor		Interventions, 1946-1992
1	United Kingdom	75
2	France	49
3	Israel	34
4	United States	30
5	China	22
6	India	19
7	Syria	19
8	Iraq	16
9	South Africa	16
10	Portugal	15
11	Soviet Union	8

Statistics like these can be very helpful in explaining the perception of others of the peacefulness of liberal democracies. Herbert Tillema, a prominent scholar in the field of interventions, defined overt military interventions as "combat-ready operations openly undertaken by a state's regular military

32 M. Krain and M. Edson Myers, "Democracy and Civil war: A Note on the Democratic Peace Proposition", *International Interactions,* vol. 23, no. 1 (1997), p. 114.

33 R.J. Rummel, *Power Kills; Democracy as a Method of Nonviolence* (New Brunswick, NJ: Transaction, 1997), p. 5.

34 Calculations by Isabelle Duyvesteyn, based on the *Overt Military Intervention File,* Herbert K. Tillema. Published in I.G.B.M. Duyvesteyn, *Wars and Military Interventions since 1945,* Arbeitspapier nr. 88/1995, Universität Hamburg-IPW.

forces within a specific foreign territory."[35] Tillema identified 690 interveners.[36] Each involvement of a state in a particular conflict was counted as one intervention. Another study identified 184 wars in the same period.[37] Both studies cover the 1945-1992 time frame. On some occasions, a considerable part of the world community was involved in a particular conflict. For example, during the 1950s, 35 countries were involved in the Korean War. For the coalition led by the United States, the target was North Korea, while others, like China, supported the war against South Korea. Between 1945 and 1992, 27 UN peace-support operations took place, including peace enforcing operations such as the intervention in the wars in Korea (1950-1953) and Congo (1960-1964).

Taking both sets of data as a starting point, some general characteristics of Western interventions can be identified. First, the data sets support the liberal peace thesis. Liberals refrained from interventions in other democracies. But at the same time, only liberal democracies carried out unilateral interventions *outside* their own region. They mostly intervened in the Middle East and Africa. Non-Western states carried out unilateral interventions *only* in their own region. The interventions of liberal democracies, except those of the United States, were mostly linked to the process of decolonization or motivated by the desire to help friendly regimes, mostly in their former colonies. Interventions by the United States had a clear ideological background and usually had geo-strategic motivations. Most US interventions took place during the 1950s and 1960s.

Second, in the absence of a clear threat, armed forces of liberal democracies have mainly been used for interventions in distant parts of the world. Western liberal democracies intervened for humanitarian reasons as well as to protect their interests. In addition, Western democracies have intervened to protect fellow countrymen, usually living in former colonies.

Third, the number of overt military interventions within the Cold War blocs was low. In absolute terms during the Cold War, the US bloc carried out more interventions than the Soviet bloc.

Fourth, there is a historical and geo-political explanation for the ranking of the four Western powers mentioned in table 2.1. Since the end of its colonial period, Portugal has no longer intervened. Of the Western pow-

35 H.K. Tillema, "Cold War Alliance and Overt Military Intervention, 1945-1991", *International Interactions*, vol. 20, no. 3 (1994), p. 251.

36 I.G.B.M. Duyvesteyn, *Wars and Military Interventions*, appendix 2, "The Overt Military Intervention File 1945-1992".

37 I.G.B.H. Duyvesteyn, "*Wars and Military Interventions*", appendix 1, the AKUF Warlist 1945-1992.

ers, only the United Kingdom and France still behave like major powers, willing to protect their worldwide interests. The US is the only remaining superpower with global responsibilities. However, most Western states are extremely reluctant to use military power. For historical reasons, Germany has been most reluctant to deploy its troops outside the NATO area. The Gulf War and the crises in Somalia and former Yugoslavia, however, triggered a debate over the future role of the German armed forces. The debate centered on the interpretation of the German constitution, the *Grundgesetz.* In 1982, the constitution was consolidated by two Federal Security Council directives which limited the *Bundeswehr* to the NATO area. These directives did not modify the constitution, but were regarded as implicit constitutional provisions. After reunification, Chancellor Kohl's Christian Democrats favored a more active German role in world politics. This led to a constitutional debate in the *Bundestag,* where the Social Democrats were of the view that the German armed forces should not participate in any military action other than low-risk UN peacekeeping. Subsequently, the matter was taken to the German Constitutional Court. On April 8, 1993, the Court condoned the participation of German pilots in enforcing the UN no-fly zone over Bosnia, which constituted the *Bundeswehr's* first combat role abroad since the Second World War. On May 1, 1993, Chancellor Kohl's cabinet approved the deployment of 1,640 troops in Somalia. In June of that year, the Constitutional Court rejected a petition from the Social Democrats that called for the withdrawal of German troops from Somalia. Nevertheless, each and every deployment of troops outside Germany has resulted in fierce political and public debates.

Fifth, during the Cold War, most interventions were *unilateral.* During this period, unilateral interventions strictly for humanitarian reasons were not executed; unilateral interventions to protect national interests were. Both the United States and the Soviet Union frequently intervened to defend their own interests.

Finally, the number of interventions has fluctuated considerably. Due to the decolonization of large parts of Asia and Africa, interventions reached a peak in the period between 1960 and 1965. After 1965, the number of interventions carried out by the United Kingdom declined sharply. This was in stark contrast to France, which continued to intervene in its former colonies after independence. Usually, French interventions were based on treaties with the ruling class. During the second wave of decolonization, from 1974 to 1979, interventions again reached a peak. An explanation of this peak is the attempts of the Soviet Union to increase its influence in Asia (Afghanistan) and Africa (Angola and Mozambique). This peak was followed by a steep decline in the 1980s. Between 1974 and 1979, 20% of those states initiating military interventions were democracies. This figure rose to 50% in the 1986-1991 time period.

Democracies and interventions: the post-Cold War era

During the 1990s, the percentage of interventions by democracies rose from 50 to 60%. Of the 39 military interventions listed in table 2.2, 23 were carried out by Western liberal democracies; one by a non-Western democracy (India), and six by the Soviet Union and its successor state, Russia. It should be mentioned the vast majority of America's coalition partners in Afghanistan and Iraq were liberal democracies. These statistics not only underpin the conclusions regarding the activist nature of Western civilization, but also help to explain why many non-Western states doubt the nonviolent stance of liberal democracies.

Table 2.2 Selected interventions after the end of the Cold War

Date	Intervener	Opponent	Objective
1986	United States	Regime of Libya	End support of terrorism
1989	United States	Regime of Panama	Regime change
1987-1990	India	Sri Lanka	Restoring peace and security
1989	Burkina Faso	Liberia	Interfere in internal politics
1991	Soviet Union	Tajikistan	Deny independence
1991	Soviet Union	Azerbaijan/ Nagorno-Karabakh	Before 1991: deny independence; after 1991: sustain CSCE cease-fire
January-March 1991	UN, lead nation: United States	Iraq, *Operation Desert Storm*	Restore international peace and security
End of 1991-early 2003	United States and United Kingdom	Iraq, protection of no-fly zones	Enforcing UN resolutions
1991-1993	ECOMOG	Sierra Leone	Halt factional fighting; enhance stability
1991-1995	UN, NATO	Former Yugoslavia, *Operation Deny Flight* and *Operation Sharp Guard*	Enforcing UN resolutions during UNPROFOR; contain conflict

Date	Intervener	Opponent	Objective
1991-1999	Liberia	Sierra Leone	Access to diamonds, political control
1992-1994	Armenia	Azerbaijan/ Nagorno-Karabakh	Protection of ethnic groups and border dispute
November-December 1992	Uzbekistan	Tajikistan	Border security and supporting neo-Soviet rule
End 1992-beginning 1993	United States	Somalia, *Operation Restore Hope*	Humanitarian intervention
July-August 1993	Russia	Afghanistan	Counterinsurgency (Tajik Rebels)
June 1994	France	Rwanda, *Operation Turquoise*	Humanitarian intervention
September 1994	United States	Haiti, *Operation Uphold Democracy*	Regime change
August 1995	NATO	Bosnia, *Operation Deliberate Force*	Coerce Serbs to cease fire and accept negotiations
1995-present	Russia	Chechnya	Counterinsurgency
April 1996	Israel	Lebanon *Operation Grapes of Wrath*	Counterterror
June 1996	France	Central African Republic	Restore order and support peace agreement and African peacekeeping force
1996-1997	Rwanda, Uganda, Burundi, Libya, Chad, Sudan, Angola, Namibia, Zimbabwe	1st Congo War	Regime change
December 1998	United States and United Kingdom	Iraq, *Operation Desert Fox*	Punishment
August 1998	United States	Afghanistan and Sudan, *Operation Infinite Reach*	Counterterror
1999-2008	Russia	Second Chechnya War in response to the intervention by Dagestan	Counterterror / separatism
March-June 1999	NATO	Yugoslavia (Kosovo), *Operation Allied Force*	Humanitarian intervention
May-June 1999	Ethiopia	Somalia	Territorial integrity

Date	Intervener	Opponent	Objective
1998-2000	Rwanda, Uganda, Burundi, Libya, Chad, Sudan, Angola, Namibia, Zimbabwe	2nd Congo War	Regime change
September 2001	NATO	Macedonia, *Operation Amber Fox*	Stability
October 2001	United States, supported by approximately 60 coalition partners	Afghanistan, *Operation Enduring Freedom*	Regime change, counterterror, followed by the NATO ISAF stabilization and reconstruction Operation (2014)
January 2002	United States	Philippines *Operation Enduring Freedom*	Counterterror
2002	Russia	Georgia against Chechen Rebels	Counterterror / insurgency
March-May 2003	United States, UK, Australia	Iraq *Operation Iraqi Freedom*	Regime change, followed by stabilization and reconstruction until 2011
August 2008	Georgia	South Ossetia	Counterseparatism
December 2008-January 2009	Israel	Gaza, *Operation Cast Lead*	Counterterror, protection against missile attacks
March 2010	Israel	Gaza, *Operation Returning Echo*	Counterterror, protection against missile attacks
March-October 2011	NATO, led by France and the UK. Initial coalition of Belgium, Canada, Denmark, France, Italy, Norway, Qatar, Spain, UK and US. The operation expanded to 19 coalition partners	Libya, *Opération Harmattan* (France); *Operation Ellamy* (UK); *Operation Mobile* (Canadian); *Operation Odyssey Dawn* (US)	No-fly zone; protection of the populace; arms embargo; ultimately regime change
November 2012	Israel	Gaza, *Operation Pillar of Defense*	Counterterror, protection against missile attacks
January 2013	France	Mali, *Opération Serval*	Counterterror

The geopolitical changes of the 1990s explain the increased number of interventions carried out by liberal democracies. As spheres of influence disappeared, interventions could be carried out without fear of escalation to superpower confrontation. Moreover, during the early 1990s, former adversaries cooperated closely in the UN Security Council. Three main categories of objectives can be identified: regime change; counterterror and counterinsurgency; and interventions in support of international peace and stability, including the protection of internationally agreed norms and values.

During the first half of the 1990s, multinational interventions under a UN mandate were the norm for liberal democracies. A distinction should be made in this regard between small and middle-sized powers on the one hand, and great and superpowers on the other. In those days UN peacekeeping operations were usually the domain of the middle-sized powers, such as Canada, Scandinavian countries, and the Netherlands. Small liberal democracies have limited capabilities to protect their interests, so they are likely to stress peaceful solutions and the use of the armed forces for humanitarian purposes and peacekeeping under the umbrella of the United Nations. Especially during the early 1990s, small and middle-sized powers were willing "to do something." The UN is especially important for small and middle-sized powers. They lack military might, so international rule of law and credible international organizations are considered a prerequisite for peaceful and stable international relations. But multinationality is important because it increases the legitimacy of the intervention as well.

Multinational interventions differ conceptually from unilateral interventions. The costs and benefits are divided, the objectives are broader, and more emphasis is put on the maintenance of a neutral position vis-à-vis the combating parties. The Security Council decided after 1990 to employ the instrument of sanctions on numerous occasions, and offered several mandates for the use of military force. Under the auspices of the Security Council, states like Iraq, Somalia, Haiti, and former Yugoslavia were put under pressure using military and economic measures, with varied degrees of success. In September of 1998, NATO's Secretary General, Javier Solana, declared that the alliance "cannot remain aloof" in developments in the Balkans and the Caucasus. He added that NATO did not want to be the victim of such events, and that NATO could determine the future.[38]

38 C.J. Dick, *Russia's 1999 Draft Military Doctrine* (The Conflict Studies Research Centre (CSRC) of the Royal Military Academy Sandhurst, November 16, 1999), pp. 4-5.

The decay of the non-intervention principle

Closely linked to the democratic peace thesis is the Western conviction that governments should be held accountable for the application of internationally accepted values and rules. The idea that sovereignty could be put aside temporarily when regimes terrorize the population and deny them basic human rights became firmly rooted during the 1990s.

Harvard Professor Stanley Hoffmann, presenting the Liberal school of thought, argued that "massive violations of human rights, which would encompass genocide, ethnic cleansing, brutal and large-scale repression to force a population into submission, including deliberate policies of barbarism, as well as the kinds of famines, massive breakdowns of law and order, epidemics and flights of refugees that occur when a 'failed state' collapses," could trigger military intervention.[39] Others argue that "gross abuse of the security of people could be seen as a threat to peace and international security," justifying intervention.[40] Especially in liberal democracies, criticism has been voiced against sovereignty and its corollary non-intervention, which were still associated with the system of Westphalia.

As a result, political leaders of liberal democracies called for a revision of international law to permit intervention, especially in failed or troubled states in which humanitarian disasters and gross violations of human rights occur. Indeed "failed" and "rogue" states pose a formidable challenge. In failed states, there is no functioning state to claim sovereignty, while a rogue state might constitute a threat to international peace and security. After the events of 9/11, the United States argued that preemptive action is justified for reasons of self-defense against rogue states that are in the process of acquiring weapons of mass destruction or that support international terrorism, and against failed states used by international terrorists as sanctuaries.

The central issue is under which conditions the sovereignty of states is subordinated to those of global humanity or the protection of human beings from intolerable evils. The proponents of humanitarian interventions maintained that sovereignty could not be an excuse for states abusing their populations.[41]

39 Hoffmann, "The Politics and Ethics of Military Interventions", *Survival*, vol. 37, no.4, winter 1995-1996, p. 38.

40 Commission on Global Governance, *Our Global Neighborhood* (Oxford: Oxford University Press, 1995), p. 90.

41 Stanley Hoffmann, "The Politics and Ethics of Military Interventions", *Survival*, vol. 37, no. 4 (1995-1996), pp. 29-51, p. 35. Jeffrey Herbst, "Responding to State Failure in Africa", *International Security*, vol. 21, No. 3 (1996), pp. 120-144.

The resulting refugee flows and the destabilizing of entire regions were considered a threat to international peace and security, that is, motivations for interventions. Consequently, sovereignty was no longer seen in absolute terms.

According to Hoffmann, there are three reasons why interventions are permissible.[42] First, sovereignty is not an absolute good. As Hobbes in *Leviathan* already observed, the state should protect the security and the property of its subjects. If the state fails to do so, the international community has the right to intervene. Second, the central moral issue is the weighing of conflicting ethical claims. Under certain circumstances, the moral good of sovereignty is subordinated to those of global humanity or the protection of human beings from intolerable evils such as the violation of their fundamental rights to life and security. Hoffmann argued that Christian doctrine looked for just causes of war in the relations *among* states. However, a modern version needs to define such causes for interventions *within* states. His third argument concerns order. Interventions may be necessary to prevent chaos in a world in which domestic strife and violence risk spreading rapidly across borders, thereby destabilizing entire regions.

Robert Cooper, a senior British diplomat who helped to shape Prime Minister Tony Blair's ideas for a new internationalism and a new doctrine of humanitarian intervention that would place limits on state sovereignty, even called for a new liberal imperialism. Cooper argued that postmodern states, most notably the member states of the EU, no longer think of security in terms of conquest.[43] Modern states like China, Pakistan, India, and possibly Russia still do. Postmodern states, that is, the member states of the EU, no longer rely on a balance of power politics, as modern states do. Premodern states, like Afghanistan and Somalia, are actually failed states. According to Cooper, the challenge for the postmodern states is how to deal with modern and premodern states. Defense and deterrence are the most likely options for dealing with modern states. For dealing with the premodern states, a new kind of liberal imperialism is needed to bring order and organization. Thus, human rights and other universally accepted values could also be imposed. One way of doing this is to create protectorates, preferably under UN authority. Cooper goes on to argue that, with respect to America's military responses, there is an overwhelming activity in the regions of the world that he calls the "premodern" world: "if we draw a line around the majority of those military interventions, we have

42 S. Hoffmann, "The politics and Ethics of Military Interventions", p. 35.

43 R. Cooper, "The New Liberal Imperialism", *The Guardian*, April 7, 2002.

basically mapped the non-integration gap." In his view, strategies should be developed for shrinking that gap and enlarging the zone of peace by increasing the number of free, democratic, and connected states. Other authors also argue that disconnectedness defines danger. Thomas Barnett wrote on the eve of Operation Iraqi Freedom that "Saddam Hussein's outlaw regime is dangerously disconnected from the globalizing world, from its set of rules, its norms, and all the ties that bind countries together in mutually assured dependence."[44]

Ideas like these put the UN at the center of international politics. Indeed, within the UN, the concept of sovereignty was also questioned. Secretary General Kofi Annan asked the following question during the 1999 General Assembly: "To those for whom the greatest threat to the future of international order is the use of force in the absence of a Security Council mandate, one might ask in the context of Rwanda: if in those dark days and hours leading up to the genocide, a coalition of states had been prepared to act in defense of the Tutsi population, but did not receive prompt Council authorization, should such a coalition have stood aside and allow the horror to unfold?"[45] Indeed, the debate on humanitarian intervention focused on the friction between humanitarianism and sovereignty.

As most liberal democracies saw the need for intervention in the case of an urgent humanitarian disaster or the gross violation of human rights, they tried to seek support for making interventions without a mandate of the Security Council more permissible and legitimate. One way to overcome the judicial problem of unmandated intervention was to refrain from unilateral military action. Multilateral peace support operations suggest that the international community has an interest in maintaining international peace and stability, even if no mandate of the Security Council can be obtained. Unmandated multinational interventions were considered legitimate, because they show that the interveners do not seek expansion. Multilateral interventions were also considered more permissible because it is the international community that decides to act.

This movement towards acceptance of liberal and moral norms of intervention was not universally accepted. Most non-Western states did not want to give up the cornerstones of international law – sovereignty and non-interference – because this would increase the possibility that one day they, too, would become the victim of an intervention themselves. They argued that interventions without a mandate are unlawful and they feared

44 Thomas P.M. Barnett, "The Pentagon's New Map", *Esquire*, March 2003.

45 United Nations Press Release, *SG/SM/7136 GA/9596*.

that their interests would be sacrificed to the interests of the powerful West, especially the United States.

These were the kinds of arguments Saddam Hussein used during the post-Gulf War period. Since the conclusion of the Gulf War in 1991, a multilateral force has been enforcing a no-fly zone over Northern Iraq and over the skies of Southern Iraq. Troops involved in these operations did not wear the blue helmet of the UN, but operated with the approval of the UN. Saddam Hussein saw these activities as a disregard for the principle of sovereignty. For similar reasons, he strongly opposed the work of UN inspection teams trying to find evidence for his research and development programs for weapons of mass destruction, especially biological and chemical weapons. Saddam Hussein frequently accused the United States of using the UN to mask intervention in the affairs of another state.

In December 1998, when American and British aerial forces attacked targets in Iraq, with the formal objective "to strike military and security targets in Iraq that contribute to Iraq's ability to produce, store, maintain, and deliver weapons of mass destruction,"[46] Thomas Pickering, a former Undersecretary of State for Political Affairs, argued that the United States believed that Saddam Hussein, in agreeing to accept the cease-fire and Resolution 687 – which implemented it – also agreed to accept the disarmament of his weapons of mass destruction. As he did not comply with this resolution, in the view of the United States, the underlying resolution – which authorizes the use of force at the end of November 1990, Resolution 678 – still applied.[47] The UN Security Council was divided over the issue. China, Russia, and France disapproved of the action, with Russia withdrawing its ambassadors from Washington and London. This clearly indicated that the legal basis was questionable.

The best example of the friction between sovereignty and humanitarianism is the 1999 Kosovo crisis. In 1998, the Serb President Milosevic applied a scorched earth policy in his attempts to suppress the insurgents of the Kosovo Liberation Army. Serbian police, together with ground and air forces, tried to put down a rebellion of ethnic Albanians. The Serbian forces indiscriminately bombarded villages along the Albanian border, killing many civilians. NATO ministers, motivated by public disapproval, could no longer tolerate the atrocities taking place in the Balkans. Moreover, the danger of a spillover of the conflict in the province of Kosovo to neighboring Macedonia and Albania, and consequently the possible involvement of

46 Mission statement, *Operation Desert Fox*, as could be found on the website of the Pentagon.

47 *Worldnet Dialogue* with Ambassador Thomas Pickering, February 19, 1998.

Greece, Bulgaria, and Turkey, forced American Foreign Secretary Madeleine Albright and Defense Secretary William Cohen to argue in favor of an unmandated intervention in Kosovo, calling upon Article 51 of the UN Charter, which acknowledges the right of self-defense. It was expected that China and Russia would oppose such an enabling resolution, because of their traditional stance against interference in internal affairs of states. Consequently, within the Alliance, a debate emerged about intervening without a mandate. During a NATO ministerial meeting in Copenhagen on June 13, 1998, US Defense Secretary Cohen argued that a mandate was not needed if peace and security in the region was threatened, and that NATO could base military action on Article 5 of the NATO treaty. Not all ministers shared this line of argument. Among others, his host, Danish Minister Hans Haekkerup, was opposed to intervening without a mandate, arguing that this would affect NATO-Russia relations in a very negative way.

The publication of the 2002 US National Security Strategy resulted in a new debate about the legitimacy of interventions. With this strategy, the Bush administration embraced the concept of "preemption." This has led to bitter disputes. Preemption refers to the initiation of war because an adversary's attack is believed to be imminent. Prevention refers to fighting a winnable war to avoid a risk of war later under less favorable circumstances. Strictly speaking, preemption and prevention are not coercive strategies, but controlling strategies, because they do not rely on the adversaries' decisions.

Scholars of international law do not reject preemption or anticipatory self-defense under all circumstances. They argue that preemption does not require certainty regarding time and place. Instead, they maintain that preemption is justified if there is a *near certainty* that an attack is *imminent.* Prevention does not meet the criterion of near certainty, and must consequently be rejected. An example of preventive action is the Israeli attack in 1981 against the Osirak reactor near Baghdad. There was no imminent threat. The attack was designed to delay Iraq's nuclear weapons program.

Prevention better defines what is referred to as preemption in the National Security Strategy. Deputy Secretary of Defense Paul Wolfowitz defended this position by arguing that it is impossible to know whether a threat is imminent: "Were the attacks of September 11 imminent? Certainly they were imminent on September 10, although we didn't know it."[48]

48 P. Wolfowitz, speech at the International Institute for Strategic Studies on December 2, 2002.

Weapons of mass destruction and terrorism pose threats unanticipated by international law. International law deals with relations among functioning states, not with non-state actors and rogue states. It can be very difficult to determine whether states possess weapons of mass destruction, are willing to use them and if that use is imminent. The same holds true for state-sponsored terrorism. From a legal perspective, there is a great difficulty in relaxing the principles of near-certainty and imminence. Where does one draw the line? Is it a perceived intent of a state to acquire weapons of mass destruction or to support international terrorism? Or is it the possession of these weapons or the existence of terrorist groups in a state? Thus, critics of the 2002 National Security Strategy feared that setting new standards for preemption could result in the death of the UN Charter framework.

The consequence of these divergences was a bitter transatlantic debate in 2002 and early 2003 over the path to be followed concerning Iraq. The debate reflected different approaches regarding security mentioned above. Most Europeans wanted a clear role for the UN. But mandated interventions were not exactly what President George W. Bush had in mind when he embarked on a more activist foreign policy after the events of 9/11. America now no longer felt constrained to intervene in sensitive areas like the Middle East, the Gulf Region, or Central Asia should its national security interests demand it.

Led by France, a majority within the Security Council rejected the notion that "serious consequences" mentioned in the US-British resolution 1441 of November 8, 2002, left the United States no other option but to go for war if weapons of mass destruction were not found or handed over to the UN inspectors by the Iraqi regime.

On February 9, 2003, the United States reacted furiously to a Franco-German-Russian initiative to triple the number of arms inspectors and back them up with surveillance flights. The next day, Germany, France, and Belgium rejected a request from Turkey for aid from NATO in the case of a US intervention in Iraq. Such a decision would signal endorsement of America's intention to go to war. Again the Bush administration reacted furiously, throwing the Alliance into its worst-ever crisis. Although the deadlock on NATO was broken a week later, this crisis continued. On February 24, France, Germany, and Russia put forward a counterproposal to an American-British draft resolution, which sought to gain the Security Council's approval for war. The counterproposal introduced a step-by-step program for Iraqi disarmament. At the same time, the United States and the United Kingdom lobbied among undecided UN Security Council members for acceptance of their draft resolution. Following that lobby, they agreed to set out the precise acts of disarmament that Saddam Hussein would have to undertake by March 17 to avoid war. France, willing to compromise over Iraq, was nevertheless unwilling to accept any deadline or ultimatum. Consequently, with France, Germany, and Russia opposed to attack, the United States and the United Kingdom abandoned hopes of gaining Security Council support for the intervention. The next day, President Bush gave Saddam Hussein 48 hours to leave the country. Following Saddam's refusal, war began on March 20 without a new UN Security Council resolution.

America's primacy

The year 1998 was a turning point in the post-Cold War history. In that year, the first post-Cold War intervention without a mandate by the United States took place. In response to the terrorist bombings of the American embassies in Nairobi and Dar es Salaam, the United States intervened unilaterally and without a Security Council mandate in Sudan and Afghanistan in August 1998 for the first time since the end of the Cold War. The goal was to deliver a blow against the alleged terrorist network of Osama bin Laden.

Due to the threat of terrorism, the Realist school of thought gained the upper hand. They were in favor of a more unilateralist stance and maintained that the unipolar world, which emerged after 1989, would be stable as long as the United States remained the hegemonic power. In 1998 and the year after, several more events took place indicating that the American administration was shifting to a more narrow and selective foreign and security policy of unilateralism and primacy:

- In December 1998, Operation Desert Fox took place. Together with the United Kingdom, the United States carried out bombings on Iraq. These were meant as retribution for the obstruction Saddam Hussein committed against UNSCOM, the UN inspectors regarding weapons of mass destruction. In 1999 and 2000, the bombings continued, albeit with a limited intensity.
- In 1998, after a period of decline, the US decided to increase its defense budget by 5.6%.[49] Investments to improve the expeditionary feature of the American military were said to be especially necessary. The products of the *Revolution in Military Affairs* (RMA) made this possible.

49 IISS, *Strategic Comments*, "US Military Spending", vol. 6, no. 4 (May 2000).

- In January of 1999, President Clinton announced he would ask Congress for 2.8 billion US dollars for the battle against chemical and biological terrorism.
- In July of 1999, the plan for a *National Missile Defense* (NMD) was presented to protect the American people against limited attacks with ballistic missiles by rogue states. The first phase planned the deployment of 100 antimissile weapons in Alaska against attacks from North Korea. The second phase planned the deployment of antimissile weapons against attacks from the Middle East. The plan demanded a review of the *Anti Ballistic Missile* (ABM) treaty of 1972, which allows for the deployment of a limited number of antimissile weapons for the protection of American and Russian strategic nuclear arms.
- Finally, in October 1999, the American Senate refused to ratify the *Comprehensive Test Ban Treaty* (CTBT), thereby vetoing a general prohibition of conducting nuclear tests.

Samuel Huntington dramatically argued in *Foreign Affairs* that, in the eyes of the outside world, the United States was itself developing into a "rogue superpower."[50] Up until then, the term "rogue" was only used for countries such as Iraq and North Korea. By doing so, Huntington made clear that the new policy might create a certain image of America. This is of great importance, because perceptions are often more important than facts in international relations. States often act on the basis of perceptions, rather than on an analysis of the facts.

Since 1998 in non-Western countries, the image has emerged of a superpower that, together with its close allies, wanted to change the status quo and to create a "new world order" after its own views. As there is a fundamental difference between Western and non-Western ideas, Russia, China, and Islamic countries distrust interventions that are based on normative principles, such as democracy and humanity. According to Chinese commentators, the interventions indicate that the West can impose its liberal values on the rest of the world without fear of confrontation with the Soviet Union.[51] It is apparent from official policy documents,[52] remarks

50 S.P. Huntington, "The Lonely Superpower", *Foreign Affairs*, March-April 1999.

51 J.T. Dreyer, "The PLA and the Taiwan Strait", paper prepared for the International Forum on the Peace and Security of the Taiwan Strait, Washington, D.C., July 1999.

52 For Russia those are the *Military Doctrine*, the *Security Concept* and the *Doctrine for Foreign Policy*, all of 2000. For China this is the *New Security Concept* of 1998.

from top-level officials, and the scientific literature that, after 1998, largely the same image of the West has been created in Russia and China.[53]

The way in which the United States, supported by allies, has intervened militarily, the announced improvement of the expeditionary character of their military forces, and the measures to decrease the vulnerability of the American territory, were an indication of the willingness, as well as the technical possibility, to actively interfere in domestic issues, such as Chechnya and Taiwan. In short, a unipolar situation has come about, according to Russia and China, in which especially the United States exploits Russia's and China's military and economic weaknesses and ignores their security concerns.

With the inauguration of George W. Bush as president of the United States in 2000, neo-conservatists came to power. Neo-conservatism is characterized by a combination of triumphalism about America's achievements, faith in America's economic and military power, optimism about its role in the world and the values it stands for, and pessimism about the rest of the world, especially the threat of rogue states, failed states, and international terrorism, and the future of China as a strategic competitor.

The Bush Administration represented the "primacy school," which is "unilateralist" and favors selective engagement in world politics based on a narrow interpretation of national interest. Advocates of this grand strategy see the rise of a peer competitor as the greatest danger for world stability and therefore the greatest risk of war involving the United States. Advocates of primacy are skeptical of international institutions, but believe they can be useful if they support America's interests. Within its first six months in office, the Bush Administration moved towards a unilateralist position. It decided to deploy a national missile defense system; abrogated the 1972 ABM Treaty; rejected the 1997 Kyoto Protocol; withdrew from the Biological Weapons Convention, which had been ratified by the United States in 1975;

53 See for example C.J. Dick, *Russia's Draft Military Doctrine*; S.J. Main, *Russia's Military Doctrine* (CSRC, April 2000); S.J. Blank, *Threats to Russian Security: The View from Moscow* (Carlisle: US Army War College, July 2000); C.A. Wallander, *Russian Views on Kosovo* and E.A. Stepanova, *Explaining Russia's Dissention on Kosovo* (Cambridge: Davis Center for Russian Studies, Harvard University, May 1999); O. Antonenko, "Russia, NATO and European Security after Kosovo", *Survival*, winter 1999-2000, pp. 124-144; D. Shambough, "Sino-American Strategic Relations: From Partners to Competitors", *Survival*, spring 2000, pp. 97-115; B. Gill and J. Reilly, "Sovereignty, Intervention and Peacekeeping: The View from Beijing", *Survival*, fall 2000, pp. 41-60; S. Shambaugh, "China's Military Views the World: Ambivalent Security", *International Security*, winter 1999/2000, pp. 52-79; J. Teufel Dreyer, *The PLA and the Kosovo Conflict* (Carlisle: US Army War College, May 2000).

and withdrew from the treaty on the International Criminal Court (ICC) that had been signed by his predecessor shortly before leaving office.

American Democrats usually favor a grand strategy of multilateralism. This school believes that engagement brings stability based on cooperative security. International organizations play a key role here. Actually, this debate is a debate between the two schools of thought mentioned in Chapter I; Liberals and Realists.

In 2001, however, the debate turned in another direction following the attacks on September 11 of that year on the World Trade Center in New York and the Pentagon in Washington. First of all, this led to the insight that more active policies in some parts of the world could result in risks to their own territory. This was apparent as one of the objectives of Osama bin Laden – the Saudi national who was implicated in the attacks – was the expulsion of all American influences from the Islamic world. Secondly, due to the attacks, the attention shifted to non-state actors. Thirdly, the attacks led to a profound shift in American thinking on coercion.

On September 20, 2001, President George W. Bush declared war on terrorism during a speech to Congress. This speech was the most important statement on grand strategy since President Harry Truman's speech on March 12, 1947 when the United States proposed to fight Communism worldwide. After September 11, the Administration refused an offer of help from NATO, which had invoked Article 5 (its collective defense clause), for the first time in history. Bush reluctantly accepted British military aid during the war against the Taliban and al-Qaeda in Afghanistan. A major policy change was announced during the State of the Union address on January 29, 2002. Referring to North Korea, Iran, and Iraq, Bush stated that "States like these constitute an axis of evil, arming to threaten the peace of the world. By seeking weapons of mass destruction, these regimes pose a grave and growing danger. They could provide these arms to terrorists, giving them the means to match their hatred. They could attack our allies or attempt to blackmail the United States. In any of these cases, the price of indifference would be catastrophic."[54] The President also put the issue of usable nuclear weapons on the agenda. He showed renewed interest in nuclear-armed missile interceptors in a national missile defense system and nuclear ground penetrators to destroy hardened underground bunkers and tunnel complexes because conventional means would be militarily less efficient. In this context, the *Nuclear Posture Review* of January 8, 2002,

54 G.W Bush, *The President's State of the Union Address*, Washington, D.C., January 29, 2002.

caused much unease among allies because it explicitly called for a capability for destroying "hard and deeply buried targets."[55]

Elaborating on the "axis of evil" speech, Bush announced another major policy shift during a commencement speech he gave at the US Military Academy West Point on June 1, 2002. The President argued that the US must "uncover terror cells in 60 or more countries" and that "we must take the battle to the enemy, disrupt his plans, and confront the worst threats before they emerge." In doing so, the United States must change the very foundations of strategic thought: "For much of the last century, America's defense relied on the Cold War doctrines of deterrence and containment (...). Deterrence – the promise of massive retaliation against nations – means nothing against shadowy terrorists without any nation or citizen to defend. Containment is not possible when unbalanced dictators with weapons of mass destruction can deliver those weapons on missiles or secretly provide them to terrorists (...) our security will require all Americans to be forward-looking and resolute, to be ready for preemptive action, when necessary to defend our liberty and to defend our lives."[56] Thus, a new unilateralist, first-strike policy of "defensive intervention" or "anticipatory self-defense" was announced. Vice President Dick Cheney underscored the need for such a strategy during a speech delivered to war veterans on August 26, 2002. He argued that preemption against Iraq was necessary because "there is no doubt that Saddam Hussein now has weapons of mass destruction. There is no doubt he is amassing them to use against our friends, against our allies, and against us. And there is no doubt that his aggressive regional ambitions will lead him into future confrontations with his neighbors." Quoting former Foreign Secretary Henry Kissinger, Cheney argued that this produces "an imperative for preventative action." In addition, "our job would be more difficult in the face of a nuclear armed Saddam Hussein."[57]

As has been argued before, this policy change was codified in the National Security Strategy, published in September 2002. President Bush officially put aside the doctrines of deterrence and containment and replaced them with new doctrines of preemption and preventive interventions: "We must be prepared to stop rogue states and their terrorist clients before they are able to threaten or use weapons of mass destruction against the United

55 US Department of Defense, *Nuclear Posture Review*, submitted to congress on December 31, 2000, pp. 46-47.

56 G.W. Bush, Remarks by the President at 2002 Graduation ceremony of the United States Military Academy West Point, New York, Washington, D.C., June 1, 2002.

57 D. Cheney, Remarks by the Vice President to the Veterans of Foreign Wars 103rd National Convention, Washington, D.C., August 26, 2002.

States and our allies and friends. Our response must take full advantage of strengthened alliances, the establishment of new partnerships." However, "while the United States will constantly strive to enlist the support of the international community, we will not hesitate to act alone, if necessary, to exercise our right of self-defense by acting preemptively against such terrorists, to prevent them from doing harm against our people and our country." It is a view that can be described as unilateral if necessary, and multilateral if possible.

In summary, Bush's grand strategy was based on a firm belief that the US is powerful enough to go it alone if this is in its interest. This is why the post-post Cold War period started in 1998. But in general, institutions, treaties, and rules were merely obstacles to Bush's grand strategy. The events of September 11 reinforced the arguments of those favoring this grand strategy. In addition, the Administration reformed its defenses to allow the US to deploy force from the continental US, rather than from overseas bases in Europe, Asia, and the Middle East, and to be able to deal with contemporary challenges, including asymmetric warfare.[58] Key officials such as Secretary of Defense Donald Rumsfeld, the head of the Defense Policy Board at the Pentagon, Richard Perle, and Security Advisor Condoleezza Rice clearly favored this grand strategy. They gained a victory over moderates, who favored an approach based on multilateralism, like Secretary of Defense Colin Powell. The proponents of the former strategy were convinced that the US should not take into account the views of others on how to protect the country. September 11 was an attack on America and everything it stands for. Consequently, America's vital interests were at stake. This was a very powerful motivation indeed to go it alone and to adopt a new doctrine of "preemption" and "defensive intervention." Finally, promoting democracy had become one of the key foreign policy objectives. President Bush's Security Advisor Condoleezza Rice argued that the United States should seize the moment by using its hegemonic power to model the world according to American values: "The international system has been in flux since the collapse of Soviet power. Now it is possible – indeed probable – that that transition is coming to an end. If that is right, then... that is not just a period of grave danger, but of enormous opportunity... a period akin to 1945 to 1947, when American leadership expanded the number of free and democratic states... to create a new balance of power that favored freedom."[59]

58 D.H. Rumsfeld, "Transforming the Military", *Foreign Affairs*, May-June 2002, pp. 20-32.

59 Quoted in F. FitzGerald, "George Bush & the World", *The New York Review of Books*, September 26, 2002.

Due to its unparalleled military power, the United States was in a unique position to model the world according to its preferences. According to the prevalent neo-conservative school of thought, America should seize the opportunity and bring entire regions into the modern world, that is, to impose a Western-style democracy through a combination of Wilsonian idealism and Reaganite muscularity. A consensus emerged that the best place to start would be the Middle East. Authoritarian regimes in the region support international terrorism indirectly by producing generations of unemployed and unrepresented, and therefore radicalized, young people. It was feared that dubious leaders like Osama bin Laden would draw their recruits from these dissatisfied groups.

One of the principal proponents of this idea was the United States Deputy Defense Secretary Paul D. Wolfowitz. Getting rid of Iraqi leader Saddam Hussein would allow the Americans to create a free, stable, and democratic Iraq that would serve as a source of inspiration to its neighbors. The "Wolfowitz Doctrine" finds its origin in the early 1990s. Wolfowitz was dissatisfied with Bush Sr.'s decision not to topple Saddam Hussein after the first Gulf War and with the efforts to coerce Saddam Hussein during the 1990. Annoyed with Hussein's cat-and-mouse game with UN inspectors during the 1990s, Wolfowitz stressed "the power of the democratic idea" and its applicability to a part of the world known for its authoritarian regimes.[60]

The United States was encouraged by successful interventions after 1989. As will be seen, a revolution in warfare made interventions more effective and less costly in terms of collateral damage and friendly losses. Military might has become a more useable instrument, so that it is likely that it will be used more often. America's new activist foreign policies can also be explained by the "war-weariness theory." David J. Singer and Melvin Small found that the winners of interstate wars from 1816 to 1965 were more likely to initiate future wars than losers.[61] John A. Nevin found that states that won two consecutive wars are much more likely to initiate subsequent wars than actors who have lost a similar number of wars in succession.[62] Jeffery Pickering came to a similar conclusion after testing 510 interventions from 1949 to 1996.[63] Being

60 M. Dobbs, "For Wolfowitz, a vision may be realized", *Washington Post*, April 7, 2003.

61 J.D. Singer and D. Small, "Foreign Policy Indicators: Predictions of War in History and the State of the World Message", *Policy Sciences* 5 (3), 1974, pp. 271-296.

62 J.A. Nevin, "War Initiation and Selection by Consequences", *Journal of Peace Research* 33 (I), pp. 99-108.

63 J. Pickering, "The Conflict-Prone and the Conflict-Weary: War Outcomes and Types of Military Intervention, 1946-1996", *Journal of Political and Military Sociology*, vol. 29 (Winter 2001), pp. 211-239.

successful in numerous wars during the 1990s, it was assumed that the United States would initiate new wars more easily, which it did.

Conclusion

In this chapter I have argued that liberal democracies are the most frequent interveners. They often use the argument of bringing democracy to explain or defend their interventions. Most decision makers strongly believe that democratization will lead to peaceful and stable relations among countries. There is strong empirical support for the democratic peace thesis. Some would argue that the absence of war among liberal democracies is the result of civilization. Undoubtedly, a Kantian "pacific union" has emerged with the EU, NATO, and the OSCE as its cornerstones. These institutions are important instruments for conflict prevention and conflict resolution. Integration and interdependence have created a situation where the costs of conflict among liberal democracies outweigh the benefits. Finally, war against liberal democracies is unlikely because their sheer economic and military strength makes aggression by others a highly risky undertaking.

The democratic peace thesis only applies to the relations among liberal democracies. Empirical evidence also shows that during the transition phase from autocracy to democracy, countries become more aggressive and war prone. As a consequence, liberal democracies should show some constraints in the unconditional promotion of democracy all over the world.

The idea that sovereignty should be put aside when regimes terrorize the population and deny them basic human rights and democracy had become firmly rooted in the West during the 1990s. Due to the geopolitical changes of the 1990s, thinking on sovereignty and interference entered a new stage. After 1998, a more unilateralist and confrontationist American foreign policy emerged. This was the start of the post-post-Cold War period, that is, the period where the United States started to use its hegemonic power more assertively. The emphasis shifted from interventions on moral grounds to interventions to defend vital interests. The events of September 11, 2001, became a watershed in contemporary history, because America's focus was now fully on rogue states, international terrorism, and the proliferation of weapons of mass destruction and their means of delivery. The foundations of American thinking about coercion shifted from containment and deterrence to preemption and preventive interventions.

I argued that this shift had important consequences for the perception others have of the United States. On the one hand, non-Western countries perceive interventions as a new form of imperialism, which should not simply be endorsed. They fear that once more they will be subordinated to Western powers. On the other hand, liberal democracies argue that the international legal order is dynamic and that the defense of interests and values could require unmandated interventions. At the same time, the United Nations adopted the concept of the Responsibility to Protect (R2P). States terrorizing their people lost their right of non-interference, and a new interpretation of the concept of sovereignty was accepted by the international community. However, the distinction between the promotion of fundamental humanitarian rights and the defense of vital interests is often unclear. This results in distrust and could undermine international peace and stability if not handled with care.

3 The Strategic Efficacy of Power Instruments

Although Americans and Europeans differ about why, how, and when coercion is legitimate, it will remain an essential element of liberal democracies' foreign policy. But, as has been argued before, the record of success is mixed. Failed interventions or partially successful efforts to coerce could undermine the credibility of foreign policy. As interventions usually provoke negative reactions in other countries, failed attempts to coerce an adversary could also jeopardize the stability of international relations. Especially interventions carried out solely for moral and ethical reasons are not always understood in other cultures, and therefore pose considerable challenges. To be successful, coercion could require the decisive use of force. However, states are willing to use force decisively only if vital interests are at stake. Actually, if their vital interests are at stake, liberal democracies have no alternative but to coerce others.

This chapter aims to contribute to the further development of theory. I will first deal with the development in thought that has taken place with respect to the use of power instruments in international relations. Following a description of existing theories, I argue that coercion requires a specific type of decision making, one that is based on a dynamic approach and knowledge about the instruments of power. To this end, I will provide insights into the mechanism that lies at the foundation of coercion and, subsequently, several different strategies that the intervener can use will be presented. The central question is how the instruments of power can be engaged most effectively in order to achieve political objectives. In order to assess the efficacy of power instruments, theoretical insights are required into the mechanism that lies at the foundation of coercion.

In spite of the substantial media interest in interventions in conflicts, academic research into the manner through which force can be used to coerce actors most effectively is marginal. Discouraged by disappointing results, the consensus gradually developed that strategic thought should focus more on the actual use of military force and less on deterrence, conflict prevention, and peace building. Thus, to an increasing extent, the success of military force is to be judged on the basis factual effort. The offensive use of military force, whether or not in combination with economic sanctions, demands a different way of thinking. Here, the central question is how military force, in combination with economic coercive measures, can be applied most effectively to achieve the political objectives. This requires a new approach to the sanction instrument as well.

The theoretical foundation of coercion

Coercion demands theoretical understanding of the dynamics of coercion, decision making that coincides with the theoretical understanding and results in attainable political objectives, an understanding of power instruments themselves, and a strategy that defines the manner in which power instruments will eventually be used. Unfortunately, the available literature and subsequent applicable theory is meager. Most theories of coercion were developed by American scholars, but the number of important studies is limited. None of these studies takes the transatlantic differences in political, and consequentially strategic, culture into account, nor do they make a distinction between coercive diplomacy and military coercion. An explanation is that the unmatched economic and military power possessed by the US prevented sophisticated thinking about how this power could be used best to achieve foreign policy objectives. In addition to this, during the Cold War, the philosophy with respect to the presentation of military might was predominantly concerned with the prevention of war by deterring the other alliance, the Warsaw Pact. NATO prevented Warsaw Pact aggression by envisioning unacceptable damage. Deterrence was the central concept. The theory that applied to this is currently not very relevant, since the nuclear weapon – the preeminent instrument of deterrence – has lost its significance. Furthermore, military power occupies primarily a passive role in deterrence theories. It was generally considered that the military was successful even if it only threatened, but did *not* have to perform.

Due to the geopolitical changes of the 1990s, divergent views regarding the philosophy concerning the application of power instruments in international relations became even more visible. Both scholars and decision makers concluded that asymmetrical responses could offset the West's advantage, so that new thinking was required about how new adversaries should be dealt with.

The existing theories about coercion are primarily based on the classical studies by Thomas Schelling, Alexander George, and Robert Pape.[1] As has

1 T. Schelling, *Arms and Influence* (New Haven: Yale University Press, 1966); A.L. George and W.E. Simons (eds.), *The Limits of Coercive Diplomacy* (Boulder: Westview Press, 1994); R.A. Pape, *Bombing to Win: Air Power and Coercion in War* (Ithaca and London: Cornell University Press,

been argued before, Schelling makes a distinction between "brute force" and coercion. The application of brute force is designed to enforce a military solution; in coercion the primary aim is to threaten with violence to affect a change in an actors' choices.[2] Schelling terms this "compellence." Concrete actions can only be avoided if the target gives in. To be successful, compellence requires a deadline, for without an ultimatum, one is confronted with an empty threat.[3] Schelling not only focuses on undoing or avoiding action, but also on the threat of violence to coerce an opponent to change his behavior. He formulated five conditions for success:[4]

1 The threat conveyed must convince the adversary that non-compliance is too costly.
2 The adversary must perceive the threat as credible. He must be convinced that the coercer has the will and the capacity to execute the threat in case of non-compliance.
3 The adversary must be given time to comply with the demand.
4 The coercer must assure the adversary that compliance will not lead to more future demands.
5 The conflict must not be perceived as a zero-sum game. A degree of common understanding that full-scale war must be avoided should exist. Each side must understand that it can gain more by bargaining.

Furthermore, a "risk-strategy" lies at the core of Schelling's approach. By targeting high-value targets such as the civilian population, and by having the opponent envision further atrocities, the adversary expects that the target will alter his behavior. This approach is not surprising if one considers that Schelling's famous study *Arms and Influence* appeared in 1966, in which he sought to find alternatives to the threat of mutual assured destruction if nuclear deterrence failed.

George's study was published in 1971, however, he presented a revised edition in the early 1990s in which he applied his theory to new cases. He makes a distinction between an offensive "military strategy" and defen-

1996); L. Freedman (ed.), *Strategic Coercion: Concepts and Cases* (Oxford: Oxford University Press); C.S. Gray, *Modern Strategy* (Oxford: Oxford University Press, 1999); R.N. Haas, *Intervention: The Use of Military Force in the Post-Cold War World* (Washington, D.C.: The Brookings Institution 1994); M. O'Hanlon, *Saving Lives with Force: Military Criteria for Humanitarian Intervention,* (Washington, D.C.: The Brookings Institution, 1997); B.R. Pirnie and W.E. Simons, *Soldiers for Peace: Critical Operational Issues* (Santa Monica: RAND, 1996).

2 Schelling, *Arms and Influence,* pp. 2-3.

3 Schelling, *Arms and Influence,* p. 69-91; *The Strategy of Conflict,* pp. 195-199.

4 Schelling, *Arms and Influence,* p. 1, 3-4, 69-76, 89.

sive "coercive diplomacy," implying an application of power instruments supported by diplomacy. Power instruments in the shape of threats or limited military interventions must force the target to cease his activities. An entanglement between diplomacy and power instruments in order to coerce the target to comply lies at the root of his approach.[5] In his view, a reward for complying with demands will influence the cost-benefit calculations of the target and thus contribute to successful coercive diplomacy. Finally, George concluded that the following conditions are determinants for success:[6]

- a clear disposition;
- the motivation of parties concerned;
- sense of urgency;
- strong leadership;
- sufficient national and international support;
- fear of further escalation felt by the adversary;
- clarity over the conditions by which the crisis will be terminated.

The theories of Schelling and George are predominantly directed at the latent use of power instruments. Pape's theory concerns the actual use of power instruments. He proposes that coercion is effective if it is directed at the benefit side of the tradeoff between costs and benefits that every opponent makes. The costs of complying with the demands of the intervener must be lower than the costs of resisting. Pape states that this is possible by denying the opponent military success and simultaneously envisaging a reward if the opponent complies with the demands.

The value of the studies discussed above is that they serve as a starting point for further research: an instrument of coercion demands the setting of a deadline (Schelling) and the envisaging of a reward to comply with the demands (George), by which costs of compliance become less than the costs of resistance (Pape). Finally, the authors offer conclusions by studying cases that often lead to the identification of conditions for successful interventions.[7]

Nevertheless, the works of these authors are only applicable on a limited scale for the continued formulation of theories. There are three reasons for this. First, their theories are incomplete. Schelling and George are primarily

5 George and Simon, *Coercive Diplomacy*, p.7.

6 George and Simon, *Coercive Diplomacy*, pp. 279 -287.

7 Pape, *Bombing to Win*, pp. 314 -331; Haas, *Intervention*, 67 -100; Freedman, *Strategic Coercion*, p. 72.

focused on the threat of force, whereas Pape is concerned with its actual application, but limits himself to *air power.* In all theories, the economic power instrument plays a subordinate role. But economic and military power instruments must be seen as complementary. What may begin as a symbolic imposition of economic sanctions may end in a large-scale military conflict, if the intervener wishes to alter the target's behavior at all costs.

Secondly, the theories are directed at affecting changes in the behavior of *states* during the Cold War. The theoretical insights of the authors mentioned are largely based on cases such as Korea, Vietnam, and Libya. Nevertheless, Pape, as well as George in the most recent edition of his work, have studied the case of Iraq 1991. Yet the theory should not be merely focused on states, but on actors in general. The theory should also apply to the warlord in Sierra Leone who attempts to obtain control over a diamond mine, or terrorist organizations, like al-Qaeda, with strategic objectives. Nevertheless, these non-state actors pose significant problems. Usually, they cannot be targeted with sanctions. They can only be countered physically, with measures directed against their financial infrastructure and by removing the root causes of their grievances. Coercion is important to force states to end support to, or refrain from supporting, these non-state actors. From the end of the 1990s onwards, it has been attempted, amongst other things through Security Council resolutions, to break the support of the Afghan Taliban regime for Osama bin Laden. The Taliban regime presented a very special case because there were diplomatic ties with some countries around the world. As has been argued before, one way of dealing with such a regime is through *second-order coercion*, that is, by coercing another regime that maintains diplomatic ties with a rogue state.

Third, their definitions of coercion have a narrow focus. Most studies do not make a distinction between military coercion and coercive diplomacy. In addition, the concepts of the threat to use force or the limited use of force are of little value. To be effective, coercive diplomacy implies the willingness to apply force massively and overwhelmingly, that is, to carry out a strategy of military coercion if diplomacy fails.

Decision making

A theoretical understanding of coercion is necessary, but does not imply that this understanding will or can actually be used during the decision-making process. George formulated his conditions explicitly to accommodate policymakers. In the case that a policymaker wishes to include these conditions in his considerations, there must be a significant level of rationality in the decision-making process. However, decision-making processes usually do not appear rational. Moreover, as Hein Goemans argued, "leaders in a crisis do *not* choose between a negotiated settlement now and a 'costly lottery' as war is almost always modeled. Instead, leaders in a crisis choose between a negotiated settlement now and a negotiated settlement later."[8] Rational decision making implies firstly that the political objective for the initiation of military force must be determined. Secondly, alternative options for how the initiation can contribute to achieving these objectives must be formulated. Thirdly, a choice must be made from these options. Finally, there should be understanding about the definition of success, which is measured by the extent to which political objectives are obtained. These objectives include enunciations concerning the desired behavior of the opponent. A realistic line of thought is required while formulating these objectives. If, for the achievement of the objectives, insufficient means are available, *coercion* is doomed to fail. In this sense, there is nothing new. A balance between political objectives and employable means is a precondition for success.

In practice, this format of rational decision making hardly ever takes place. That this is a well-known and acknowledged problem is apparent from the report on peace operations that was written for the Secretary General of the United Nations in 2000. A committee presided over by the former Algerian minister of Foreign Affairs, Lakhdar Brahimi, stated that prior to the dispatching of troops, an analysis of the security situation must be made to facilitate the formulation of a clear mandate with unambiguous political objectives.[9] This would provide the basis from which the necessary military units could be determined. If the desired number of troops cannot be attained, then the entire operation should not proceed, according to Brahimi's recommendations. Practice proved to show the opposite. First a decision to participate is taken, and then the voluntary contribution of each individual country is examined, finally the operation will continue, whether or not the desired size of the military is attained. In fact, this practice often leads to great operational risks.

The cause lies in the decision-making process. Policymakers appear to be preoccupied, uncertain of their ability to judge, are hastened by time pressure, are directed by different, often conflicting motives, and are influenced

8 H.E. Goemans, *War and Punishment: the Causes of War Termination and the First World War* (Princeton and Oxford: Princeton University Press, 2000), p. 319.

9 United Nations, *Report of the Panel on United Nations Peace Operations,* August 2000.

by their background and the processes that take place within the group and its followers. In addition, the nature of the challenges that are part of the initiation of military force are so dynamic, complex, and uncertain that it is difficult, sometimes even impossible, to offer succinct answers to important questions. All this demands such a large degree of knowledge from the policymaker that it is worth asking whether he is actually capable of arriving at the best decision. Indeed, although they are responsible for the execution of coercive strategies, political decision makers usually have little knowledge about the use of the instruments of power. Among decision makers, thinking in terms of deterrence is still dominant and most of them are not interested in, or could not find the time to read, new concepts of coercion. Moreover, most civil servants in departments of defense and foreign affairs are often too preoccupied with everyday issues. Finally, the military is usually hampered by conceptual conservatism. It takes years before new concepts are wholeheartedly embraced.

Only in very rare cases is a president or prime minister supported by a staff of experts. President George W. Bush's first administration is a good example. Vice President Dick Cheney, Defense Secretary Donald Rumsfeld, Foreign Secretary Colin Powell, and the National Security Advisor Condoleezza Rice all had considerable experience with foreign policy and defense matters. But even then,things would go wrong. With astonishing speed, the US removed both the Afghan and Iraqi regimes from power, but had great difficulties in winning the peace during the stabilization phase. It was thought that the Afghans and Iraqis would welcome the US-led coalition as liberators because they were longing, according to Rumsfeld, for peace and democracy. It was not lack of knowledge about military affairs that caused the problems; rather, it was an over-optimistic view based on ideology and a profound lack of understanding of cultural differences. Many followers of the old regimes and religious hardliners considered the coalition an occupying force which was to be expelled from the country. They did not long for freedom and democracy on America's terms.

In practice, the average policymaker will attempt to answer several questions, such as:

- What is the objective of the initiation of military force?
- What is an approximation of the costs and benefits of achieving the objective?
- What is the probability that the objective will be achieved?

Answering these questions is an incremental process, in which opinions can often shift. The outcome of the deliberations is not necessarily the best decision, but a decision that is acceptable in terms of risks. The acceptability of risks, however, is a subjective judgment. Moreover, decision making during a crisis is hampered by stress. This could further undermine the quality of the decisions.

The Israeli scholar Yaacov Vertzberger noted that, in all circumstances, policymakers are led by their personal convictions, based on perceptions, feelings, and beliefs.[10] Ideology, which includes values, plays an important role. Besides, a loss of reputation and credibility can be important motivational factors for decision makers. Looking at it from another viewpoint, these can also be the by-product of an intervention. After all, if the intervention is not executed successfully, the reputation and credibility of the intervener will become questionable and he will see this as an incitement to continue on the same footing. As such, President Bush's intervention in Panama in 1989 was predominantly the result of his desire to show to the American people that he was not a weakling. This example illustrates that the willingness to take risks is closely connected to the personal characteristics of the policymaker. In general, the traits of risk takers are: persistent, self-confident, opportunist, aggressive, able to manipulate, and result-oriented.

The environment in which the policymaker operates can influence someone's willingness to take risks. Policymakers who have spent most of their lives in a bureaucratic environment, like a ministry or a military staff, will be more hesitant.

Others, like President Bush Sr., who was known to be risk averse, can be forced by their new position to alter their style; however, there is no noticeable qualitative difference in decision making between those who take risks and those who avoid them.[11]

There is an undeniable relationship between the interests at stake and the willingness to take risks. The aim of Operation Desert Storm was to expel Iraq from Kuwait. American access to the oil-rich Gulf region was threatened. From the fact that American estimates took 20,000 wounded and 7,000 killed into account, it is apparent that Washington was willing to pay a high price. On the eve of the ground war, President Bush was told to expect some 5,000 casualties.[12] This was different from the humanitarian

10 Y.Y.I. Vertzberger, *Risk Taking and Decision Making: Foreign Military Intervention Decisions* (Stanford: Stanford University Press, 1998), chapter 8.

11 Vertzberger, *Risk Taking and Decision Making*, p. 77.

12 "The Secret History of the War", *Newsweek*, March 18, 1991, p. 25.

intervention in Somalia, where American participation ended after only 18 American soldiers were killed. Policymakers are willing to take great risks if the vital interests of the state are at stake. If vital interests are violated, the state is directly threatened. Some examples of this are: physical military or terrorist threats; threats to economic stability because, for instance, access to essential natural resources or trade routes is hindered; or threats to the political and social stability of a state through, for example, subversive activities, or a stream of large numbers of refugees.

Vertzberger concludes that if policymakers estimate the risks to be low or average, but vitally important interests are at stake, they will in general be willing to allocate a massive and decisive military force to achieve their political objectives. These interventions are generally successful. Operations Enduring Freedom and Iraqi Freedom serve as examples. If the risks are estimated to be high and thus the price to pay is high, and there are no vital interests at stake, usually the choice will be to slowly increase pressure. But if pressure is increased slowly and the intervention turns into a longer-term process, chances of success are much smaller, since the opponent can take the initiative. Initiative is therefore also a critical success factor for measures of coercion.[13]

Patrick Regan has demonstrated that there is a direct relationship between the intensity of a conflict, the accompanying risks to the intervener, and the willingness to intervene: the more intense the conflict, the smaller the chances are of an intervention. However, one must include that if vital interests are at stake, a state will be more easily prepared to act with risk. Yet, vital interests are only rarely at stake. In addition, Regan noticed a paradox: policymakers generally do not want to intervene if the conditions for an intervention are bad; yet, on the other hand, they have little *ex ante* knowledge to determine whether the intervention will be successful. In short, if the "feeling" is not right, there will not be an intervention.[14]

However, as has been argued before, success in consecutive wars could make decision makers more war-minded. Victories seem to enhance the winning state's physical capabilities and create optimism about war. Successive victories could bring to power hawkish politicians associated with success in wars.

13 Vertzberger, *Risk Taking and Decision making*, p. 394

14 P.M. Regan, *Civil Wars and Foreign Powers* (Michigan: University of Michigan Press, 2002), p. 140.

Vertzberger notes on the basis of a number of cases that policymakers develop different techniques to reduce the complexity of the question at hand and to increase the clarity of the solutions:

- Available information is consciously or unconsciously excluded from the decision-making process.
- Simplified historical analogies are applied (what worked then, will also work now).
- Standardized techniques and schedules are used to ascertain the truth.

Standardized techniques structure the decision-making process and could thus result in more rational decision making. The "just war" doctrine can be seen as the oldest "standardized technique." For a war to be just, it must meet several criteria:

- War can only be waged as a last resort, with all nonviolent options exhausted.
- The violence must be proportionate to the injury suffered.
- The weapons used must discriminate between combatants and non-combatants.
- The peace following the war must be a clear improvement over what currently exists.
- The interveners must have legitimate authority sanctioned by the society they represent. In practice, this will be the UN.

Former US President Jimmy Carter argued on the eve of Operation Iraqi Freedom that war against Iraq did not meet these criteria.[15]

Usually, standardized techniques involve a mixture of moral justifications and criteria related to military effectiveness. An example of such a standardized technique is the Weinberger-Powell doctrine. In 1984, US Secretary of Defense Caspar Weinberger and the Chairman of the Joint Chiefs of Staff General Colin Powell argued that the tenets of force employment are:

- the existence of specific national interests;
- the objective to win;
- clear political and military objectives;
- an exit strategy;
- overwhelming the enemy with superior firepower;
- the support of the American people and the Congress.

15 J. Carter, *Just War – or a Just War?* March 9, 2003.

While the Weinberger-Powell doctrine focused on war fighting, President Clinton's *1994 Presidential Decision Directive (PDD) 25* focused on peace operations. The document mentioned the following criteria:
- UN involvement advances US interests.
- There is a threat to or a breach of international peace and security.
- There are clear objectives.
- The means to accomplish the mission are available.
- The political, economic, and humanitarian consequences of inaction have been weighed and are considered unacceptable.
- The operation's anticipated duration is tied to clear objectives and realistic criteria for ending the operation.

There is a striking resemblance between this approach and the determinants of success mentioned by George. A significant problem is that, in practice, policymakers only rarely make integral use of these criteria. Moreover, risks appear to be characterized as "sensible" if participation is considered highly desired. Political and military aims will then become more attainable. Finally, as will be seen, strategy is the most important factor contributing to the success. Formulating strategy is a creative process, which cannot be guided by standardized techniques and schedules.

Nevertheless, many policymakers expect that the quality of decision making remains guaranteed and success automatically follows if all conditions are met. This conclusion is erroneous. These factors are the wrong point of departure for decision making. They are useful to give more content to the decision-making process when there is understanding concerning the strategic effectiveness of power instruments in a given situation.

The instruments of coercion

Decision makers should not have an exaggerated view of what can be achieved with the instruments of power. In his ground-breaking study, Patrick Regan found that only 30% of all interventions were considered successful.[16] Strictly military interventions which accounted for 70% of all interventions were the most common. Economic interventions accounted for 7%, while mixed interventions accounted for 23%. The study concluded that a mixed strategy has been the most successful (35%); strictly military

16 P.M. Regan, "Conditions of Successful Third-Party Intervention in Intrastate Conflicts", *Journal of Conflict Resolution*, vol. 40, no. 2, 1996, p. 345.

interventions have succeeded about 30% of the time; and purely economic interventions have succeeded 23% of the time.

There are three different coercive instruments: political measures, economic sanctions, and military force. The EU emphasizes political and economic action, while the United States, usually supported by a small number of allies, tends to military action.

The political instrument

Political isolation is the most commonly used form of coercion. It involves forms of political protest such as diplomatic *demarches,* the withdrawal of ambassadors, denial of visas to officials, UN resolutions, and cultural and travel boycotts. Due to political isolation, a regime could become a pariah. As this is not an attractive prospect, it is hoped that the regime will revise its course. In practice, political isolation is a low-cost, declaratory tool that is not very effective. First, if not backed up by pressure, it means little for a regime that does not have the goodwill of the international community as a foreign policy goal. Second, political isolation is likely to strengthen rather than weaken the regime. Some regimes have used international outrage to gain the support of the population for their policies. This was done by the Iranian revolutionary leadership, Slobodan Milosevic, Saddam Hussein, and the North Korean Kim dynasty. They all pointed to an outside threat to gain the support of the population. In summary, political isolation alone is unlikely to be effective if not backed up by the threat of economic or military force.

The economic instrument

Economic sanctions were first used by the ancient Greeks. In response to the kidnapping of three Aspasian women, Pericles enforced a decree in 432 BC, banning the Megarians from the market. Sanctions are certainly attractive, because they could be more humane than using military force. Economic sanctions are politically less risky than military interventions.

From ancient Greece through to the 19th century, sanctions went hand in hand with war. It was only after the First World War that attention was given to the notion that economic sanctions might be a substitute for war. But even between the two world wars, sanctions were usually linked to military action. Sanctions were imposed to complement the war effort or to disrupt a military campaign. In the period following the Second World War, sanctions were imposed to prevent target countries from exercising military power. For example, during the years immediately following the Second World War, the United States tried to coerce colonial powers such as the Netherlands, France and the United Kingdom to abandon their former colonies in a peaceful way. Since the 1960s, sanctions have been imposed to strengthen efforts to protect human rights and to halt nuclear proliferation. The Carter administration was the first to frequently impose sanctions to protect human rights in Latin America and elsewhere. Since the 1970s, the United States and Canada have tried to coerce India and Pakistan not to develop nuclear weapons. Ultimately, they failed, because in May 1998 both countries carried out a series of nuclear tests. Sanctions were also imposed to combat international terrorism. The best-known case is Libya, where sanctions have covered all trade and finance since the mid-1980s until 2004.

From the mid-1990s, sanctions have also been imposed on parties to a conflict, rather than on a state. Sanctions were also applied to non-state actors. The first such case concerned sanctions imposed on UNITA, a rebel group in Angola. Sanctions were also imposed on rebel groups in Sierra Leone and Liberia.

It should be kept in mind that only rich countries can use the economic instrument of power. Usually only liberal democracies use sanctions. In very rare cases, non-Western countries tried to use the sanction instrument. In 1974, the members of OPEC, mostly Arabic states, issued an oil boycott to coerce the Netherlands into giving up its pro-Israel policies.

The measures chosen can be economic (e.g., the prohibition to buy or sell certain goods) or financial (e.g., blocking bank accounts). States may use two broad categories of economic pressure: trade restrictions and financial restrictions. Trade sanctions affect the target country in terms of lost exports, lost markets, denial of crucial imports, lower prices received from embargoed import, and higher prices paid for substitute imports. In extreme cases, trade may be suspended completely and financial flows may be blocked. In practice, economic weapons will be used in a selective way to:

- indicate that the behavior of an actor is not to be tolerated;
- deter future behavior of the actor;
- act as a surrogate for military measures.[17]

Thus, sanctions may persuade a government that the issues at stake are not worth the price, or may result in popular pressure to force the government to concede. The hope is that sanctions will result in a popular revolt,

17 H.C. Hufbauer, J.J. Scott and K.A. Elliot, *Economic Sanctions Reconsidered* (Washington, D.C.: Institute for International Economics, 1990), p. 36.

overthrowing the government, resulting in a new government that will make the concessions. The most important measure of the intensity of sanctions is the loss of gross national product (GNP).

Sanctions are primarily intended to affect the prosperity and well-being of the state against which they are directed. This pressure is expected to influence the target's behavior, for instance by undermining its power structure. Therefore, sanctions can be targeted to:

- incur damage to the military potential of the target (oil and weapons embargoes);
- end undesired behavior against the target's population or other states;
- undermine the government.

If sanctions could be as effective as military force, then policymakers would obviously choose the instrument of economic sanctions. However, measuring the success of a sanction is difficult. One of the most important criteria is that the target state concedes to a significant part of the coercer's demands.

During the 1960s and 1970s, scholars became increasingly pessimistic about the usefulness of economic sanctions. However, over the past decade, both scholars and policymakers have become more optimistic. In the mid-1980s, they began to argue that sanctions have been underrated by policymakers because too much attention had been given to a relatively limited number of failures. Indeed, neither many years of economic sanctions nor a military intervention could end the Communist regime of Cuba's Fidel Castro. Iraq has been subjected to one of the most extreme sanctions in history, but Saddam Hussein remained in power until he was removed by military force.

Gary Hufbauer, Jeffrey Schott, and Kimberly Ann Elliot studied 115 cases from 1914 to 1990 (the "HSE study").[18] They found that in 40 cases, or 34%, sanctions were successful; a higher figure than the 23% mentioned earlier. These empirical data suggest that the effectiveness of economic sanctions is limited. Sanctions fail because there is a weak relation between economic deterioration and the willingness to incur behavioral change. There are several explanations for this:

- A state always has alternatives, like smuggling, and coalitions with like-minded states, to minimize or even nullify the effects of the sanctions.
- Sanctions form an external threat. Sanctions provide the target state with an opportunity to unite the population against the outside threat. This could even strengthen an extremely unattractive regime.

18 Hufbauer, Schott and Elliot, *Economic Sanctions Reconsidered.*

- Multilateral sanctions are difficult to execute, since countries often hold different opinions on their execution. Sanctions can even lead to the situation where countries become compassionate to the sanctioned state and aid it in order to nullify the sanctions.
- Sanctions can lead to high costs for the sanctioner. Target states are often able to shift the economic burden of sanctions onto the sender. Trade interests can be damaged, companies can pressure the government to alleviate or postpone the sanctions, or circumvent sanctions through sister companies.

Sanctions usually have little effect on the GNP. Some sanctions had no effect at all, most had limited effects: less than 1%. Iraq is one of the few cases where sanctions resulted in a dramatic decrease of the GNP. Nevertheless, it appears that the sanctions have strengthened, rather than weakened, Saddam Hussein's position.[19] Another case is the sanctions the United States and the United Kingdom issued against Iran in 1951 when Iran's Prime Minister Mohammed Massadegh nationalized the Anglo-Iranian Oil Company and ousted Shah Mohammad Reza Pahlavi from power. The Western powers boycotted the purchase of Iranian oil and demanded a fifty-fifty% profit-sharing deal on oil and the return from exile of the Shah. Economic sanctions resulted in a more than 14% decrease of the Iranian GNP. Equally, US and British sanctions against Rhodesia in 1965 resulted in a loss of more than 13% GNP. Sanctions were established after Rhodesia's Prime Minister Ian Smith declared his country independent from the British Commonwealth.

In general, if the targeted leaders can fuel (latent) nationalism, ethnicity or fundamentalism, they can easily organize resistance against the source of external pressure. Thus, even weak or badly organized states are able to counter the pressure. Consequently, sanctions can even be counterproductive. To impose sanctions is often seen politically to be a low-cost option to which no great political risks are attached. They seem a humane alternative to the use of military force. Yet the Iraq experience demonstrates that appearances can be deceptive. Indeed, policymakers often have a false image of the possible effects of sanctions. The thought at the root of the sanction instrument is that populations hold their leaders responsible for the misery caused by the sanctions. This will then result in pressure on the leaders, who will have to revise their behavior. Sanctions may lead to popular revolts, which forces leaders to clear the political arena. The sanctions against the

19 *The Economist*, "Making Monkeys of the UN", July 10, 1993, p. 34.

Federal Republic of Yugoslavia during the greater part of the 1990s, did not contribute to the departure of Slobodan Milosevic, who was held responsible by the international community for the instability in the Balkans and the suffering brought upon the population.

A serious weakness of the sanction instrument is that sanctions tend to have a too limited effect to realize ambitious political objectives. According to the HSE study, sanctions can only be successful if:
- allies are pressured;
- costs for the sanctioned (the receiver) are high;
- costs for the sanctioner (the sender) are low;
- the objectives and sanctions are proportionately related.

Nevertheless, critics have argued that the HSE study is seriously flawed. Robert Pape considered only five of the 115 cases as being clearly successful.[20] Closer examination of the 40 success stories revealed that practically none could stand up to examination. Pape argued that in eighteen cases the dispute was determined by force, in eight cases the target state never conceded to the demands, six cases were trade disputes as opposed to economic sanctions, and three cases were indeterminate. Of the five cases that were successful, three were over trivial issues. In 1933, the Soviet Union agreed to release six prisoners; in 1979 Canada agreed not to move its embassy from Tel Aviv to Jerusalem; and in 1987 El Salvador agreed not to release three prisoners convicted of murdering US citizens. The most successful was India's coercion of Nepal in 1989-1990. Thirteen months after India partially closed its border with Nepal in retaliation for Nepal's purchase of anti-aircraft guns from China, King Birenda surrendered power to a pro-democratic government that agreed to consult India on defense matters. The other success was the cancellation of a reprocessing plant by North Korea in 1975.

Pape argued that the key reasons that sanctions fail are related to the nature of the target state: "Nationalism often makes states and societies willing to endure considerable punishment rather than abandon their national interests. States often accept high costs, including civilian suffering, to achieve their objectives. Democratization further imbues individual

20 R.A. Pape, "Why Economic Sanctions Do Not Work", *International Security,* Autumn 1997, vol. 22, no. 2, pp. 90-136. Also: K.A. Elliott, "The Sanctions Glass: Half Full or Completely Empty", *International Security,* Summer 1998, vol. 23, no. 1, pp. 50-65; R.A. Pape, "Why Economic Sanctions *Still* Do Not Work", *International Security,* Summer 1998, vol. 23, no. 1, pp. 66-77.

citizens with a personal attachment to national goals. Even in the weakest and most fractured states, external pressure is more likely to enhance the nationalist's legitimacy of rulers than to undermine it. In some situations advances in communication further improve the ability of governments to enhance the legitimacy of the state and its policies. Even much more severe punishment than economic sanction can possibly inflict rarely coerces."[21] Regarding the latter, Pape referred to the limited success of strategic bombing campaigns that damaged the economies of North Korea, North Vietnam, and Iraq without their populations rising up against their regimes.

The recognition that sanctions are mostly ineffective, but increase the suffering of the population, has led to a debate about *smart sanctions,* which do not target the population, but rather the leaders personally. Smart sanctions are directed at, for instance, the freezing of foreign financial assets, the denial of loans and credit, and travel restrictions. Even with these sanctions, success is expected to be limited, since actors that possess large sums of money can find a way to bring their assets into safety, and there are always countries that are sympathetic to an actor who has been targeted by smart sanctions.

Zimbabwe serves as an example. In an attempt to get reelected, President Robert Mugabe promised the poor black farmers that he would take land from the white farmers for redistribution. Mugabe not only decided to take the land by force, but to expel the white farmers as well. In an attempt to stop the atrocities, in 2001 the EU applied smart sanctions, denying the regime access to its European bank accounts; travel restrictions were also imposed. The result was a further isolation of the regime, but the effect could not be measured; however, after his reelection, Mugabe did soften his tone.

Another example is Libya. During the Arab uprisings, which started in December 2010, the UN Security Council resolution froze Libyan assets. More than $100 billion, including Gadhafi family assets, were captured. It is unclear to what extent this damaged Gadhafi's ability to wage war. In the case of Syria, smart sanctions were imposed by an international coalition of more than 60 countries spearheaded by Arab states and known as the Friends of the Syrian People International Working Group on Sanctions. The group reflected consensus among more than 60 countries who imposed sanctions without approval of the UN Security Council because of a possible Russian veto. In November 2011, the Arab League imposed its

21 Pape, "Why sanctions do not work", p. 107.

own set of sanctions.[22] The sanctions sapped $4bn of oil revenues from the economy and caused fuel shortages and power blackouts. Although inflation increased more than 50%, the Syrian pound dropped more than 30%, and the GDP contracted significantly, sanctions did not affect the regime's ability to fight.

Smart sanctions could also be directed at non-state actors such as warlords with their militias and terrorist movements. For example, following the events of 9/11, a global campaign to block al-Qaeda's access to money was started. In the months that followed, more than $112 million in "rogue capital" was frozen. It turned out, however, that before September 11, al-Qaeda had already removed its money from the banks and invested it in commodities such as diamonds and gold that were transferred to failed states like Somalia.

In conclusion, empirical data suggest that the effectiveness of economic sanctions is limited. Consequently, economic sanctions cannot be a credible alternative for military force and can only be used when vital interests of the sender are not at stake.

Military power

Successful coercion could require the application of military force. Statistically, however, as has been argued, military interventions are only marginally more successful than sanctions. The reason for this is a lack of political will to use military power in a decisive manner, which can be explained by risk avoidance and lack of understanding of how military power can best be used. The successful application of military force requires recognition of the connection between interests at stake and the level of force used, and a knowledge of some of the basic principles of military doctrine, which will be discussed in part two of this book.

Because of its characteristics, air power appears to be the prime instrument of coercion. Air power is used against strategic targets to decapitate the adversary or against tactical, mobile targets to deny the opponent the use of its armed forces. Being a low-risk and low-cost option, a coercer might even try to coerce the adversary by air power alone. Air power is delivered by aircraft dropping free-fall bombs or firing stand-off weapons and armed drones. Land attack missiles fired from navy vessels and aircraft launched

22 *International New York Times*, "Isolating Syria, Arab League Imposes Broad Sanctions", November 27, 2011.

from carriers play an increasingly important role in the delivering of air power. The same holds true for land-based missiles fired by ground forces. In other words, air power is no longer the exclusive domain of air forces. For the Obama Administration, Unmanned Aerial Vehicles (UAV) or drones of the Central Intelligence Agency (CIA) and Special Operations Forces (SOF) became the weapons of choice. The President used armed drones and SOF against the training camps and the hiding places of terrorists mainly in Pakistan and Yemen. During his first term in office, the President authorized six times more than the number of attacks authorized by his predecessor's eight years in office. CNN reported that, "Under Bush, al-Qaeda members accounted for 25% of all drone targets compared to 40% for Taliban targets. Under Obama, only 8% of targets were al-Qaeda, compared to just over 50% for Taliban targets."[23] According to the New America Foundation, there were 420 strikes between 2004 and February 2013. Of these, only 49 occurred under President Bush.[24] These strikes killed between 2,424 and 3,967 people; between 395 and 562 of these deaths occurred under President Bush. Between 1,967 and 3,236 militants were killed, and there were between 276 and 368 civilian fatalities. During a speech at the National Defense University, the President defended the use of armed drones, arguing that the strikes are legal because the US was attacked on September 11, 2001. But, he argued, "America's legitimate claim of self-defense cannot be the end of the discussion. To say a military tactic is legal, or even effective, is not to say it is wise or moral in every instance. (...) And that's why, over the last four years, my administration has worked vigorously to establish a framework that governs our use of force against terrorists – insisting upon clear guidelines, oversight, and accountability that is now codified in Presidential Policy Guidance."[25]

Due to its long range, air power is relatively invulnerable, especially if stand-off weapons, which are capable of hitting targets at long distances are used. In addition, air power is extremely accurate and there are a whole set of systems, from fixed-wing aircraft and helicopters to missiles. Most likely, political objectives could only be achieved by joint naval, air, and land operations. How this is done, is analyzed in depth in the second part of this book.

23 Peter Bergen, "Drone is Obama's weapon of choice", http://edition.cnn.com/2012/09/05/opinion/bergen-obama-drone/

24 http://natsec.newamerica.net/drones/pakistan/analysis

25 http://www.whitehouse.gov/the-press-office/2013/05/23/remarks-president-national-defense-university (May 23, 2013).

If territory must be physically occupied, ground forces will be employed. Air power is indispensable to facilitate effective dispatching of regular land forces facing acceptable risks and to support them during the operation. In this way, Operation Desert Storm was preceded by an ongoing air offensive, after which the ground forces finished the job in 100 hours.

In most cases, ground forces will first have to establish a bridgehead and give priority to self-defense. Subsequently, step-by-step control over an area will be gained. Finally, the area must be searched for remaining combatants. This concept is applied both for conventional and unconventional warfare. Only the scale and the tactics will differ.

Nevertheless, conventional warfare operations involving regular units are to the advantage of technologically advanced and well-trained Western forces. Due to their superiority, Western powers have escalation dominance, or the ability to increase the threatened costs to the adversary while denying the adversary the opportunity to negate those costs or to counterescalate.[26] Western forces are less well trained to fight unconventional wars against irregular units, such as guerillas and terrorists. These fighters are hard to hit, especially with air power. For example, the Israeli government frequently used fighter aircraft and armed helicopters during the intifada to confront Palestinian organizations and their leaders in urbanized areas with limited success.

As will be argued in chapter 6, the development of "smart" precision weapons, advanced computerized systems for command, communication, and information gathering, and networks of sensors, increases the potential of Western military forces to fight and win against both regular and irregular forces. New technologies and doctrines should make it possible to deploy military forces decisively, under all conditions and against acceptable risks and costs, anywhere in the world. This constitutes a paradigm shift in the way wars are conducted. Until the end of the 1980s, it was expected that the costs, risks, and problems that are related to the deployment of military force would continuously increase, while the benefits would only decrease.[27] The assumption was that, through this development, military force had become a useless option in international relations. This assumption is no

26 D. Byman and M. Waxman, *The Dynamics of Coercion: American Foreign Policy and the Limits of Military Might* (Cambridge: Cambridge University Press, 2002), p. 38.

27 For example: K. Knorr, *The Power of Nations* (New York: Basic Books, 1975); J. Mueller, *Retreat from Doomsday: The Obsolescence of Major War* (New York: Basic Books, 1989); R. Ullman, *Securing Europe* (Princeton: Princeton University Press, 1991); R. Rosecrance, *The Rise of the Trading State: Commerce and Conquest in the Modern World* (New York: Basic Books, 1986); F. Fukuyama, *The End of History and the Last Man* (New York: Avon, 1992).

longer valid. During the 1990s and the early 21st century, interventions were carried out within a short time-frame and with astonishingly low levels of friendly losses and acceptable levels of collateral damage.

The dynamics of coercion

The efficacy, along with the justification, of an intervention demands a strategy based on a dynamic approach. This will determine the method in which power instruments are employed to achieve political objectives. The effective use of force requires a strategy. Strategy is defined as the link between political objectives and the military means available. The formulation of a strategy therefore starts with defining political objectives. Alexander George and William Simons have concluded that "clarity and consistency in what is demanded help persuade the adversary of the coercing power's strength of purpose."[28]

Clear political objectives are a prerequisite to define military objectives. If political and military objectives have been achieved, victory has been achieved. Unclear political objectives make it impossible to declare victory, but politicians usually desire some flexibility. To avoid the definition of success in absolute, almost binary terms, they are likely to define political objectives in rather vague terms. Especially if vital interests are not at stake, it could be tempting to declare success if, for whatever reasons, the intervention must stop.

On March 24, 1999, at the start of Operation Allied Force, numerous objectives were formulated by different political leaders. NATO Secretary General Javier Solana mentioned three clear objectives: to end the human tragedy; Milosevic's acceptance of the Rambouillet peace agreement; and to end the instability in the Balkans. President Clinton mentioned three unclear objectives: to demonstrate NATO's desire for peace; to deter further violence; and to degrade Serbia's military capabilities. Clinton's objectives formed a weak basis for operational planning. For example, the actual meaning of "to degrade Serbia's military capabilities" is unclear. If one or two Serbian tanks were destroyed, Serb forces would be "degraded," but the effects on the battlefield situation would be minimal.

Nevertheless, the military objectives as defined by NATO's Supreme Allied Commander Wesley Clark and the Chairman of the Joint Chiefs of Staff Hugh Shelton were clear: to create favorable conditions for the actual

28 George and Simons, *Coercive Diplomacy*, p. 280.

air campaign by destroying the enemy's air defenses; to isolate Serbian forces outside the Kosovo theater of operations; and to attack forces in the Kosovo theater of operations. So, despite an unclear political framework, the military was able to define clear operational objectives.

In some cases, objectives change during the conflict. In March 2011, UN Resolution 1973 authorized a no-fly zone to stop the Gadhafi regime's attacks from the air, and further authorized all necessary measures to protect the Libyan people. In a speech on March 28, 2011, President Obama stated that "our military mission is narrowly focused on saving lives."[29] Initially coalition partners denied that regime change was the objective of the intervention. But in April, the Obama Administration, together with the heads of state and government of France and Great Britain, published an open letter printed simultaneously in the *Washington Post*, the *Times* of London, and *Le Figaro,* openly acknowledging that the purpose of the intervention was regime change, and that they would be committing an "unconscionable betrayal" if the Libyan leader were left in government.[30]

The employment of military means will be misguided and doomed to fail without the use of strategy. Yet one must note that in the decision-making process, the appropriate strategy is only rarely adhered to. Richard Betts suggested that policymakers are not capable of strategic considerations because of political, psychological, and organizational reasons and therefore interventions are doomed to fail.[31] Colin Gray argued that because of the complexity of the subject at large, the "strategist" is required to possess a number of intellectual capabilities that are rarely found in one individual.[32] Regan's findings, which concluded that the strategy of the intervener is the single most important factor of success, have demonstrated that the quality of strategic thought is a serious problem.[33] The lack of an adequate strategy can additionally explain why the percentage of successful interventions is so low.

In addition, the strategy should take into account that the intervention passes through different phases. For example, Operation Enduring Freedom succeeded in removing the Taliban from power and stopped al-Qaeda from

29 "Remarks by the President in Address to the Nation on Libya", National Defense University, Washington, D.C., March 28, 2011.

30 Libya letter of April 15, 2011: http://www.bbc.co.uk/news/world-africa-13090646.

31 R. Betts, "Is Strategy an Illusion?" *International Security,* vol. 25, no. 2, 2000, pp. 5-50.

32 C.S. Gray, *Modern Strategy* (Oxford: Oxford University Press, 1999), pp. 49-54.

33 Regan, *Civil Wars and Foreign Powers,* p. 141.

using the entire country as a sanctuary. This first phase of military coercion clearly was a victory for the United States and its allies. Following regime change, during the stabilization phase, the initial success of the coercive efforts was jeopardized. The lesson learned is that without a proper exit strategy or a comprehensive concept for dealing with the subsequent stabilization phase, the coercer could get caught up in an ongoing conflict.

Formulating a strategy is very demanding of the cognitive qualities of policymakers. It demands great imagination and the willingness not to overlook any scenario. Creativity and a flexible mind are essential. Strategy is not an exact science. It is not the miracle about which the great Chinese strategic thinker Sun Tzu wrote in a book on the art of war more than two thousand years ago. Fiascoes predominantly occur when policymakers do not have the willingness or the intellect to take all possible future situations into account and to put themselves into the mind of the opponent. This usually happens because they are prisoners of traditional thinking. One of the biggest problems has been that, since the end of the Second World War, Western powers have been prepared for conventional war against regular forces, while present tasks primarily need to be executed in areas where irregular forces are using unconventional methods such as guerilla warfare and terrorism. This explains, in part, failures in former Yugoslavia, the withdrawal from Somalia, and the disillusionment among policymakers with the stabilization phases in Afghanistan and Iraq following Operation Enduring Freedom and Operation Iraqi freedom.

A different problem is the result of self-imposed limitations or caveats, such as the refusal to accept undesired collateral damage, which may lead to the insufficient employment of military force and could jeopardize the entire strategy. This was the case during Operation Allied Force in 1999. NATO chose to slowly increase pressure on Kosovo. Targets in or close to populated areas were avoided, enabling Milosevic to increase the intensity of his terror campaign against the Albanian population in Kosovo, in order to obstruct the alliance to end the humanitarian tragedy which justified the intervention.

Caveats had a detrimental effect on commanders's planning and flexibility during ISAF. Caveats included the refusal to conduct night-time combat, refusal to transport Afghan personnel via helicopter, the refusal to fight after snowfall and the prohibition against allowing trained police forces to be deployed outside their province. Especially German forces were criticized because they were not allowed to leave their armored personnel carriers while on patrol, or their bases at night. In Kunduz, the Dutch were criticized because of the numerous caveats that severely restricted the training of Afghan police forces. One particular point of criticism was the restriction that police forces trained by the Dutch were not allowed to carry out combat operations except for self defense. This was the result of a compromise in Parliament where left-wing politicians rejected Dutch involvement with combat operations.

As noted above, decision making, by definition, is based on subjective considerations. This may lead to the perception that decision making is irrational or leads to great operational risks. Working through focal points or taking success factors into consideration can improve this state of affairs. However, even this does not automatically result in success, because this approach is mechanical and based on the exact sciences.

A bad strategy could result in the prolongation of the conflict or defeat. Long-lasting interventions are accompanied by great political and military risks. If an intervention takes too much time, the credibility and reliability of the policymakers will be reduced and public and political support for further measures will erode. Operational planners at NATO predicted that Operation Allied Force would last five days; in the end it became 78. In this period, support for the air campaign crumbled to such an extent in countries such as Germany and Italy that NATO feared for the collapse of the coalition. The strategy of Operation Allied Force, based on the idea of a phased air campaign with gradual escalation, was simply wrong. It left the initiative to the opponent, allowing the Serbs to kill more Albanians during the war than before. A successful strategy provides a clear link between political objectives and military means.

Two strategies of coercion

To decide on the right strategy, first must be understood from which strategies can be chosen. The difference between *coercive diplomacy* and *military coercion* is the weight and emphasis accorded to diplomacy and military force in efforts to coerce the opponent. Although seemingly trivial, these strategies are entirely distinct, and opting for one entails very different consequences for the actions of the coercer. In coercive diplomacy, economic sanctions and the threat or limited use of military force are used to add weight to diplomatic activities. The military power instrument is used as a deterrent or a punishment; either by threatening its use, or by its limited employment but always by being subordinate to the diplomatic effort. In coercive diplomacy, the military instrument is complemented with other power instruments, and achieving military success is of secondary concern. A strategy of coercive diplomacy is built around a deterrent *threat* to use force, economic *sanctions*, political *isolation,* and *inducements.* If the adversary does not comply, measures to *punish* the opponent with military means should be the next step. If coercive diplomacy fails or has been rendered obsolete, the coercer may have no other choice but to turn to a strategy of military coercion. Here, the instrument of military power is assigned priority, and preference is given to achieving military success, possibly necessitating intensive use thereof. Diplomacy moves to the background, or diplomatic channels are closed altogether. Military coercion is a strategy that uses the armed forces as a stick to exact political objectives. It is an integral component of the dynamic of coercion.

Successful military coercion or coercive diplomacy requires a dynamic approach, based on creativity, flexibility in the methods to achieve the objectives and knowledge of the dynamics of coercion. In addition, an understanding of the power instruments themselves is required. The strategy should take threats, possibilities, perceptions, and improbabilities into account. It must be a reflection of the expected dynamic resulting from the interaction between the actors involved. The balance between costs and benefits for both coercer and opponent determines the dynamic and guides the choice of strategy. The opponent is only willing to change his behavior if the costs of complying with the demands of the coercer are lower than the costs of resistance. This implies that the coercer must not only have an understanding of his own costs and benefits, but also of those of the opponent. Carl von Clausewitz formulated it as follows: "If our opponent is to be made to comply with our will, we must place him in a situation which is more oppressive to him than the sacrifice which we demand."[34]

There must be a clear link between political objectives and means used. Political isolation and sanctions are useful instruments for a strategy of *coercive diplomacy.* When used in isolation, however, sanctions are predominantly used to express a political signal of discord and to demonstrate to the domestic constituency that "something" is being done. For that reason, the objectives that are to be achieved through an exclusive reliance on sanctions should never be ambitious. To be effective, sanctions should be part of a broader strategy in which diplomacy, sanctions, rewards, and military force are complementary and mutually reinforcing. The threat of or use of limited military means may help to enforce sanctions by carrying out an embargo or a blockade. There must, however, be a willingness to escalate, and for the opponent, this must be clear. This requires the coercer to speak with one

34 C. von Clausewitz, *On War* (London: Penguin Books 1968), p. 104.

voice and follow a consistent course and do so persistently. This may require escalation to a strategy of *military coercion*. In that event, diplomacy plays a subordinate role at best; military means should be employed decisively to achieve the political goals. Credible escalation dominance thereby becomes a prerequisite for success.

The choice of coercion strategy informs the way in which the military is used. Several possible applications of military force exist ranging from *punishment* to *decapitation* and from *control* to *attrition*. Their choice determines how the opponent is targeted and is dependent on whether military coercion or coercive diplomacy takes place and the type of opponent the coercer is confronting.

Thirteen of the twenty-eight cases studies listed in the appendix were deemed successful in meeting the declared political objectives. In some cases, including Kosovo (1999) and Libya (2011), politicians declared victory, but this claim cannot be sustained if one measures the outcome of both NATO operations against the objectives set. In both cases, NATO was unable to quickly end humanitarian suffering, while more people were killed during the military operations than in the months preceding the intervention. Some authors measure success differently. James Dobbins and Laurel Miller measured progress in 20 post-conflict nation-building missions conducted by NATO, the UN, and ad hoc coalitions.[35] They used the Freedom House Index, data from the International Monetary Fund, and the UN's Human Development Index. Dobbins and Lauren concluded that sixteen of these societies achieved peace in 2012, and that all but two saw improvements in democratization, but they did not establish a direct link between the data and the interventions. In cases where no intervention took place, such as Rwanda, a similar development happened. In other words, using successful examples of state building as a justification for interventions should be rejected on empirical grounds.

In twelve of the thirteen successful cases listed in the appendix, use was made of military coercion, six of which started out as interventions of coercive diplomacy but later changed to instances of military coercion. Only two cases of coercive diplomacy were successful, Operation *Deliberate Force* in Bosnia and Operation *Uphold Democracy* in Haiti. Regarding the military strategy used, in all cases of successful military coercion (the threat of) the physical *control* of territory with ground forces was instrumental

35 James Dobbins and Laurel Miller, "Overcoming obstacles to peace", *Survival*, February-March 2013, pp. 103-120.

to success. In Operation *Allied Force* no actual use was made of elements of *control*. However, in this case, the threat of physical *control* of territory is widely considered to have contributed to Milosevic's collapse. *Control* as a military strategy seems essential for successful coercion, however, it is not a guarantee. For instance, the two Chechen wars failed because Russia incompetently applied doctrine and the tactics of *control* and *attrition*. In ten of the fifteen unsuccessful cases, there was a mismatch between means and objectives.

Another conclusion is that asymmetry in interests is to the advantage of the party which interests are more at stake. During Operation Continued Hope in Somalia and Operation Turquoise in Rwanda, no real interests were at stake for the coercer. As such, in its military strategies, it was reluctant to apply force decisively, and both operations failed.

In conclusion, to be successful, the coercer should be willing to employ force decisively; this is motivated by the interests at stake. When opting for military coercion, the military strategy should contain significant elements of *control*, and limited objectives are a prerequisite for balancing military means and political ends.

In choosing for military coercion or coercive diplomacy, policymakers need to be aware of three generic mechanisms that, when combined, determine the strategic efficacy of power instruments. Derived from the twenty-eight case studies listed in the appendix, these mechanisms apply to both coercer and opponent. They are intentionally broadly formulated, as they relate both to the preparation of regime-change operations as well as relatively easy and risk-free peacekeeping operations. Finally, these mechanisms can be applied to activities facing non-state actors, as the struggle against militias and terrorist organizations also demands a solid balance between means and objectives and costs and benefits.

Coercive mechanism 1: The intensity with which the coercer is prepared to use power instruments is proportional to the interests at stake.

The case studies reveal that the interests of the coercer ($I^{Coercer}$ in Fig. 3.1) are directly related to the intensity with which the coercer is prepared to use his power instruments (in Fig. 1 identified by the letter *p*). The interests at stake for the coercer (or coercers) are translated into a willingness to use military force – the ultimate power broker in coercion – and a willingness to incur costs in the process. If the interests at stake are high or vital, a coercer will be more inclined to turn to military means, display greater resolve, and accept higher costs. These costs are generally defined in terms of financial capital, and material and human costs. If the interests at stake are low or non-vital, the willingness to use force will be low and there will be a limited ability to absorb friendly casualties and other costs. In that case, the coercer will generally turn to diplomatic or economic power instruments, which are relatively risk free. The intensity with which power instruments are employed by the coercer is thereby a product of the willingness to use force and the willingness to incur costs. Schematically this can be captured in the following coercion equation:

$I^{Coercer} = p$:
the intensity with which power instruments are used is related to the interests at stake and;

$I^{Coercer} = F + C$:
the interests at stake determine the coercer's willingness to use force (F) and incur costs (C).

Therefore: $p = F + C$:
The willingness to use power instruments is determined by the willingness to use force and incur costs.

Figure 3.1 demonstrates this mechanism by plotting several interventions by Western states. For the United States, the threat posed by the Taliban regime in 2001 was considered a vital interest. The 9/11 attacks shook the United States, which then mobilized significant military resources to remove the Taliban from power and ensure that Afghanistan would no longer be a terrorist sanctuary. At the other end of the scale, we find operation *Continued Hope* in Somalia in 1993, where the United States withdrew its forces following the loss of eighteen Rangers. No vital interests were at stake and the United States was not willing to incur the human cost. A similar dynamic has been at play in recent years regarding a possible Western intervention in the humanitarian crisis in the region of Darfur in Sudan. While human rights are violated, they are not perceived to constitute a threat to vital interests warranting a decisive employment of power instruments.

Figure 3.1 Assessment of Coercion Function and several interventions by Western states (see appendix)

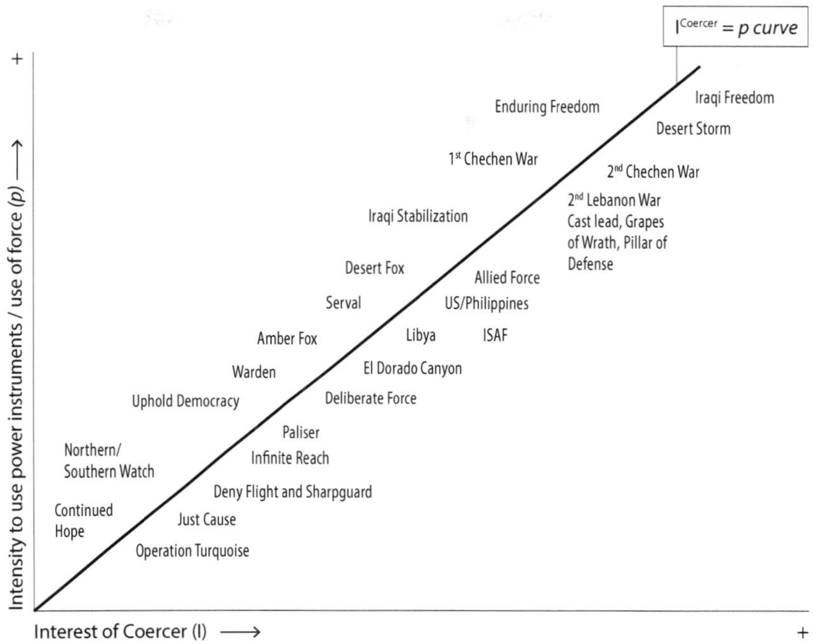

The coercion function also helps understand the behavior of states during or prior to coalition operations. In the run-up to Operation Iraqi Freedom, the United States requested the support of the Netherlands for its intervention in Iraq. The Netherlands however, was only willing to support operation *Iraqi Freedom* politically, not militarily. The interests at stake for the US government were dissimilar to the interests at stake for the Dutch government. The Iraqi regime was not seen by the Dutch as threatening its interests to a similar degree. The Netherlands did not perceive the Iraqi regime as constituting a vital security threat warranting the mobilization of substantial military resources. The Dutch and US governments had a different appreciation regarding the use of power instruments and, subsequently, this resulted in different behavior. Coalition operations are an effort to deal with interest differentials among allies. This impacts the overall willingness to apply power instruments decisively. During operation Allied Force, political negotiation among allies took place throughout the military operation. Allies had differing interests at stake and therefore had their own separate position on the coercion function. Political motivations, combined with military-operational necessities, prescribe a preference for coalition operations; however,they may jeopardize effective coercion.

Effective coercion demands a willingness to employ power instruments decisively. Escalation dominance is a necessity intervening states must be willing to adhere to, but this will only occur when the interests at stake are sufficiently high and, in the case of coalition operations, when interests are defined similarly. When vital interests are threatened and the coercer is willing to apply power instruments decisively, usually the interests at stake are related to the security or survival of the state. However, for Western states, these interests are seldom at risk. Governments will not be willing to pay a high price to coerce others. In the model, p will be small or close to zero. Consequently, political leaders may choose to "do something"; because for domestic political reasons the political price of doing nothing could be too high. This clearly is a dilemma. The chance that what they've done will be successful is low, because the opponent will not be impressed by the coercive measures. If force is not applied decisively, the role of inducements becomes important. Alexander George and William Simons have argued that inducements, combined with more traditional forms of coercion, make resolution of a conflict more likely.[36] The most commonly used inducement is economic aid or the lifting of sanctions as a reward for compliance.

During the conflict, the perception of interests at stake may change, resulting in a new cost-benefit calculus for the coercer. This could occur in case of a half-hearted or unsuccessful intervention. Lack of success could lead to a situation where the credibility of the coercer is at risk; the interests thereby increase. This occurred during the months preceding the war on Kosovo. Economic sanctions were put in place (p was low, because the interests at stake were low), yet they had little effect. NATO warned Milosevic numerous times before commencing operation *Allied Force*. But Milosevic did not comply. If this situation had continued, NATO would have suffered loss of face. This was considered unacceptable. The interests at stake increased, influencing the intensity with which power instruments were willing to be used. The Alliance started the war, and then-British Prime Minister Blair put the credibility of the alliance forward as one of the reasons for the intervention. "Just as I believe there was no alternative to military action [in Kosovo], now it has started I am convinced there is no alternative to continuing until we succeed. On its 50th birthday, NATO

36 George and Simons, *The Limits of Coercive Diplomacy*, pp. 28-29.

must prevail," Tony Blair said on April 24, 1999.[37] As interests had increased, so had the intensity with which power instruments were used, and NATO shifted to a strategy of military coercion. During the operation, as Milosevic defied NATO by not complying with the demands it had set, interests at stake further increased for the alliance. NATO's credibility was put at risk. As losing was no option, towards the end of the intervention, decision makers in a number of countries were willing to execute a "ground option."[38]

From *Allied Force* we have learned that during an intervention that starts out with initially no vital risks at stake, *not losing* could become a vital interest itself. The objective of the intervention is redefined, resulting in an escalation of the conflict. This phenomenon is called *entrapment*: the policymaker becomes a prisoner of his own decisions. He cannot retreat, because this will lead to loss of face and affect his credibility. Interests at stake increase, having their effect on the willingness to use force and to incur costs, leading to a greater intensity in the use of power instruments. This situation can occur when the opponent's motivation, opportunities to resist and willingness to take blows is underestimated or misunderstood. Therefore the second essential coercive mechanism focuses on the opponent.

Coercive mechanism 2: The opponent attempts to confront costs following from the intervention that are directly proportional to his interests at stake.

For the opponent, the same calculus holds as for the coercer. The interests at stake are the determinants for his motivation, in this case, for resisting the coercer. Economic sanctions can threaten his economic safety, a military intervention his territorial integrity, and a combination of both can undermine the political and social stability in his territory and compromise his regime. In the ultimate case, an intervention can threaten the life of the opponent.

For the opponent, the interests at stake translate into a willingness to incur costs as well.[39]

37 Prime Minister Tony Blair, "Doctrine of the International Community", address at the Economic Club, Chicago (IL), April 24, 1999.

38 See, for instance: D. Priest, "Kosovo Land Threat May Have Won the War", *Washington Post*, September 19, 1999.

39 This is a variant to Robert Pape's model presented in *Bombing to Win* which reads: "R + Bp(B) – Cp(C), where: R = value of resistance, B = potential benefits, p(B) = probability of attaining benefits by continued resistance, C = potential costs of resistance, p (C)= probability of suffering costs," p. 16.

If a government feels that its continuation or existence is threatened, it will be inclined to accept higher costs than if the objective of the intervention of the coercer is limited.[40] An intervention intent on "regime change" is, for instance, directly targeted at the government itself and leaves little room for maneuver. The reaction of the opponent is likely to be a "nothing to lose" strategy. This is especially the case when dictators or autocratic leaders are concerned. Such a strategy can only be pursued when the interests involved for the coercer are high, so that he is willing to use force decisively and pursue regime change vigorously or when the target is substantially weaker and has lost control over the state's power instruments, such as was the case with Noriega in Panama and Cedras in Haiti.

The appendix shows that interests at stake for the opponent have generally been larger than for the coercer creating asymmetries of interest and yielding insights into the course of action pursued by both sides. The low level of interest the US accorded to al-Qaeda in 1998 helps understand why *Infinite Reach* was limited to a risk-free salvo of cruise missiles. During the regime change operation *Iraqi Freedom* and the counterterrorist operation *Enduring Freedom* the interests at stake for the United States were closely aligned with those of the opponent and led to a dedicated effort involving substantial military forces. Figure 3.1 illustrates why the United States withdrew its troops following the incident in 1993 with Task Force Ranger in Somalia (limited interests at stake), and why it accepted significant casualties and costs during *Desert Storm* (significant interests at stake). Also, it is indicative of the problems the United States was encountering in Iraq in the stabilization phase following the regime change in 2003. The interests at stake in Iraq were perceived as lower than during Operation *Allied Force* in 1999. This is a reason why the US government was facing strong domestic pressure to withdraw from Iraq; the willingness to incur costs had been surpassed.

It should not be surprising that the interests at stake for the opponent mostly outweigh those of the coercer. The opponent oftentimes has much more to lose. If vital interests are at stake for the opponent, but not for the coercer, the opponent is willing to make larger sacrifices than the coercer, which diminishes the likelihood of quick success. An intervention will then, in the most advantageous case, proceed tediously, and in the worst

40 See also Jeffrey Record, "The Limits and Temptations of America's Conventional Military Primacy", *Survival*, vol. 97, no. 1 (Spring 2005), pp. 36-37.

case, fail.[41] When there are asymmetries of interest in favor of the opponent, the coercer should be aware that the opponent will be willing to employ his power instruments with greater intensity and tenacity than the coercer. Ignoring the opponent's interests is dangerous when the opponent's tactics are ignored as well. The failed humanitarian intervention in Somalia provides an excellent example. Unfortunately, in most interventions, there is an asymmetry of interests. If there are no vital interests at stake for the coercer, caution is advised.

The key is to accurately assess the interests of the opponent. The logic of coercion ensures that the calculus of the coercer and the opponent are intimately connected. They are locked together in a dynamic. The coercer shapes his action based on the perceived interests at stake. For the coercer, the interests at stake – caused by the opponent's actions – are the starting point. The coercer perceives the world around him and identifies threats to his interests. These affect his willingness to incur costs and determine the intensity with which he is willing to use power instruments to defend or promote those interests. The opponent's willingness to incur costs is dependent on his interests at stake, which are derived from the course of action the coercer adopts. The logic of action and reaction ensues. If the opponent feels that vital interests are threatened he will be willing to accept a higher cost and will be more resilient. The interest and cost calculus of the opponent is dependent on the action taken by the coercer. This is an aspect that has been little understood by policymakers. Instead, Western leaders rarely take the interests of the opponent into account or only do so marginally. The first explanation for this is a lack of empathy, generally for domestic political purposes. There is an almost uncontrollable tendency to demonize the opponent, often to obtain public support for an intervention. Yet this blinds decision makers to the strategic options of the opponent. Furthermore, there is a widespread sense of moral superiority. Interventions are often portrayed as battles between good and evil or as a new *mission civilisatrice*; the means and resources of the 21st century are employed to act against institutions of "medieval barbarism." Prior to the first Gulf War, one way President George H.W. Bush justified military action was on the basis that Saddam was worse than Hitler: "This morning, right now, over three hundred innocent Americans – civilians – are held against their will in Iraq. Many of them are reportedly staked out as human shields near pos-

41 Exceptions are the interventions in Haiti and Panama, where military operations removed leaders that had become isolated and were unable to mount significant opposition against US coercion.

sible military targets, something that even Adolf Hitler didn't do."[42] During the war on Kosovo, Milosevic was demonized by Western politicians and commentators, charged with genocide and indicted by the International Criminal Tribunal for the former Yugoslavia for crimes against humanity.[43] Similarly, with respect to the NATO operation in Afghanistan, Secretary General Jaap de Hoop Scheffer spoke about NATO not being "in the same moral category" as the Taliban.[44] By advocating moral superiority, the organization runs the risk of underestimating the opponent.

Secondly, the cultural context in which coercion occurs is often neglected. This applies to understanding the interests of the opponent as well as his ensuing behavior. Assuming irrationality because he does not behave conform to Western assumptions of rationality is a recipe for disaster.[45] Arab ethics, for instance, revolve around self-esteem and mutual respect. The concepts of "honor" and "pride" are of crucial importance. After the arrest of Saddam Hussein, many Iraqis protested against pictures of their former leader undergoing dental examinations, because this left him with no honor. In the West this was met with unbelief and instead the examination was an opportunity to bring the "Butcher of Baghdad" back to human proportions.[46] This defamation fueled Baathist loyalist anger against the coalition. Similarly, actions by coalition forces in Afghanistan that offend the traditions or culture of the local population are likely to be counterproductive. Cultural intelligence is a necessity for successful coercion.

Sometimes, however, perceptions of the interests on both sides are correct. During the Cuban Missile Crisis, President Kennedy had judged his opponent Khrushchev correctly. For the Americans, there were vital interests at stake and US armed forces were militarily superior in the region. For Khrushchev, there were reasons to believe that Kennedy would indeed use these assets. Kennedy estimated that his opponent would retreat when

42 President George H.W. Bush, Remarks at a Republican Fundraiser in Burlingon, MA, November 1, 1990.

43 The International Criminal Tribunal for the Former Yugoslavia, case IT-99-37, May 22, 1999.

44 J. de Hoop Scheffer, Joint press availability with President George W. Bush, Crawford (TX), May 21, 2007.

45 Kenneth Pollack, for instance, in *The Threatening Storm: The Case for Invading Iraq* (New York: Random House, 2002), concluded that Saddam Hussein was irrational or a "serial miscalculator" and therefore could not be deterred, necessitating an intervention.

46 In the media, Saddam Hussein was frequently referred to as "the Butcher of Baghdad" or the "'Baghdad Butcher". See: *The Daily Mirror*, "Our Boys Blast the Butcher from Baghdad", December 18, 1998; The *Observer*, "From a Tikrit Boy to the Butcher of Baghdad", December 13, 2006.

the risks became too high, because for the Soviet Union no vital interests were at stake.[47]

The final and perhaps most important explanation is the conventional military might of the West and particularly the United States' role as the world's only military superpower. With unmatched military capabilities, it seems futile for opponents to resist US demands, and objectives appear easily attainable. With relatively weak opponents, the United States could even afford to ignore the economic and military power of others and simply issue demands. If these demands are not met, the US could take measures with horrendous consequences for its opponents, resulting in a new world order based on American military primacy,[48] or so the reasoning goes. This, however, fails to take account of the willingness on both sides to incur costs and to use force. In short, the assumption that interventions in all circumstances will succeed due to overmatching conventional military power ignores the logic of coercion. The US could make demands of any state, but is it able and willing to follow up on these demands if military coercion is required? As the next section will demonstrate, this fails to take asymmetric warfare into account.

Coercive mechanism 3: Asymmetry in interests or military capabilities lead to asymmetrical reactions.

This brings us to the role of military capability as it translates into coercive power. A key factor essential to understanding coercion is the relationship between the coercer's capabilities and those of the opponent. By operating asymmetrically, opponents are able to discount the advantage of Western militaries partially or entirely. Asymmetric reactions offset the advantage of superior conventional capabilities by increasing the impact of power instruments. In the event that vital interests are at stake for the opponent, its full military response will be mobilized to obtain the maximum effect of its power instruments. However, given the military superiority of the West, targets of coercion are unlikely to respond by fielding conventional forces. They would be immediately crushed. Instead, the adversary will exploit asymmetries in the coercer's willingness to incur costs by confronting him

47 Graham T. Allison and Philip Zelikow, *Essence of Decision: Explaining the Cuban Missile Crisis* (New York: Longman, 1999, 2nd ed.).

48 See, for instance: "Excerpts from the Pentagon's Plans: Prevent the Re-emergence of a New Rival", *The New York Times*, March 8, 1992, and The White House, "National Security Strategy of the United States", Washington, D.C.: 2002.

non-conventionally.[49] In so doing, he is increasing the effect of his power instruments. The Fedayeen of Saddam Hussein during *Iraqi Freedom* are an example. Although the United States' armed forces were very capable in dealing with the Iraqi Republican Guard, the surgical guerilla-style attacks on supply routes by the Saddam Fedayeen, a loosely organized group of combatants that functioned more like guerillas than soldiers, proved more troubling. By operating non-conventionally, they started to level the playing field. If the Fedayeen had been organized into regular divisions and confronted the US in the open, like the Iraqi Republican Guard, it would not have stood a chance. The insurgency in Iraq that followed the phase of military coercion is an illustration of an asymmetrical confrontation, one where the United States has substantial difficulty in achieving even limited success. The greater willingness to incur costs by the opponent is reflected by the number of insurgents that are killed opposed to coalition forces, yet they still persist. Asymmetries in interests and capabilities lead to a leveled playing field by spawning non-conventional responses to coercion. Non-state actors such as terrorist organizations and guerilla movements use these asymmetries as the basis of their strategy.[50]

To be successful in achieving an asymmetric response and to upgrade the efficacy of its military capabilities, the opponent must try to deny the coercer his strategic objectives by targeting weak spots and affect the coercer's willingness to incur costs. In itself, this is not a new concept; it is the classic strategy of the guerilla warrior and the terrorist. Those weak spots of the West are the following:

- zero tolerance to friendly casualties if no or limited interests are at stake;
- the short time horizons of Western policymakers and the desire to reach quick solutions;
- a preference for the use of airpower and conventional maneuver warfare;
- the wish to minimize collateral damage;
- the necessity to abide by the law of war and other internationally accepted norms;
- the desire to keep a coalition together;
- an emphasis on technological solutions;
- a conceptual division between the military and the civilian realm;

49 See, for instance: Qiao Liang & Wang Xiangsui, *Unrestricted Warfare* (Beijing: PLA Literature and Arts Publishing House, 1999).

50 See also Col. T.X. Hammes, USMC, *The Sling and the Stone: On War in the 21st Century* (St. Paul: Zenith Press, 2004).

- the tendency to be very confident of one's own capabilities while underestimating the opponent's motivations and opportunities of resistance;
- the economic and social vulnerability of open Western societies;
- intensive media coverage.

An effective opponent will design his response on the basis of these characteristics and, in addition to conventional responses, he has a number of asymmetric strategies of countercoercion available. From the case studies we have derived the following. The first strategy is based on countering American conventional military superiority on the battlefield and increasing the number of victims amongst the intervening forces. Western forces are vulnerable against irregular opponents who employ non-conventional combat tactics. Neither the Americans in Vietnam and Somalia, nor the Russians in Afghanistan and Chechnya could withstand guerrillas and insurgents using terror and hit-and-run actions. After NATO started enforcing a no-fly zone above Bosnia in April 1993, the Serbs reacted by holding UNPROFOR peacekeepers hostage, who were thereafter used as human shields. Hostage taking can be extremely effective, especially if the coercer's populace does not wholeheartedly support the intervention. Similarly, the opponent can draw the coercer into a battle which he is not prepared to fight, like an urban counterinsurgency or operations in dense or mountainous terrain. Traditionally, Western forces are trained and equipped for mechanized, conventional performance against a regular opponent. Hand-to-hand combat in demanding counterinsurgency and counterterror operations does not fit this framework. In the conventional combat phase of *Iraqi Freedom,* 140 Americans died; in the subsequent counterinsurgency phase this number increased to 4,488 killed and 32,222 wounded. The Western way of warfare relies on the use of air power to support ground forces or reach strategic objectives. Deploying a sophisticated air defense system constitutes a significant obstacle to Western planners. Also operating in small, mobile units makes fighting with airpower for the coercer difficult. Furthermore, ground forces are generally concentrated at specific points of debarkation and forward operating bases upon deployment. By mining harbors or deploying theater ballistic or cruise missiles adversaries can create "anti-access" or "area-denial" environments troubling an intervention or deterring it all together. The threat of CBRN attacks on military forces also fits within this category.[51] Unconventional capabilities can thereby weaken Western conventional military strength.

51 For more on the Western way of warfare and operations in these contested zones, see Barry Posen, "Command of the Commons", *International Security*, vol. 28, no. 1 (Summer 2003), pp. 5-46.

The second strategy is aimed at increasing the suffering of one's own population, either by increasing the likelihood of collateral damage or of spreading death and destruction among the civilian population through other means. It is based on the premise that Western coercers make a strict distinction between combatants and noncombatants, or civilians, and that by increasing the suffering of the own population, the opponent can question the legality of the intervention and its employed means. Autocratic leaders appear to be very capable in this: Saddam Hussein passed the consequences of the sanctions, to the horror of the West, on to the Iraqi population. Subsequently, the international community cried for a revision of the Iraq sanction regime. Saddam, as well as Milosevic, placed military installations in highly populated areas, or introduced "human shields" so that the population might become the victim of aerial bombings.[52] Oftentimes this meant that the installations were not targeted altogether.

The third strategy is directed at the population of the coercer himself. This strategy implies terrorism in those countries participating in the intervention. The attacks on the World Trade Center and the Pentagon on September 11, 2001, also fall in this category. The problem lies in the perception among Western populations and policymakers that war only takes place on the battlefield, and thus the further the geographic distance from the battlefield the safer one is. Instead, opponents can try to move the battlefield from their territory to that of the coercer.

The fourth strategy is that of partial passivity. This strategy was also put into practice by Milosevic. NATO's calculations indicated that when Milosevic would use his air force and air defenses, he would be defeated within a few days. But Milosevic hid his fighter planes and merely used them once in a while. Air defenses were also only periodically operated. The result was that during the entire air campaign, threats to NATO airplanes persisted, because the opponent retained the capability to come into action.[53] NATO could not obtain complete air supremacy and had to bomb from 15,000 feet. This visibly delayed the air campaign and increased the chances of collateral damage or errors. A strategy of partial passivity could also imply that the opponent does not resist an intervention with land forces if he is convinced that he cannot win. Instead, the adversary

52 See, for instance: Richard Norton-Taylor, "Air strikes hampered by human shields", *The Guardian*, Tuesday, May 18, 1999.

53 This situation was further exacerbated through Milosevic's extensive use of decoys. Joseph Fitchett, "But Generals Say Air War achieved Alliance's Goal: NATO Misjudged Bombing Damage", *International Herald Tribune*, June 23, 1999.

could try to fight the coercer as an insurgency during the stabilization and reconstruction phase. The situation in Iraq following the toppling of Saddam Hussein is reminiscent of this.

The fifth strategy the opponent can choose is horizontal escalation. In reaction to an intervention, the struggle can be pursued on a different front. During the 1991 Gulf War, Saddam Hussein launched missiles at Tel Aviv and threatened to initiate a second front against Turkey. It took the Alliance a lot of effort to keep the Israelis at bay, as an Israeli intervention in Iraq would potentially have broken the coalition. During the Kosovo War, Milosevic seemed willing to mobilize the Bosnian Serbs. The result was that the strategic reserve of SFOR was brought into the highest state of alert. Even *information warfare* – hackers that try to disrupt or disable the computer systems of the coercer – can be seen as a form of horizontal escalation.

The last strategy embodies denying the coercer the use of vital infrastructure, raw materials, and other strategic assets. Scorched earth tactics are the most likely method. This is what Saddam Hussein did in 1991 and – to lesser success – in 2003. He attempted to make the military victory of the allies a severe economic and ecological loss by setting oil wells on fire.

A consequence of these strategies is the ability of the opponent to prolong the conflict. Western states want short interventions. Colonel Hammes observed that: "The United States wants to fight short, well-defined wars. We went into Vietnam, Bosnia, Kosovo, Afghanistan, and Iraq convinced we could 'clean it up' quickly. In each conflict, our leaders told the people we would be out in a year or so. They felt this was important to convince the American people to go to war."[54]

Through these asymmetric strategies, the opponent is increasing the effectiveness of his power instruments. By employing these strategies, the opponent attempts to make the coercer pay a high price for achieving his political objectives. It is thereby testing the coercer to see how far the coercer is willing to go to reach those objectives.

The opponent's countercoercion is therefore not directed at achieving a military victory, but rather to avoid a defeat, and undermining the willingness of the coercer to continue. When the opponent avoids a defeat, he has effectively won. The Chinese authors of "Unrestricted Warfare" were correct in stating that the unquestionable military superiority of Western power leads to no other options except asymmetric reactions. This requires shifts

54 Col. T.X. Hammes, USMC, *The Sling and the Stone: On War in the 21st Century* (St. Paul: Zenith Press, 2004), p. 221.

in thought by Western leaders, who appear driven by the idea that superior economic and military force is key to success in interventions. Thinking in the West about asymmetric warfare has progressed since past interventions, and some have even come to encapsulate asymmetric countercoercion strategies as a new generation of warfare.[55] Yet, without a strategy, it is a type of warfare to which Western policymakers have little response. Superior force and differences in interests trigger asymmetric reactions. Only when vital interests are at stake are Western intervening powers able to muster the will to sustain operations to confront asymmetric countercoercion.

Applications of military force in coercion strategies

Now to turn to the question how military force can be applied by the coercer. The coercer's strategy needs to take account of the expected reaction of the opponent and be able to counter it. In any coercion strategy using military force, a coercer must have a clear definition of the opponent and understand what the opponent values. And he must decide what he is willing to put at risk to reach the objective. There are a limited number of options for the use of military force in strategies of coercive diplomacy or military coercion.

First of all, it may have the direct effect of creating civil unrest, forcing the opponent government to concede, or triggering popular revolt – resulting in the establishment of a new government that is willing to steer a different course. Traditionally, sanctions are aimed at the population. Military force can be as well. This is the core of Schelling's reasoning; a slow increase of pressure by envisaging the prospect of further and increased damage to civilian targets. This is termed a *risk strategy*. Coercion focused on risk is a watered-down version of punishment, whereby a population is punished for the actions of its government. The rationale of targeting the population finds its roots in the concepts of early theoreticians concerning the deployment of air power. Giulio Douhet is the archetypical punishment strategist.[56] He firmly believed that large-scale bombings of cities and economic infrastructure would induce enough pain and fear among the populace that the government would make concessions. Pape, however, argued that there is no historical evidence to prove that these campaigns have ever led to capitulation, the collapse of a regime, or the stagnation

55 Ibid.
56 See G. Douhet, *The Command of the Air* (Washington, D.C.: US War Department, 1921).

of industrial production resulting from a shortage of labor.[57] His explanation is that conventional bombings produce insufficient damage to the civilian population to warrant a change in a government's actions. Among historians and air power experts, there still is disagreement as to whether the strategic bombing campaigns in Germany and Japan were critical in ending the Second World War. Some, like Richard Overy, argued that it is fundamentally implausible that massive strikes against Germany and Japan would not have made a significant contribution to the Allies' victory.[58] It may therefore be safe to conclude that strategic bombing campaigns exclusively are not decisive, but could contribute to the overall success.

Secondly, the use of the military by the coercer can target the political and military leadership directly in order to replace it. Smart sanctions and military force could be involved to isolate the regime. A coercive strategy focused on decapitation through precision strikes is attractive, because it is theoretically quick, clean, and simple and it exclusively focuses on those responsible. In a number of cases decapitation, capturing or killing a leader, did weaken the opponent. A prime example was the removal of the Hamas leadership by Israel in 2004. Firstly its founder, Sheikh Ahmed Yassin was killed by a missile fired from an attack helicopter. Subsequently, his successor, Dr. Abdel Azziz Rantisi, was killed in a similar way. After the latter's killing, the Hamas leadership appointed a new, unnamed leader. With this, Israel effectively deprived Hamas in the short term of visible, charismatic leaders. However, the effects of decapitations should not be overstated. Stephen T. Hosmer analyzed 24 cases and concluded that the results of such attacks were poor.[59] The assassination of Chechnya's president, Dzhokhar Dudayev, did not affect the war. And Hamas to-date remains a potent militant adversary of Israel. Baathists in Iraq persisted in killing American soldiers while Saddam was dead and the Taliban in Afghanistan have continued to hurt coalition forces and sow instability in the absence of strong, public leadership.

Decapitation strikes have historically not resulted in massive revolts and protests by the population against their leaders. In fact, precision strikes tend to result in the population backing the regime. As such, the population's response to both risk/ punishment or decapitation is similar. Aerial strikes create a prime opportunity for leaders to obtain the support of the population and to mobilize resistance. Especially if aerial strikes go awry

57 Pape, *Bombing to Win*, p. 23.

58 R. Overy, *Why the Allies Won* (New York: Norton, 1995), p. 133.

59 S.T. Hosmer, *Operations against Enemy Leaders* (Santa Monica: RAND, 2001), pp. xi-xvii.

and collateral damage is the result. The successor to Milosevic, Vojislav Kostunica, testified that Western interventions in Yugoslavia considerably prolonged Milosevic's political life. According to him, Milosevic would have had to clear the political field in the beginning of the 1990s if it were not for the interventions.[60]

Thirdly, military force can be directed at the state as a system. A coercion strategy of weakening or incapacitation targets the power base of the adversary, not the leadership per se. The founder of modern theory on weakening or incapacitation was the American air force colonel, J.A. Warden.[61] Warden assumed that the destruction of the power base would lead to the collapse of a regime. His prescribed strategy was put to practice during operations *Desert Storm* and *Allied Force*, and by the Israeli Defense Forces against Hezbollah's power base in Southern Lebanon in 2006. Headquarters of the military and political leadership, communication nodes, radio and television stations, vital industrial complexes and the barracks of loyal military and paramilitary units were bombed. Incapacitation targets important backers of a regime, critical infrastructure, communications and other institutions that make up a country's economic strength and political cohesion.

Finally, the military strategy of the coercer can be directed at the opponent's ability to wage war. This concerns denying the opponent battlefield success through preventing him the use of his military means (denial), through the physical occupation of the territory (control) or by the destruction of vast areas (attrition or brute force). Denial requires an air campaign, bombing military targets, including infrastructure, barracks and headquarters, to deny the opponent the use of his military and to prevent him from reinforcing troops in the battle area.[62] Denial can be a "stick" as part of a strategy of coercive diplomacy, such as the targeting of Iraqi radar stations and air defense systems as part of enforcing the no-fly zones over Iraq in the 1990s. Control is very demanding as it requires vast amounts of ground forces and material to physically occupy the territory. *Iraqi Freedom* and *Enduring Freedom* contained important elements of denial and control. Attrition or brute force brings with it moral and

60 S. Erlanger, "A Key Issue Hangs Over Serbian Election: Legacy of U.S. Actions", *International Herald Tribune*, December 23-24, 2000.

61 J.A. Warden III, "Employing Air Power in the Twenty-First Century", in R.H. Shultz, Jr. and R.L. Pfalzgraff Jr., *The Future of Air Power in the Aftermath of the Gulf War* (Air University Press: Maxwell Air Force Base, Alabama, 1992).

62 Robert A. Pape, "The Limits of Precision-Guided Air Power", *Security Studies*, Winter 1997/98, p. 97.

military obstacles. Attrition through aerial bombings or scorched earth tactics bear little risks for the coercer. However, due to its adverse effects it is a desperate act, one that is chosen only when all other options have failed and the coercer does not want to run risks. The destruction of vast rural and urban areas will lead to international protests and is likely to strengthen, rather than undermine, the morale of the population. The destruction of Grozny by the Russians during the wars in Chechnya was a form of attrition.

While many of the applications of military force are based on air power, air power alone is insufficient to cause the collapse of a regime.[63] Nevertheless, the belief otherwise is remarkably persistent in Western thought, because through the development of advanced weapons systems such as stealth, stand-off missiles, and precision-guided munitions it is a relatively risk-free and "clean" means of waging war and makes use of the technological superiority of Western forces. Yet, as operations *Iraqi Freedom* and *Enduring Freedom* demonstrate, it is when air power is employed jointly with ground forces that military coercion is successful.[64] Success will often contain elements of multiple military strategies. Of the ten successful interventions studied, half relied on a combination of weakening, denial, and control and included the deployment of ground forces.

63 For a discussion on the use of air power in the Second Lebanon War, see P.H. Gordon, "Air Power won't do it", *Washington Post*, July 25, 2006.

64 See Robert A. Pape, "The True Worth of Air Power", *Foreign Affairs*, vol. 83, no. 2 (March/April 2004), pp. 116-130.

Strategies and Opponents

Table 3.1 Summary of use of force in different strategies

	Coercive Diplomacy *Diplomatic and economic measures + Risk/Punishment*	**Coercive Diplomacy and Military Enforcement** *Weakening/ incapacitation*	**Coercive Diplomacy and Military Enforcement** *Denial*	**Military Coercion** *Decapitation*	**Military Coercion** *Control*	**Military Coercion** *Attrition*
State actor with regular forces	Applicable, low-cost option	Applicable, low-cost option	Applicable, low-cost option	Applicable, unlikely to be conclusive	Applicable, high-cost option, substantial ground forces needed	Applicable, low-cost option, but usually unacceptable
State actor with irregular forces	Applicable, low-cost option	Applicable, but unlikely to be effective	Usually not applicable, unlikely to be effective	Applicable, unlikely to be conclusive	Applicable, usually only option, substantial ground forces needed	Applicable, usually unacceptable
Non state actor with irregular forces	Applicable, but unlikely to be conclusive. Symbolic measure	Not applicable. No target system	Usually not applicable, unlikely to be effective	Applicable, ground forces usually needed. Unlikely to be conclusive	Applicable, usually only option, substantial ground forces needed	Applicable, but unlikely to be effective. Usually unacceptable

Table 3.1 summarizes how different military and diplomatic strategies impact different adversarys. It shows that most opportunities for successful coercion occur when Western forces act against an opponent that possesses regular combat forces and is trained for conventional warfare. Regular

forces require extensive support structures which, together with the fielded forces, form lucrative targets for Western firepower. The chances of success are smaller when action is taken against irregular forces, guerillas, and terrorists. These forces are difficult to localize and do not rely on substantial support structures. They possess few heavy weapons, if any, and they move by foot or use civilian means of transport. Therefore a strategy based on denial or weakening is not sufficient. During the Kosovo campaign, Serb actions were executed by irregular fighters, like Arkan's Tigers, and the paramilitary units of the ministry of internal affairs. These units were relatively invulnerable to NATO's bombs. The case studies used in the appendix show that successful coercion against non-state actors always contained elements of control, aimed at physically occupying territory and sweeping it for the opponent's forces. While decapitation could also be effective, it is only partial to reaching the objective. Non-state actors have the tendency to be able to continue operating following the removal of a leader. Control, however, creates considerable problems when confronting irregular forces. Western militaries have very limited capacities for counterinsurgency and counterterror operations, such as *clear and hold* or *search and destroy* missions. Additionally, Western military institutions lack the size and the organization to sustain long deployments. Success requires the restructuring of Western armed forces. The great risks that accompany a strategy of control imply that Western leaders are hesitant to use military force in this way and only do so when the interests at stake are high. The strategy of control was used in 21 of the case studies used in the appendix, and in 11 of those cases, the interests at stake were high. If the contingency concerns a non-state actor with ties to a state actor; such as a terrorist organization sponsored by a state, second-order coercion is appropriate. Following the attacks of 9/11, the Taliban was pressured by the United States through coercive diplomacy to extradite Bin Laden and remove al-Qaeda from its soil. Having failed to do so, Washington placed the Taliban in the same category as al-Qaeda, and both became the object of a military campaign based on weakening, denial and control. Although the focus was on al-Qaeda, the US pressured the Taliban because its regime was al-Qaeda's lifeline in Afghanistan. Second-order coercion occurred as al-Qaeda could not maintain its powerbase with the Taliban removed from power. Finally, dealing with state-sponsored terrorist organizations requires an integral strategy of second-order coercion. It includes targeting the financial infrastructure (economic sanctions), possibly addressing perceived grievances or "root causes" (rewards), and the willingness to initiate military control to target the terrorist infrastructure and operatives.

Policy implications

In conclusion, the coercive mechanisms suggest that, regardless of the interests at stake, a militarily superior coercer will prevail if the balance between military means and political objectives is right, and if control with ground forces is not ruled out. In four cases, the model incorrectly predicted success. The two Chechen wars failed because of the incompetent application of strategy by the Russian military leadership. Israel's operations Grapes of Wrath and Cast Lead were terminated before the threat could be removed.

Another conclusion is that any intervention strategy needs to be based on the dynamic interaction between coercer and opponent. It is essential to understand this dynamic and take the opponent's perspective fully and honestly into account to be able to create a strategy that can lead to a successful intervention. The interests that are at stake for both the coercer and opponent determine the intensity with which both will use their power instruments. The interests at stake determine the willingness of both parties to use force and incur costs during the intervention. As such, it informs which strategy fits the coercer best.

The three coercion mechanisms mentioned, together with the delineation of strategies and counterstrategies, lead to the following policy implications for coercers.

First, limited interests require limited political and military objectives. If vital interests are not at stake, Western countries are unwilling to pay a high price for an intervention. When a state opponent is concerned, coercive diplomacy with military force supporting diplomacy is the preferred strategy. The threat to use force should go hand in hand with diplomatic activities and inducements or rewards. Diplomatic channels should remain open and the demonization of the opponent should be avoided at all costs. The opponent must be offered a way out. If there is no other option but to use force, the coercer should choose a method that maintains the opportunity for the opponent to find a suitable and honorable way out. It must be avoided that through the intervention vital interests of the opponent become threatened. When this is the case, he will make the ultimate effort to resist, and do so asymmetrically. Denial, punishment, and weakening are the preferred military options. Weakening and punishment serve as a clear signal of the coercer's resolve; so does denial and deprives the opponent of some military options as well. The credibility of coercive diplomacy is ultimately dependent upon the willingness to escalate and to eventually act rapidly, decisively and if necessary massively. Military coercion could then follow if coercive diplomacy has failed and all diplomatic means have been exhausted. The entrapment of Western allies in the run-up to operation *Allied Force* comes to mind. If there isn't a willingness to shift to military coercion, this may lead to the political decision to let the situation crawl on, or to refrain from pursuing further actions by simply stating that the objectives have been reached.

Second, if vital interests are at stake, decisive use of force is required and a strategy of military coercion with diplomacy in a subordinate role is preferred. Diplomatic activities, including those by a third party, should not be ruled out but are not a prerequisite for success. A strategy of military coercion requires the decisive and resolute use of force. There is a direct correlation between successful military coercion and a coercer's perception that the interests at stake are high. Six out of ten successful interventions under scrutiny in the case studies used in the appendix took place when the coercer's interests were considered to be high.[65] There is a similar correlation between successful military coercion and the military strategies used. Of the interventions that obtained their objectives, most relied completely on or contained significant elements of control. Decapitation, system warfare through incapacitation, and denial can be applicable elements, yet when acting against a non-state actor or a state actor using irregular forces, there is no other choice but to take physical control of territory. All successful interventions against non-state actors either relied completely on, or contained significant elements of, control. It follows that military coercion is most effective when ground forces are introduced.

Third, traditional military superiority is not a prerequisite for successful coercion, as asymmetries of interest lead to asymmetric reactions that can potentially offset Western conventional military power. Asymmetric reactions lead to increases in the costs for the coercer to achieve his objectives. It must be assumed that with any intervention the response of the opponent will be asymmetric. If no vital interests are at stake for the coercer, the political willingness to escalate the conflict and use military power decisively will be absent. Then great caution must be exercised with rhetoric and threats. If for vital interests are perceived to be at stake for the opponent and not for the coercer, the West's military superiority hardly matters. As such, the chance of a successful intervention is higher when similar interests are at stake for the opponent and coercer than if there are asymmetries of interest. The asymmetric response of a militarily weaker

65 In the other four cases, the interests at stake for the coercer were medium.

opponent can lead to a reevaluation of the coercer's interests and require the shift to a strategy of military coercion.

Fourth, clear strategic objectives and appropriate means for achieving them are required. In an intervention, the coercer can make two cardinal mistakes. The first is that he wishes to achieve the objectives of military coercion by employing force designed for a strategy of coercive diplomacy. The second mistake is that, due to political reasons, symbolic measures are chosen instead of a strategy. While potentially necessary for domestic political purposes, symbolic measures are not credible in the eyes of the opponent and he will continue his activities. This can lead to the coercer's loss of credibility. Either he will have to cease his symbolic activities or, on the other hand, escalate the situation to coerce the opponent to change his behavior. A symbolic measure might provide political satisfaction in the short term, but may prove disastrous and costly in the long run. The risk of entrapment is present, especially during the phase of coercive diplomacy. Unsuccessful efforts to influence the strategic choices of an actor could result in loss of credibility. Over the course of the conflict, preserving credibility could become a vital interest itself, requiring more force than anticipated.

Fifth, coercive diplomacy is rarely a viable strategy against state or non-state actors when the willingness to shift to a strategy of military coercion is absent. The only two successful instances of coercion based on coercive diplomacy were against the young and instable regime of Raoul Cedras in the small state of Haiti, and against the Serbian leadership in operation *Deliberate Force*. In the case of the former, Cedras had little sway over the country's power instruments to confront the United States. *Deliberate Force* was successful due to the willingness to employ military means selectively, avoiding antagonizing the opponent and stating limited political objectives, namely the reopening of negotiations. This should be seen as a lesson when opting for this strategy. Success against non-state actors is only possible – although not guaranteed – through a strategy of military coercion based on control that possibly includes elements of denial and weakening. Coercing non-state actors may only be effective when there are vital interests at stake for the coercer. A hybrid version is the battle against terrorist organizations with state sponsors. Here, second-order coercive diplomacy can be used to coerce a host state to give up its support for the terrorist movement, and subsequently, a strategy of military coercion to deal with the terrorist movement itself and expanding it to the host-state if coercive diplomacy fails.

Sixth, successful interventions require the willingness to eventually take control of the territory of the opponent. Because Western countries are in general not willing to do this, great caution is required when formulating demanding political objectives. Any strategy is useless if escalation is not prepared for. Because the opponent's perception of the coercer is vital, the credibility of the coercer's strategy is paramount.

Seventh, the protection of values is very important to Western governments. However, the protection of human rights, freedom, and democracy will usually not affect the vital interests of Western coercers. In those cases it is unlikely that the coercer is willing to pay a high price for the intervention and use force decisively. This conclusion is of great importance for "humanitarian" interventions, which precisely require the rapid and decisive deployment of military means to end human suffering quickly.

Eight, even when a strategy of control is chosen, however, asymmetric responses will make the coercion difficult. As the Chechen Wars have shown, a strategy of control is not a guarantee for success. A hesitant, conservative approach to interventions based on a careful assessment of vital interests at stake is therefore warranted.

Finally, successful interventions become possible when in formulating a strategy the interests of both parties are taken into account. In the end, a strategy must be formulated that is simple and straightforward. An ancient truth says that if the strategist needs more than a minute to explain his strategy, it is doomed to fail. The next chapter deals with Western military culture. The issue at stake is how the military thinks wars should be fought. As will be seen, there is a clear mismatch between the requirements of coercive strategies, doctrine, and, consequently, the military means available.

Part 2
Strategic Culture: How the West Coerces

In analogy with political culture, strategic culture is defined as traditions, values, attitudes, patterns of behavior, habits, symbols, achievements, and ways of solving problems with respect to the use of force. As strategic culture is expressed through doctrine, I will analyze the evolution of military doctrine since the end of the Second World War. Doctrine defines the nature and the characteristics of current and future military operations, preparations for those operations in peace time, and the methods for successfully completing military operations in times of conflict. A large part of doctrine is based on military experience gained during past operations. Doctrine is codified in "how to fight" manuals, it is general in nature, and reflects the mind-set of modern soldiers. It describes the fundamentals, principles, and preconditions for military operations at different levels. This part of the study primarily deals with the strategic and operational levels.

I argue that for decades, probably for centuries, doctrine has been founded on some clearly identifiable principles, which make them perfectly suitable for conventional warfare. Therefore, the question of whether these doctrines are applicable to modern challenges as well becomes relevant. If this is not the case, the efficacy of coercion is likely to diminish. Given the differences in political and, consequently, strategic culture, most of the innovative doctrinal thinking took place in the United States. Due to the differences in political and strategic cultures, Europeans – except for the British, the French and, to a lesser extent, the Germans – contributed very little to the development of doctrine. Some member states reluctantly accepted NATO doctrine, which was derived from American documents, but they were unwilling to use them as a basis for procurement. For NATO, interoperability has been an enduring problem, reinforced by the differences in strategic culture on both sides of the Atlantic.

4 The Evolution of Modern Military Doctrine

Geography, history, and technology have determined the way in which modern Western armed forces fight. Norman Davies wrote that the inhabitants of the Great European Plain, which stretches from the Atlantic to the Urals, could find no natural limits to the territory they chose to occupy. The peoples who settled on the plain had to fight for it. They had to learn the art of systematic military organization, so it comes as no surprise that the plain nourished the greatest military powers in Europe's history: France, Prussia, and Russia.[1]

The modern system of states, and the characteristics of Western civilization, contributed greatly to the shaping of modern armed forces. Territorial expansion and survival of the state became the objectives of war. The Peace of Westphalia (1648), which gave birth to the modern state system, and the French revolution (1795) provided the political condition for armies based on militarized conscription. Conscription provided the state with an instrument to quickly mobilize mass armies for the defense of the homeland. Industrialization and the rapid rise in population in the decades following the French revolution provided the material basis for mass armies. Nevertheless, after the restoration of autocratic regimes in the early 19th century, the ruling classes feared the consequences of armed citizens. Particularly in France, Prussia, and Austria, this gave rise to a class of longer-serving professional officers who represented the autocratic political structures. This pattern became widespread throughout Europe. Conscription enabled the emerging industrialized liberal democracies to view their military potential in terms of national population size. Both geography and the system of Westphalia required large, standing armies. Conscripts became the most important source of manpower. Consequently, temporary armies led by nobles were gradually replaced by standing armies led by professionals.

The system was further developed with new technological and organizational innovations. The railway system made mass movement, or "strategic lift" in contemporary jargon, possible. The electric telegraph was part of a new communications network. Political control over mass armies from great distances, and tactical control of deployed forces, was thus greatly enhanced. Other innovations, such as bureaucratic staffs and national

1 Davis, *Europe*, p. 52.

census systems, made possible the organization of mass armies. In the words of C. Dandeker, "a powerful bureaucratized war machine emerged."[2]

This "war machine" was no match for colonies and other less developed countries. During the 20th century, some industrially underdeveloped autocracies, such as the Soviet Union, were able to build up mass armies as well. Due to the absence of an innovative industrial base, its Red Army could rely only on its superiority in numbers, while the West had no other option but to compensate for this with superior technology.

The West's focus on technology had a tremendous impact on its armed forces. The Industrial Revolution radically changed the nature of warfare. Alvin and Heidi Toffler wrote that the most dramatic changes in war came from the new standardized weaponry that was produced by mass production methods.[3] Rapid-firing rifles, with their increased accuracy and greater range, replaced the old musket. Artillery, which was produced by advanced metal working industries, challenged the primacy of infantry. The machine gun and artillery contributed immensely to the firepower of modern armies. New weapons systems led inevitably to new tactics such as mobile warfare with mechanized units. Technology was increasingly being used to gain advantage over the adversary.

Until the end of the Cold War, large standing armies with mechanized units, innovative tactical doctrines such as mobile warfare, and dependence on technology to increase firepower were the dominant characteristics of modern Western armies. After the end of the Cold War, however, the armed forces of most West European states were rapidly transformed. The need to defend the homeland against a large-scale attack had disappeared. Consequently, in most countries, defense was now considered in terms of the defense of interests, that is, the political, social, and economic stability and well-being of the state. This new mission could also require crisis management and peace support operations in far-off places. As a result, most West European states abolished conscription and transformed their tactically mobile armed forces into strategically mobile expeditionary armed forces. It goes without saying that an expeditionary role for the armed forces had enormous consequences for doctrine as well.

In the West, there are important differences in military thinking. In the absence of a traditional threat, the United States has emphasized the expeditionary character of its armed forces ever since the First World War.

2 C. Dandeker, *Surveillance, Power and Modernity* (London: Polity Press, 1990), reprinted in Freedman, *War*, p. 118-122.

3 A. and H. Toffler, *War and Anti-War* (New York: Warner Books) 1993, p. 41.

Moreover, as a superpower, it had worldwide responsibilities. To a lesser extent, this also holds true for the former major colonial powers of France and the United Kingdom. This explains why these countries are more advanced in their doctrinal thinking than most other Western nations.

Flexible response

Contemporary doctrinal thinking about conventional and nuclear warfare is dominated by the US and is based on principles which mainly have their origin in the strategy of *flexible response*. Actually, the shaping of the contemporary Western mind-set began with the adoption of this strategy in 1967 by NATO. The strategy was developed in the US as a reaction to its predecessor, the strategy of *massive retaliation* of the 1950s. The critics of massive retaliation claimed that this strategy focused too much on nuclear weapons, which meant that it had only two options: suicide or surrender. This was related to changes in the balance of power. In the 1950s, the Warsaw Pact was superior in the area of conventional forces. The conventional Western inferiority was compensated by the superiority in nuclear weapons, and as a result, there was a plausible balance of terror. In the 1960s, American nuclear superiority disappeared. According to critics, this left the West with just one possible reaction to a conventional attack – the use of virtually its entire nuclear arsenal. As massive retaliation would come close to suicide, it seriously reduced the strategy's credibility. Credibility could be regained by controlled and limited use of nuclear weapons. This became an important basis for the new strategy. Should deterrence fail, there were, according to MC14/3 – the secret document drawn up by NATO's Military Committee – three types of military response open to NATO:

1 Direct defense seeks to defeat the aggression on the level at which the enemy chooses to fight. (...) Successful direct defense either defeats the aggression, or places upon the aggressor the burden of escalation. (...) The direct defense concept includes the use of such nuclear weapons as may be authorized.
2 Deliberate escalation seeks to defend aggression by deliberately raising, but where possible, controlling, the scope and intensity of combat, making the costs and the risks disproportionate to the aggressor's objectives. (...) Depending on the level at which the aggression starts (...), escalatory steps might be selected from among the following examples (...):
   - broadening or intensifying a non-nuclear engagement, possibly by opening another front or initiating action at sea in response to low-intensity aggression;

- use of nuclear defense and denial weapons;
- demonstrative use of nuclear weapons;
- selective nuclear strikes on interdiction targets;
- selective nuclear strikes against other suitable military targets.

3 General nuclear response contemplates massive nuclear strikes against the total nuclear threat, other military targets, and urban-industrial targets as required. (...) It is both the ultimate deterrent and, infused, the ultimate military response.[4]

The adoption of flexibility in response solved, at least on paper, NATO's "suicide or surrender" dilemma. The strategy, which provided guidance for national defense planners and the development of national "how to fight" doctrines, was based to a significant degree on the idea that Western technological superiority would actually make the controlled and limited use of nuclear weapons possible. The technological superiority of the West's conventional armed forces was also considered to partly compensate for the Warsaw Pact's numerical superiority. Conflicting views, however, continued to dominate the debate over its implementation. As will be seen, the debate was marked by confusion. A basic dilemma thwarted attempts to resolve questions using traditional methods of defense planning. The major problem was tactical nuclear weapons. Political leaders and US military planners argued that tactical nuclear firepower was organic to NATO's conventional forces. In Europe, however, many argued that tactical nuclear weapons could not serve national objectives in the same way conventional military forces could, but both superpowers maintained large nuclear forces, and for that reason it was imperative to plan their use. But how should one use nuclear weapons? Basically, the debate over the implementation of flexibility of response was a debate over the nature of deterrence. US defense planners advocated deterrence by denial of objectives. They tried to use traditional methods of defense planning to integrate nuclear weapons in the conventional battle. On the one hand, they considered tactical nuclear weapons as an extreme form of firepower that could provide the urgently needed tactical edge in combat power that would be required to win the war. On the other hand, they were aware of the many uncertainties that the use of nuclear weapons would involve. Consequently, the prevailing notion was that nuclear weapons should not be employed before conventional defenses had been severely tested and found inadequate. Many European

4 NATO, *Overall Strategic Concept for the Defense of the North Atlantic Organization Area* (MC 14/3), 22 December 1967, section 17.

political leaders, however, favored a policy based on deterrence by the threat of punishment. They suggested a rather early resort to tactical nuclear weapons in a limited and demonstrative mode. It was argued that early first use might enhance deterrence because it would threaten the adversary with nuclear escalation. The latter, however, was precisely what nuclear "war fighters" tried to avoid. NATO's strategy of flexibility in response was ambiguous enough to be interpreted in both ways.

Active defense

The flexibility in response strategy guided the development of doctrines such as active defense, AirLand Battle, and Follow On Forces Attack (FOFA). By 1974, the United States had regained its decisive influence regarding doctrinal matters, and took the lead in implementing NATO strategy. A major doctrinal reassessment of the US Army had already taken place in the early 1970s. It reflected a reorientation from the infantry and air mobile war in Vietnam to conventional nuclear war in Europe. The 1973 Yom Kippur War had a tremendous impact on this reorientation. For the first time since the Second World War, a major battle was fought between forces equipped with conventional weapons quite similar to those of NATO and Warsaw Pact countries. As a result, the US Army drew a number of important conclusions with regard to a major war in Europe. The Yom Kippur War made clear that the conventional battlefield had changed both in tempo and lethality. The US Army's Training and Doctrine Command (TRADOC) was tasked to summarize the lessons learned and incorporate them in a new "how to fight" manual. The most important lesson was that modern weapons were vastly more lethal than conventional weapons had been in the past. Improvements in range, accuracy, and lethality made TRADOC conclude that anything that can be seen on the battlefield can be hit, and almost certainly destroyed. The Yom Kippur War awoke new interest in exploiting new weapons technologies. Increased accuracy was obtained from precision guidance techniques. New electronic data links permitted the execution of more complex missions and new technologies greatly enhanced the lethality of munitions, combined with reduction of unwanted side effects. Improved target identification and acquisition techniques enhanced the effectiveness of conventional weapons as well, as did improved command, control, communications, and intelligence (C3I) systems. The latter could provide a better overall picture of the battlefield. After the Yom Kippur War, increased lethality through better accuracy and intelligence became a major focus for US defense planners. Another important development was the abolition of the draft, since it was acknowledged that only an army of professionals was able to conduct high-tech expeditionary operations.

In late 1974, TRADOC set out to develop and publish the revised edition of the basic "how to fight" manual, which was published in June 1976. According to the manual, the US Army's primary objective was to win land battles.[5] It seems that the US Army's definition of "winning" was the unconditional surrender of the enemy. US planners assumed that the Warsaw Pact forces would be superior, both in troops and in equipment. It was recognized that for economic and political reasons the US Army, like the armed forces of the NATO allies, could not hope to match the numerically superior armed forces of the Warsaw Pact states. The solution, it was argued, lay in fielding a US Army qualitatively better equipped and trained than the potential enemy. Thus the most important question was how the Army should fight and win when outnumbered on an armor-dominated battlefield.

It was assumed that any wars being fought would be of short duration, intense, and extraordinarily violent. Losses would occur in short periods, and entire forces could be destroyed quickly if they were improperly deployed. The manual concluded that "the first battle of our next war could well be its last battle: belligerents could be quickly exhausted, and international measures to stop fighting could bring about an early cessation of hostilities."[6]

The key chapter of the manual dealt with "modern weapons on the modern battlefield." It began with an analysis of the Yom Kippur War, and compared modern land combat with campaigns during the Second World War. Since then, the emphasis on precision-guided munitions has only increased. Against this technological background, the manual explained the principles of modern combat.[7] To win a war, adequate forces and weapons must be concentrated at critical times and places. The combination is combat power. Moreover, the battle must be controlled and directed so that the maximum effect of fire and maneuver is concentrated at decisive locations. Thus, improving maneuver and combat power by making use of new technologies became the cornerstone of modern warfare.

Understanding the enemy was also among the fundamentals of defensive operations. It was considered an absolute priority to study Warsaw

5 US Army, Field Manual (FM) 100-5 *Operations* (Washington, D.C., 1976), p. i.

6 FM 100-5 (1976), p. 1-1.

7 FM 100-5 (1976), p. 3-4.

Pact weapons systems and tactics. Soviet military doctrine and strategy, operational art and tactics, as well as the consequences of the introduction of mobile surface-to-air missiles, were extensively analyzed for the first time. Part of the effort to obtain a better understanding of Soviet plans was the translation of various Soviet military literature. The manual observed that "the time to study and think is now."[8] Only after some 30 years, the US Army analysts started to try to understand the enemy. An explanation for this was the preoccupation with nuclear strategy. Nevertheless, until today, understanding the adversary has always been a weak link in US doctrine. As has been argued before, during Operation Allied Force – the war on Kosovo in 1999 – the Americans displayed little understanding of Slobodan Milosevic. As a result, both the assessment of the campaign's duration and the way it was fought turned out to be wrong.

Another fundamental of defensive operations was that the commander must "see" the battlefield because an "outnumbered defender must know where to concentrate."[9] This requires superior battlefield command, control, communications, and intelligence, although it was acknowledged that its electronic components might be vulnerable on the integrated battlefield.

Of great importance was that the manual stated that in defending against breakthrough tactics, division commanders should not only concentrate their forces at the right time and place, but they should also be prepared to take risks at the flanks: "A defense which spreads two brigades thinly across a wide area and holds one brigade in reserve for counterattack will be defeated by a breakthrough attack."[10] The requirement to take risks on the flanks and the relative static defense tactics became known as *active defense.*

Surprisingly, this manual largely ignored the integrated conventional and nuclear battlefield. In terms of planning, it was assumed that a Warsaw Pact offensive would be non-nuclear and would be countered by non-nuclear means. Only one small chapter dealt with nuclear operations, but it did not contain a nuclear war fighting doctrine, although nuclear weapons played a crucial role in NATO's strategy of flexibility in response. The manual only dealt with the effects of nuclear explosions on the battlefield, the control and release procedures, and some aspects of nuclear planning. In fact, this manual and other relevant manuals made clear that the US Army had no idea how to fight and win a tactical nuclear war.

8 FM 100-5 (1976), p. 5-2.

9 FM 100-5 (1976), p. 5-2.

10 FM 100-5 (1976), p. 5-3.

Interoperability

During the 1960s, the European allies were concerned with minimizing the risks of unilateral US troop reductions under the pressure of both Vietnam and "Mansfieldism." A European fear that the United States would unilaterally withdraw troops was certainly justified. As a direct consequence of the unpopularity of the Vietnam War, the Nixon doctrine was proclaimed. In 1969, President Richard Nixon stated that with regard to "our Asian friends," the United States would try to keep its treaty commitments, but also, "as far as the problems of international security are concerned, as far as the problems of military defense, except for the threat of a major power involving nuclear weapons, that the United States is going to encourage and has the right to expect that this problem will be increasingly handled by, and the responsibility for it taken by, the Asian nations themselves."[11] Beginning in 1969, troop withdrawals from Vietnam were undertaken, one of the two US Army divisions in South Korea was withdrawn, and a ground unit and a tactical air unit were withdrawn from Thailand.

Nixon stated in his 1970 foreign policy report that a "one-and-a-half war concept" was required to fight back a full-scale Warsaw Pact attack in Europe, and a major conflict elsewhere. Both President Gerald Ford and President Jimmy Carter accepted the concept as a basis for force planning. Nevertheless, these developments raised fears in Europe that the United States would eventually reduce its commitment. This prospect convinced the European allies that Europe should take a greater share of the burden of common defense and strive after a greater interoperability. This resulted in the "AD 70" study on allied defense, initiated in December 1970. The resulting report listed eight priority areas: "armed anti-armor potential; the air situation including aircraft protection; overall maritime capabilities, with special reference to anti-submarine forces; the situation on NATO's flanks; the peacetime deployment of ground forces; further improvements in Allied mobilization and reinforcement capabilities as well as in NATO communications, for crisis management purposes."[12] In 1971, a ninth priority was added: electronic warfare. At the same time, NATO's European defense ministers launched a European Defense Improvement Program designed to rectify the deficiencies listed above. It soon became clear that the AD 70 list was too broad. Consequently, it was narrowed to six basic

11 Kissinger, *The White House Years* (New York: Simon and Schuster, 1979), p. 224.

12 North Atlantic Council, *Alliance Defense for the Seventies*, annex to the final communiqué, Brussels, September 3-4, 1970.

issues: aircraft shelters; anti-armor weapons; war reserve stocks; electronic warfare; mobile air defense; and modern air-delivered munitions. The AD 70 exercise resulted in a plea to Nixon not to withdraw troops from Europe, except in the context of negotiated reductions with the Warsaw pact.

By the mid-1970s, however, the effort had failed. Apart from a common infrastructure program and NATO's integrated communications system, both established in 1971, all proposed projects were national programs. Each country decided for itself what it was prepared to do, thus ignoring NATO's overall objective of improving efficiency and interoperability. AD 70 represented NATO's first of many failed attempts to define a common defense program.

A major complication for the execution of NATO's conventional defense improvement program was based on economic grounds. Following the 1973 Middle East war and the first oil crisis, Western Europe and the United States were facing economic recession. In 1973, the percentage of gross domestic product (GDP) devoted to defense in the United States dropped from 7.9% in 1970 to 6% in 1973, and to under 5% in 1976. The percentage for NATO Europe remained virtually constant in the range of 2.6% to 3.8%. Between 1973 and 1975, however, the GDP declined both in the United States and in NATO Europe.

In the US Army field manual, special emphasis was given to operations in the NATO area. Interoperability was considered to be a major problem because all allies used different "how to fight" manuals. In contrast to the Warsaw Pact, no single NATO doctrine existed, and there was no formal NATO guidance for the development of national doctrines. To harmonize the doctrinal efforts, NATO developed Allied Publications (APs) providing the national authorities with information pertaining to tactics, intelligence, doctrine, security rules, exercise procedures, and technical and administrative matters. These documents provided a basis for the improvement of interoperability. In 1976, two important Allied Tactical Publications (ATPs) were made available: the *land force tactical doctrine* and the *tactical air doctrine*.

Before examining the development of the ATPs, it is useful to have a detailed look at the events leading to the Supreme Allied Commander Europe's (SACEUR's) request to attempt such a standardization. Central to the AD 70 initiative was the desire to make more efficient use of existing resources. Its objective was to make progress towards a "total force concept," in other words, bringing all elements of NATO defense into the fullest and most balanced coordination possible. This effort would be most successful if tactical doctrine was standardized as well. Against this background, in 1971,

SACEUR General Andrew J. Goodpaster requested that NATO's political authorities attempt to standardize his Supreme Headquarters Allied Powers Europe (SHAPE) in this way. Consequently, the resulting Allied Tactical Publication, which contained guidelines for the member states' doctrine writers, contained most key elements of the new US Army manual FM 100-5.

By the end of 1977, it was decided to promulgate Edition 1 of the ATP-35 NATO land force tactical doctrine. The similarities with FM 100-5 were striking. The ATP emphasized active defense-style tactics. It was clear that the doctrinal debate was largely dominated by American and German officers. The publication of the ATP-35 can be considered as a landmark, because it provided a starting point for the development of national "how to fight" manuals, although the document stated, "It is understood and accepted that the land force doctrine of any nation may go beyond and expand ATP-35."[13]

Attrition warfare versus maneuver warfare

The doctrinal debate of the 1970s was dominated by the question whether emerging technologies (ET) could offset the numerical superiority of the Warsaw Pact. In the Pentagon, both the research and development community and the tactical nuclear community were interested in the application of ET and the development of new defense concepts. Under Secretary of Defense for Defense Research & Engineering, Richard De Lauer, and his predecessor, William Perry, were articulate proponents. According to Steven Canby, a representative of the "military reform" movement, the view of these technicians was simple: "there is an opposing target array and each weapon has an associated Pk [*probability of kill*-RdW]. The greater the Pk, the better."[14] This concept had reached its peak with the doctrine of active defense, which was a typical attrition concept. Canby wrote that their view is simply stated: "Electronics is the leading edge of military technology; the West holds a substantial lead in these associated technologies; by exploiting their potential, Western superiority in technology can offset Eastern superiority in numbers."

In contrast to the research and development community, the tactical nuclear community knew about strategy and policy. But their understand-

13 NATO Military Agency for Standardization, *Land Force Tactical Doctrine* (Allied Tactical Publication 35, 1977).

14 S. Canby, *The New Technologies* (unpublished paper, November 1993), p. 8.

ing was based on strategic nuclear war, and they knew little about tactical concepts and conventional nuclear war, which are conceptually different. The Defense Nuclear Agency funded numerous studies by analysts from the strategic nuclear community on aspects of conventional war, which might affect, escalate, or impact on nuclear use. Their view was similar to that of De Lauer's: attrition oriented. Firepower was the key to success. The studies by these proponents of attrition warfare finally led to a method of interdiction called "holding the second echelon at risk."

At NATO's military headquarters SHAPE, similar studies were undertaken. During the mid-1970s, SACEUR General Alexander Haig initiated a series of studies on the selective use of nuclear weapons in the European theater. By 1976, no one at SHAPE knew precisely how MC 14/3's requirement of selective use should be implemented. There was no single SHAPE document on selective use, so that the question of how to employ nuclear weapons in Europe without risking uncontrollable escalation had yet to be answered. Studies indicated that one should first consider the employment of nuclear weapons as a top-down decision instead of a bottom-up request. This would allow for greater control over the employment of tactical nuclear weapons. Second, deep strike fires against East European targets far behind the forward edge of the battlefield and even against targets in the Soviet Union would probably be the best way to convince the Soviets that war termination was in their best interests. It was argued that these deep attacks should have some military value. Choke points and bridges were considered good targets for the initial use of tactical nuclear weapons. A major problem, however, was the lack of deep strike assets, both conventional and nuclear. This operational requirement was one of the origins of the debate on intermediate-range nuclear forces (INF) that dominated the 1980s. In summary, the conventional nuclear strike concepts and the INF debate had the same intellectual background.

The problem for the nuclear war fighters was how to get support for their plans. The support would never be approved under the heading of nuclear war fighting, because "it would not sell in the US and it was absolutely antithetical to Europeans."[15] According to analyst Steven Canby, the nuclear war fighters' "brilliance was in nudging the Army into its own predilections for the 'extended' and 'integrated' battlefields and then subsuming their own efforts under these headings. In this way the cost attributable to tactical nuclear warfare is reduced to the mere marginal cost of replacing conventional with nuclear warheads."

15 S. Canby, *New Technologies*, p. 9.

General Bernard Rogers was the leading US Army proponent of attrition warfare and nuclear war fighting. He saw deep attack as an expansion of the 1976 active defense doctrine, codified in FM 100-5 "Operations." Before he was appointed SACEUR in 1979, he was the US Army's Chief of Staff. Rogers, facing the problem of declining budgets, recognized the growing interest in ET in the Pentagon, the Congress, and the public. Thus ET became the forerunner of the debate on the Revolution in Military Affairs (RMA).

There was, however, a second school of thought, emphasizing maneuver warfare. Most of its proponents belonged to the "military reform movement." It was a heterogeneous group of military and civilian experts, congressmen, and former military and Pentagon officials. They were principally united in believing that there had to be a better way to allocate scarce resources to defense needs. Many of them agreed that NATO should reduce its dependence on nuclear weapons by strengthening conventional defenses. With regard to the latter, the application of ET offered new opportunities. Beyond these points, it is impossible to summarize the views of the military reform movement since there was considerable disagreement regarding how to accomplish this task. Civilian analysts, like Canby and Luttwak, were among the principal reformers. Most of the doctrine-writing work, however, was done by a small number of experts in the US Army.

The doctrinal debate of the late 1970s was highly confusing, since both schools developed new defense concepts that had little in common with each other. *AirLand Battle 2000* was the brainchild of a group of senior generals, who carried the US Army active defense doctrine to its logical extreme. It was a concept for the future, encompassing the period from 1995 to 2015. The characteristics of the future battlefield would be: large quantities of sophisticated combat systems; difficult command and control; no single dominant weapon systems; no significant advantage available; battle expanded into the air space and depth of enemy formations (more than 300 km.); and intensive battles at decisive points. From these characteristics, an operational concept, AirLand Battle 2000, was developed. The concept emphasized initiative, deep attack, agility, time, and synchronization. The key ingredient of AirLand Battle 2000 was initiative, "not just by traditional means but extensive use of emphasizing maneuver is a blend of fire and movement plus use of all combat assets in a truly integrated effort."[16]

With regard to tactics, firepower and attrition were the key elements of AirLand Battle 2000. In September 1981, Army Chief of Staff General Edward C. Meyer approved the basic concept. The individual concepts for

16 US Army, Training and Doctrine Command, *AirLand Battle 2000,* 4 September 1981, p. 5.

the functional divisions of AirLand Battle 2000 were worked out in 1981 and 1982 and published by TRADOC in August 1982. In late 1983, TRADOC renamed the concept *Army 21* to avoid further confusion with the AirLand Battle concept. Army 21 elaborated on the original concepts set out in AirLand Battle 2000, but sought greater specificity in ideas.

AirLand Battle represented a compromise between the thinking of the attrition warfare school and emphasizing maneuver warfare school. It featured a highly mobile type of emphasizing maneuver warfare and deep strike. The deep strike element represented the influence of the attrition warfare school. In attrition warfare, firepower dominates and emphasizing maneuver is movement to gain a better firing position. As a result, the US Army's 1976 active defense doctrine would lead to static warfare. In maneuver warfare, however, the role of firepower is suppressive and the enemy should be defeated by the crushing impact of sudden and unexpected moves.

These divergent opinions dominated the doctrinal debate of the late 1970s. Over the years, however, Army 21 incorporated many ideas from the US Army AirLand Battle doctrine, including the concept of a highly mobile type of maneuver warfare. Thus, Army 21 became the US Army's future concept along the lines set out in AirLand Battle.

In summary, the strategy of flexibility in response and the doctrines that were derived from it shaped the mind-set of senior American military officers, while the Europeans reluctantly accepted some of the new doctrinal principles. Their main preoccupation was interoperability and the application of new technologies to increase the performance of their armed forces.

The debate on active defense

From 1976 onwards, TRADOC elaborated on the doctrine of active defense. In 1979, however, the Army Headquarters in Washington intervened and countermanded TRADOC. It seemed that Army Chief Meyer was not satisfied with the work being done. There was much criticism of active defense both inside and outside the Army. In early June 1979, immediately after General Bernhard Rogers was appointed SACEUR, Meyer suggested to General Donn A. Starry that TRADOC should begin to consider revising the 1977 manual along new lines. In principle, Meyer agreed with the critics of active defense, but he had two other concerns. First, the manual was written for the battle in Europe and lacked worldwide application. Meyer believed that a war outside Europe was more likely. Second, Meyer was concerned with the defensive orientation of active defense doctrine. Indeed, events in Iran and Afghanistan had an immediate impact on US Army doctrine.[17] In addition, the principal author of the resulting doctrine, Colonel Huba Wass de Czege, argued that, "Army commanders became convinced as a result of their field training and war games that they would be unable to defeat the Soviets using the doctrine of 1976. These commanders believed that even if they could beat the leading Soviet echelon using 'active defense,' the initial battle would render their units ineffective while leaving Soviet follow-on forces intact with complete freedom of action."[18]

De Czege referred to the work of General Starry, the commander of the US V Corps in Europe in 1976 and 1977. An analysis by the V Corps of 150 battle situations revealed that follow-on forces would be the key element of the Warsaw Pact breakthrough operations. Among the first to discover the "tactical revolution" in Soviet military strategy was Philip Karber. The 1976 doctrine was especially vulnerable on the point of the Soviet breakthrough maneuver. It assumed a classic massed armor breakthrough, but Karber wrote in 1976 that a "major shift in tactical operational concepts" had occurred.[19] One year later, Karber wrote that the Soviets were concerned about NATO's anti-tank guided missiles.[20] According to Karber, it produced a strong awareness of their armored infantry fighting vehicle (the BMP). The latter was an indispensable support element to the concept of the massed armor breakthrough. Consequently, the Soviets exercised another breakthrough maneuver: the concept of multi-pronged attacks by BMP regiments, reinforced with armor across the entire battlefront seeking weak spots and holes.

William Lind, a member of Senator Gary Hart's congressional staff, wrote the first extensive critique of the 1976 manual.[21] He argued that the doctrine paid insufficient attention to the offensive. The doctrine was regarded as

17 J.L. Romjue, *From Active Defense to AirLand Battle: the Development of Army Doctrine 1973-1982* (Fort Monroe: Virginia, June 1984), pp. 30-32.

18 H. Wass de Czege, *The US Army's Doctrinal Reforms*, unpublished paper, November 3, 1982, p. 2.

19 P.A. Karber, "Soviet Lessons of Middle East War", *Army Research and development,* November-December 1976, pp. 11-15.

20 P.A. Karber, "The Tactical Doctrine in Soviet Military Doctrine", *Military Review,* November 1977, pp. 33-34.

21 W.S. Lind, "FM 100-5 Operations: Some Doctrinal Questions for the United States Army", *Military Review,* March 1977, pp. 54-65.

reactive, ceding the initiative to the attacker by discouraging maneuver or forces against enemy vulnerabilities. Offensive action was de-emphasized because of the perception that the US Army should fight and win when outnumbered. Another weak point of the 1976 manual was the assumption that the US Army had to fight and win the first battle of the next war. Lind noted a preoccupation with the first battle. He argued that the organization of the Soviet forces in echelons would permit the US to lose the first battle. If necessary, they could go on to win the second battle.

The weakest point of active defense was the focus on massing firepower toward the point of an attempted Warsaw Pact breakthrough. Active defense maintained that the key to success would be in massing all available firepower against the enemy at the point of attack; withholding any forces from the battle was considered risky. It was assumed that the enemy attack was best defeated by massing lightly engaged elements from either flank or threatened penetration against the front of the enemy's main attack to achieve at least the ratio of one defender for every three attackers. This tactic was considered to be dangerous because of the lateral movement of NATO troops in the face of Warsaw Pact massed formations and because combat force ratios in these areas have continuously and overwhelmingly favored the attacker. Related to this was the notion that what counted in the defense was the number of weapons systems sited forward to "service enemy targets." This notion supported the conclusion that few elements should be kept in reserve. Finally, the doctrine was attrition oriented. It stressed firepower at the expense of maneuver. This could lead to an early exhaustion of forward defense by subjecting it to the momentum built by Warsaw Pact follow-on forces. It was clear, however, that Soviet changes in tactical concepts urged the revision of US Army tactical doctrine. Moreover, it was still believed that the US Army should fight and win, even if it was outnumbered. As TRADOC put it: "if we can't always be stronger, then we must be smarter."

Thus, a new doctrine should be developed, exploiting the weak points of Soviet tactics. Two developments in Soviet military strategy attracted considerable attention: the revival of the Second World War "mobile group" as an "operational maneuver group" (OMG), and the Soviet concept of echeloning.

Soviet doctrine held that, if war broke out in Europe, it must be won very quickly, if it is to be won at all. A quick victory would prevent the war from escalating into a catastrophic nuclear exchange. Moreover, the strains of a prolonged battle might destroy the Soviet bloc from the inside. If a war is to be won quickly, surprise is essential. If NATO were given a long preparation time, the Western forces would be strong and well entrenched so that a quick victory was unlikely. Furthermore, Soviet planners seemed to be aware that an early and effective use of NATO's tactical nuclear weapons would cause a disastrous disruption to their offensive. To achieve a quick victory, while preventing NATO nuclear use, the Soviet General Staff developed a plan that would accomplish a rapid collapse of the NATO political and military system. To achieve this objective, Soviet military strategy called for an echeloned force structure and OMG.

According to NATO analysts, follow-on forces – all reserve forces, reinforcements and OMGs not committed to the front battle – would be used to build up momentum.[22] By keeping the momentum of the attack and continuously pouring fresh combat forces onto NATO's defensive positions, the Warsaw Pact sought to create major breakthroughs along NATO's defensive line, to try to destroy NATO's forward defense. OMGs – the term itself appeared in the Polish military press in 1982 – would try to push through any weakness in NATO's forward defense and operate independently behind NATO's lines to overrun important targets. These attacks were likely to be directed against NATO's weakest corps sections, notably the British, Dutch, and Belgian sectors. The objective of OMG operations was to destroy, disrupt, or seize NATO's nuclear weapons, C3I systems, air defenses, airfields, and lines of communications. Moreover, these OMGs would assist the advance of Warsaw Pact forces by seizing, for example, bridgeheads and road junctions. Finally, OMGs would prevent NATO not just from recovering and stabilizing a second line of defense, but also prevent the employment of its reinforcements and reserves.

The concept of echeloning led to a dramatic change in the US Army's basic tactical concept. The new US Army doctrine codified in Field Manual 100-5 "Operations" was promulgated on 20 August 1982. According to the manual, success on the battlefield would depend on the four basic tenets of AirLand Battle 2000, namely initiative, depth, agility, and synchronization.[23] Also, similar to AirLand Battle 2000, the new manual emphasized mission tactics.

As the new doctrine was a compromise between the two schools of attrition warfare and maneuver warfare, it contained elements of both. In fact, the manual called for two battles to be fought at the same time: a forward

22 B.W. Rogers, "Follow-on Forces Attack (FOFA): Myths and Realities", *NATO Review,* December 1982, p. 2. See also: AS Congress, Office of Technology Assessment, *New Technology for NATO: Implementing Follow-on Forces Attack* (Washington, D.C., June 1987) p. 16.

23 US Army, *Field Manual 100-5* Operations (Washington, D.C., August 20, 1982), p. 2-2.

battle against committed forces, and a deep battle against uncommitted or follow-on forces. The deep strike concept was designed to counter the threat of follow-on forces in order to maintain NATO and Warsaw Pact forces along the forward edge of the battlefield at a manageable level. If follow-on forces could be kept out of the forward battle, the US Army could provide a credible forward defense at the conventional level. AirLand Battle envisioned deep strike approximately 130 kilometers behind the forward edge of the battlefield.

The battle against committed forces was assumed to be highly mobile. Maneuver warfare was the second main innovation of the new doctrine. According to the manual, "maneuver warfare is the dynamic element of combat, the means of concentrating forces in critical areas to gain and to use the advantages of surprise, shock position, and momentum, which enable smaller forces to defeat larger ones."[24] The manual defined maneuver as the employment of forces through movement supported by fire to achieve a position of advantage from which to destroy or to threaten destruction of the enemy.

In contrast to the old doctrine, the counteroffensive was emphasized. Offensive operations were characterized by aggressive initiatives on the part of the subordinate commanders by speed and violence, by seeking soft spots, by rapid shifts in the main efforts to take advantage of opportunities, by momentum, and by the deepest, most rapid destruction of the enemy defense possible. According to the manual "the offense is the decisive form of war, the commander's only means of attaining a positive goal or of completely destroying an enemy force."[25] The offensive spirit was also found in the doctrine's defensive concepts. The manual stated that there is often little distinction between the offensive and the defense: "To win, one must attack. However, the distinctions between defensive and offensive operations of large formations are made primarily on their intended purposes rather than on the types of combat actions they undertake. Offensive combat is as much part of defensive operations as strong point defenses or delaying actions."[26]

The controversial aspects of the lateral movement by elements of the defending force of active defense had now disappeared. There was no single defensive technique. Defensive techniques could range from a static positional defense to a deeper, more dynamic force-oriented defense or maneuver.

Nuclear weapons and chemical weapons played a dominant role in the 1982 manual. For the first time since the adoption of the NATO strategy of

24 FM 100-5 (1982), p. 2-4.
25 FM 100-5 (1982), p. 8-1.
26 FM 100-5 (1982), p. 10-1.

flexible response, the US Army doctrine described an integrated battlefield. It seemed now that the non-nuclear battlefield was history. An integrated approach would be the answer to the dilemma of the military requirement for a timely release and the political requirement for time-consuming deliberations. Commanders should plan for preemptive nuclear strikes, and release procedures had to be simplified. In short, the use of tactical nuclear weapons should be preplanned so that tactical nuclear weapons would be available during the first hours of the battle.

The manual did not contain a single chapter on the use of tactical nuclear weapons. Instead, the use of these weapons was integrated into all tactical situations. They were to be employed as soon as possible. The manual emphasized selective nuclear employment and a deep strike role with nuclear weapons: "Nuclear weapons are particularly effective in engaging follow-on formations in depth because of their inherent power and because of reduced concern about troop safety and collateral damage."[27] The use of tactical nuclear weapons would be crucial for victory, because on "the modern battlefield, nuclear fires may become the predominant expression of combat power, and small tactical forces will exploit their effects." According to the manual, key nuclear targets would be "enemy nuclear delivery systems, key command and control elements, support forces in the rear of committed element, follow-on or deep echeloned forces, reserves."[28]

In conclusion, the doctrinal debate of the 1960s and 1970s established some important principles. With the exception of the idea that nuclear weapons were considered as an extreme form of firepower, most principles still play a key role in contemporary military thinking:
- Technology is to be exploited to better allocate scarce resources to defense needs. Especially electronics were seen to be at the leading edge of Western military technology.
- Offensive maneuver and combat power by making use of modern technology became the cornerstone of modern combat.
- Deep strike with stand-off weaponry became methods of interdiction to deny the enemy the opportunity to reinforce and supply its forward deployed troops.
- Interoperability in terms of doctrine, procedures, and assets became a prerequisite for coalition warfare.

27 FM 100-5 (1982), p. 7-15.
28 FM 100-5 (1982), p. 1-3.

The European reactions

On the one hand, the impact of the German "how to fight" manual HDv 100-100 on the development of the AirLand Battle doctrine was strong. It featured some elements that were incorporated in the new US Army manual. Starry and his doctrine writers were not only obsessed with *Auftragstaktik* or mission tactics, but also with the German concept of the *Schwerpunkt*: the center of gravity or point of main effort. The idea was to designate and sustain the main effort at the point of enemy vulnerability. This concept was also introduced in the new manual.

On the other hand, NATO's political headquarters in Brussels, national governments, and parliaments, paid little attention to these developments. NATO's political leadership dealt with everyday issues such as budgets, arms control, and East-West relations. Moreover, there was a physical barrier between NATO's political headquarters in Brussels and its military headquarters in Mons. Most European political leaders considered the developments as being strictly American business and having no consequences for Europe. This is hardly surprising, given the differences in political and strategic cultures between the US and the majority of its European allies. Thus, an inner circle of the US defense establishment developed new concepts for the defense of Europe, which were finally adopted by the allies. Nonetheless, the new approach met with some serious political opposition.

The language used caused much of the confusion and critique about the new US Army doctrine. It was blunt and straightforward. The doctrine writers did not worry about political sensibilities. The offensive and aggressive spirit, the integrated battlefield, the highly mobile type of maneuver warfare, the emphasis on striking deep, met with hostile reactions in Europe. The manual was widely distributed in Europe. Peace movements, political parties, and defense analysts used the manual to make obvious the aggressiveness of the US Army. Its publication coincided with the debate on the deployment of intermediate range nuclear forces (INF) in Europe, which marked the nadir of US-European relations. The INF debate, however, led the discussion away from the tactical implementation of flexibility in response.

The maneuver aspects of the new doctrine caused some political disturbance as well, especially in the Federal Republic of Germany (FRG). This comes as no surprise because, as has been argued before, Germany had developed a distinct political culture with pacifist tendencies. Moreover, being a frontline state, it had much to fear from war between NATO and the Warsaw Pact. Indeed, American and German views on defense matters were almost diametrically opposed to each other.

Although the German "how to fight" manual was important for the drafting process, the German government rejected the new US Army doctrine. It was feared that the maneuver orientation of AirLand Battle might mean that the depth needed would not only be found on enemy territory, but also more to the West. This would mean a violation of forward defense. Moreover, it was argued that preparing both for a close and a deep battle would cause great budgetary problems.

The deep strike aspects of AirLand Battle also caused some disquiet in the FRG.[29] It was feared that the geographical extension of the battlefield might result in undesired escalation, because the attacker could conclude that the most sensible course of action would be to opt for an all-out offense. Finally, some feared that the US Army would use deep strike as an excuse for "liberating" Eastern Europe. NATO's "parliament," the North Atlantic Assembly, rejected the new doctrine with the following argument: "The recently adopted US Army AirLand Battle doctrine argues for the development of an offensive terrain-seizing capability for US forces of Warsaw Pact territory. This would be neither prudent nor appropriate for the alliance. It would not be prudent militarily because such deep attack forces would have to be taken from currently earmarked reserve or counterattack forces; thereby leaving alliance forces in a very exposed position should the deep attack be frustrated. It would not be appropriate politically inasmuch as NATO is a defensive alliance. There is an essential distinction to be drawn between terrain seizing and force-oriented interdiction. NATO has long engaged in planning for operations against Warsaw Pact air bases and key fixed military targets in Warsaw Pact territory. From the Soviet viewpoint, the ability of NATO to seize terrain well into Eastern European territory would represent a political instrument to exploit lack of cohesion within the Warsaw Pact and could be perceived as part of a political and military offensive strategy for NATO."[30]

In short, according to the assembly, AirLand Battle would undermine crisis stability. The military, however, welcomed the concepts of maneuver warfare and deep strike. Former NORTHAG commander Sir Nigel Bagnall argued that NATO's problem was the "over-literal interpretation of forward

29 The German debate between Stratmann, Lubkemeier, and Nikutta in *Aussenpolitik und Zeitgeschichte* (February 16, 1986); R. Nikutta, *Eine Offensive Kriegsführungsdoktrine für das Schlachtfeld Europa: AirLand Battle und Rogers Plan*, Arbeitspapiere aus dem Berliner Projektverbund der Berghof-Stiftung für Konfliktforschung, January 1984.

30 North Atlantic Assembly, Military Committee, *Interim Report of the Sub-Committee on Conventional Defense in Europe* (Brussels, November 1983), p. 13.

defense and the defensive nature of the alliance."[31] According to Bagnall, the "result is that we tend to try and defend passively and right up to the inter-German border regardless of whether or not this is feasible." Accordingly, he emphasized a defense concept of maneuver warfare.

Although politicians did not agree with the military, no major changes were introduced in the concepts.

On May 6, 1986, a new version of the AirLand Battle manual was published. The language was much more diplomatic. Distribution of the manual was limited to US government agencies, and other requests for release of the document could only be made under the Freedom of Information Act. Thus it was hoped that a public debate on the new manual could be avoided. In fact, the 1986 manual was a refinement and update of the 1982 AirLand Battle doctrine, not a revision. It did not change the basic doctrine.

Although the effects of deep strike on space and time were better defined, the message remained the same: observe and attack deep. Under German pressure, however, deep strike was reduced from 130 kilometers to approximately 30 to 100 kilometers. Thus, deep strike was hoped to be less provocative.

In an attempt to enhance crisis stability, the offensive was de-emphasized and the balance between offensive and defensive operations was more clearly defined. The role of both nuclear and chemical weapons was de-emphasized. While the 1982 manual assumed the use of nuclear weapons right from the start of the conflict, the 1986 version argued that it was not certain that tactical nuclear weapons would be employed during the conflict. Thus, the role of conventional forces was emphasized. The role of tactical nuclear weapons was not emphasized throughout the manual. Instead, small sections in a number of paragraphs dealt with employment considerations.

Its main innovation was that it elaborated the concept of the operational level of war. Moreover it emphasized low-intensity conflict, thus making the manual better applicable to contingencies outside the European theater. The manual was "both more theoretical and more general so as to meet US needs in other theatres."[32]

31 N. Bagnall, "Concepts for Land/Air Operations in the Central Region", Part I, *RUSI* journal, vol. 129, no. 3, p. 46.

32 US Army, *Field Manual 100-5:* Operations (Washington, D.C., 1986) p. i.

AirLand Battle and NATO tactical doctrine

On the one hand, many European political leaders maintained that AirLand Battle was merely a US Army doctrine that did not apply to the other nations' armies. Besides the INF debate, this was another important reason why NATO Europe did not discuss the new concept thoroughly. SACEUR General Rogers confirmed this view when stating that AirLand Battle did not coincide with the doctrine of Allied Command Europe (ACE). Thus Rogers suggested that he rejected the new doctrine. On the other hand, Secretary of Defense Caspar Weinberger stated that the doctrine had been discussed extensively with the allies. Moreover, Rogers had initiated a study on the integration of AirLand Battle in NATO doctrine. Finally, Rogers, as commander in chief of US forces in Europe, was committed to the doctrine. In February 1986 he endorsed the new manual.

In summary, there was much confusion about the status of the new doctrine. The absence of a political debate on the tactical implementation of flexibility in response suggests that NATO's political leaders had no idea how US Army doctrine might influence the development of national "how to fight" doctrines. They were not aware of the fact that the basic concept of the US Army doctrine was already "leaking" into national doctrines.

According to the 1986 manual, it was itself consistent with NATO's land force doctrine.[33] In fact, the new manual had a profound impact on the development of NATO's doctrine. As already stated, the similarities between NATO's 1977 land force doctrine and the US Army's 1976 active defense doctrine were striking. So were the similarities between the two new documents.

After having agreed on the promulgation of the NATO doctrine for land forces in December 1979, the Tactical Working Party set to work to prepare a second edition of the document, incorporating the lessons of major exercises. Initially, the working group did not envision major changes in the concept, but "a minimum of two years is needed for users to apply doctrine in major exercises conducted by NATO commands, and one year for review and processing of users' comments and recommendations."[34] Nevertheless, in June 1979 it was decided that a new structure for the document was needed "somewhat along the lines of the German manual 100-100." The basic objective of the restructuring was to make it easier for the reader to consult doctrine. As already stated, the exercise was an attempt to come

33 As codified in Allied Tactical Publication-35(A), *Land Force Tactical Doctrine,* March 1984.

34 This section is based on the Tactical Working Party's historical file.

to greater standardization and harmonization. In this respect, the exercise was quite successful, although there were "several areas of concern." The standardization lessons from exercises were presented by the member countries and by SHAPE. For example, the US VII Corps noted that the areas of concern "both related to the differences in the national doctrines of defense, i.e., active and position of defense. Problems centered on rear boundary coordination and exchanges of information between German and US units." In short, the main problem was that the national doctrines were still not fully in compliance with the ATP. The new ATP-35(A) was published and distributed to the nations and NATO commands by the end of June 1984. The similarities with the US Army AirLand Battle doctrine were striking. Following a discussion on the implementation of the new Allied Tactical Publication, the American delegation pointed out that NATO's new doctrine had already been implemented in FM 100-5 and that the primary difference between the two were ones of omission rather than conflict. In other words, the US Army field manual had served as a framework for the development of NATO's new doctrine. The latter incorporated all major concepts of the US Army doctrine of 1982. The new NATO document also regarded maneuver as the key principle of defense and the decisive element at all levels. It also emphasized an offensive spirit. The defender should not be passive and wait, but must seize and create any opportunity to surprise the enemy and force him to depart from his plans, and at every level he must take offensive action to harass the "enemy." "The defense should, therefore, be fought with imagination, energy, and aggressive spirit with the aim to seize the initiative, wherever and whenever possible."[35]

The new ATP also called for an integrated battlefield: "Whatever concept of defense is employed it must be immediately adaptable to nuclear conditions," and, "When nuclear release is given, it is still important to use all resources including non-nuclear fire, air attacks, barriers, and troop in contact, in order to force the enemy to concentrate, thereby creating worthwhile targets."[36] Like the 1982 US Army doctrine, it called for the early use of tactical nuclear weapons: "If nuclear weapons have been released, it will be important to use them at an early stage, to destroy enemy forces during the employment."[37]

The new NATO doctrine provided a revised framework for the development of national "how to fight" doctrines. After some time, national

35 ATP 35(A), section 0312.

36 ATP 35(A), section 0316.

37 ATP 35(A), section 0414.

doctrines were quite similar indeed. There are, however, some differences. The revised 1983 British manual sought to redefine the space that would be required for maneuver warfare more in depth on NATO territory. The Dutch manual was revised in 1985 along similar lines. In Germany there was little political support for a revision of the Field Manual 100-100 similar to the Dutch and British manuals, since this would violate the concept of forward defense. Consequently, there was some support for solving this problem by extending the battlefield eastward, as the Americans did in their FM 100-5. Ultimately, it was agreed that Warsaw Pact lead forces would be dealt with by maneuver on FRG territory, aided by air-mobile operational reserves and complemented by obstacles and by firepower attacks on second echelon units, rather than maneuvers against these units.

Follow-on Forces Attack

In 1979, SACEUR General Rogers tasked the SHAPE staff to study the conventional strength of Allied Command Europe (ACE) and to study "Attack and destroy second echelon forces." In fact, the new studies used the SHAPE studies on selective nuclear use as a starting point. Moreover, there were strong links with the American doctrinal debate. Although it was developed over the same rough time scale as the US AirLand Battle concepts, it was a SHAPE initiative and was not an attempt to simply incorporate US ideas.[38]

Nevertheless, the best elements of these American studies were incorporated in a new "sub-concept of operations" called Follow-on Forces Attack (FOFA). Initially, the work was especially influenced by the AirLand Battle 2000 concept. Rogers was Army chief during its genesis and he was especially interested in the application of ET.

In 1983, FOFA became an agreed concept of operations for ACE. On November 9, 1984, the defense ministers formally approved the new doctrine, thus making FOFA officially part of NATO strategy.

According to the Office of Technology Assessment, three major factors came together to produce FOFA, and make it a major part of NATO's strategy.[39] First, it has been recognized that successfully attacking follow-on forces could have a profound effect on the ability of the Warsaw Pact to execute its offensive strategy. Second, there was a new emphasis on directly

38 NATO, Supreme Headquarters Allied Powers Europe, *FOFA Statement to TACWP.*

39 Office of Technology Assessment, *New Technologies for NATO: Implementing Follow-on Forces Attack* (Washington, D.C.: May 1979), p. 16.

attacking ground forces themselves, in addition to facilities such as air bases that would support them. Finally, there was a recognition that achieving a significant capability to attack forces would depend strongly on exploiting new technologies. With regard to the latter, FOFA would provide the West with the opportunity to exploit its technological advantage to offset the Warsaw Pact's numerical superiority, their use of follow-on forces, and their ability to use their strategically mobile offense against a much-less mobile defense. By attacking the follow-on forces, SACEUR hoped to decrease their ability to effect the front battle. With regard to NATO's strategically less mobile battle, the FOFA capability would be used to compensate for this by directing the firepower of longer-range weapons and interdiction aircraft along the front. Both mobile and fixed targets were to be attacked. According to Rogers, most follow-on movements would depend on the East European railway system, which is vulnerable to attack on electrical power supplies, central command and control facilities, communications systems, computer stations, switching stations, on-and-offloading sites, railway beds, and river crossing sites. Moreover, road movement would be vulnerable to disruption from attacks on choke points. Rogers also pointed out that logistic sites and assembly areas of combat forces would be targets for deep strike operations.

There were great differences between AirLand Battle and FOFA, although the rationale behind the two concepts is similar, that is, destroying or disrupting follow-on forces before they engage the main battle. FOFA dealt with the application of deep strike firepower by echelons above corps. It was a multinational concept which sought to centralize deep strike firepower. It did not contain guidelines for the ground commander to fight his close battle. The latter was the responsibility of the national commander, who would fight according to national doctrine. With regard to AirLand Battle, the US commander sought to synchronize the deep battle with the ground commander's scheme of maneuver, which leads to a decentralized application of deep strike firepower. The same held true for NATO's doctrine for land forces, codified in the NATO Land Force Doctrine.

Doubts about the feasibility of AirLand Battle

During the 1980s, critics argued that the new defense concepts could not be implemented. One author clearly indicated that the US Army AirLand Battle doctrine was merely a procurement concept, when stating that because "the Army realizes that attrition warfare with the Soviets cannot be won, weapon and combat support systems are now being developed which exploit emerging technology and will assist in the successful execution of concepts of the AirLand Battle doctrine."[40] The greatest shortfall would be C3I. Maneuver warfare required advanced C3I technologies that were still under development.

The Office of Technology Assessment observed that in implementing FOFA, NATO should overcome many limitations: NATO's current reconnaissance and command, control, and communication systems and procedures are not designed to provide timely information on the precise location of mobile targets; most existing air-delivered weapons cannot destroy armored vehicles in significant numbers; few NATO aircraft are capable of operating well at night or in bad weather, and all will face competing demands from other missions, including opposing enemy air forces, close air support, and nuclear standby; additionally, ground-launched weapons, which would complement aircraft at times when few aircraft are available, have little to offer.

The first real test for AirLand Battle came during the Gulf War. Operation Desert Storm was an unparalleled success. On the one hand, the victory was a great boost to morale and was instrumental in further shaping the mind-set of soldiers, politicians, and civil strategists. On the other hand, this was the kind of warfare the US and its allies had prepared for, for many decades. Moreover, the terrain was ideally suited for the Western way of war. Like the North German plain, the terrain was ideal for the deployment of large mechanized formations. Finally, Saddam Hussein applied Soviet-style tactics, while AirLand Battle was developed to deal with such tactics in Europe. Nevertheless, AirLand Battle is now considered as a turning point in the history of warfare. It was the ultimate triumph of Western technology and the proof that the West could gain quick victories with few casualties, at least on the coalition side, and little collateral damage.

Until today, most of the shortfalls identified by NATO and the Office of Technology Assessment have not been solved. But ET was reincarnated as network-centric warfare in the early 2000s. AirLand Battle survived the Cold War, and maneuver remained the key element of ground operations. FOFA was abolished, because Russian military doctrine was no longer taken into account in operational planning. But deep strike resurfaced prominently in the AirSea Battle concept of 2012.

40 J.F. Rybicki, "Emerging Technologies and the AirLand Battle", *Military Technology, 10* (1984), p. 25.

The doctrinal mess of the 1990s

Until 1990, there was a lack of hard evidence as to how the new technologies might work in practice. Due to Vietnam, there was little confidence that US armed forces could fight and win wars quickly and decisively without too many losses, but the Gulf War demonstrated the virtues of modern technology. Soon after the Gulf War, the US and its allies started to restructure their armed forces. The restructuring process was far from a radical departure. The main innovation was not doctrinal, but technological. The debate was largely about the revolution in military affairs (RMA) and the virtues of air power. The term "revolution" was misleading, because most of the core RMA technologies had been developed in the 1970s. As pointed out, most of the debates on the impact of precision and remote guidance target identification and acquisition, and the importance of command, control, and communication started after the Yom Kippur War of 1973. Due to the large-scale introduction of computers based on microelectronics, warfare evolved further and resulted in the debate on ET. Reinforced by the "information revolution" of the early 1990s, the RMA now depended on the interaction between systems that collect, process, fuse, and communicate information and those that apply military force.

To be successful on the battlefield, dominant battle space knowledge was achieved through superior command, control, communications, computers, intelligence and surveillance, target acquisition and reconnaissance (C4ISTAR). This made continued precision strike possible. Together with the ability to strike with precision over great distances, time and space considerations would become less of a constraint. Precision strike would require fewer munitions with smaller yields and consequently fewer sorties. This would not only reduce logistical demands of expeditionary armed forces, but it would decrease collateral damage as well. Moreover, fewer sorties meant fewer risks for pilots. Nevertheless, soon after the Gulf War, serious doubts emerged about both doctrine and military effectiveness in conflicts with different characteristics than those of the Gulf War.

In the US, two schools of thought emerged, both predicting a paradigm shift in the Western way of warfare. The first maintained that statistical evidence showed that most conflicts were not fought by regular armed forces practicing conventional warfare techniques. They maintained that the Gulf War was an exceptional case, and that it was unlikely that future conflicts would be fought in a similar way. Future wars were likely to be fought against irregular forces, using unconventional warfare techniques. As there are no peer competitors in the new security environment, concepts such as maneuver warfare and deep strike would have little meaning. This school put emphasis on what was called "asymmetric wars," which took the strategies of the weak into account.

The second school of thought argued that the Gulf War was the ultimate triumph of air power. As explained previously, after a six-week air campaign, ground forces were able to do the job within 100 hours. For the first time in history, the use of air power brought an enemy to its knees. In a report to the US Congress, the Pentagon wrote that "air power was the principle instrument of military force during the first 38 days of Operation Desert Storm" and "according to the Air Force, over 80% of the precision-guided bombs released were hits."[41] CNN had shown cruise missiles following predetermined routes to their targets and videos from onboard cameras of smart bombs hitting bridges and bunkers with great precision, thus contributing to the idea that the nature of warfare had changed dramatically. In practice, only 7% of the total tonnage dropped was smart bombs. Moreover, it was unclear what the various strikes were meant to achieve.

During the 1990s, the air power school became dominant. As has been argued in chapter 3, some considered air power the ideal instrument for coercion. Air power could save the lives of soldiers on the ground; stand-off and precision strikes would reduce collateral damage, so that using force would be morally more acceptable. During the 1990s, it became common wisdom that air power was now so lethal and US air power so dominant that victories could be won at little cost. As decisive battles would be won from the air, the US and its NATO allies should radically alter their procurement strategies and invest more heavily in air power.

After the war on Kosovo, the British historian John Keegan stated that the time had come to redefine how victory in war may be won. If Keegan were right, Pape would be wrong. In *Bombing to Win,* he concluded that air power alone could not do the job. Moreover, he had little faith in the RMA because, he concluded, "the 'precision-guided missile revolution' is not likely to enhance the coercive effects of strategic bombing."[42]

To examine these propositions, it is first necessary to have a closer look at air power. Its traditional roles include:

- Counterair operations, i.e., operations conducted to attain and maintain a degree of air superiority. Operations involve attacks against airfields, air defense assets, and command and control facilities. Gaining air

41 Department of Defense, *Conduct of the Persian Gulf Operation,* pp. 6-1 and 6-2.

42 Pape, *Bombing to Win,* pp. 314-316.

superiority in the initial phase of the war is crucial because it provides freedom to attack as well as freedom from attack.

- Strategic attack, i.e., actions carried out against the adversary's centers of gravity and other vital targets, to affect a level of destruction and disintegration of his military capability to a point where he can no longer retain the ability to wage war. Strategic attack could involve air interdiction, i.e., air operations to destroy, neutralize, or delay the adversary's military forces before they can be brought to bear effectively against friendly forces.
- Tactical operations, i.e., attacks against fielded forces, usually in support of ground forces. Traditional missions include close air support, i.e., attacks against hostile targets in close proximity to friendly forces.

The key innovation was precision engagement, or the ability to forgo the brute force-on-force tactics of previous wars, and apply discriminate force precisely where required. As modern air forces have global reach, techniques of precision engagement can be applied anywhere around the world in a matter of hours and minutes. Information superiority enables precision engagement around the globe. It is the ability to collect, control, exploit, and defend information, while denying the adversary the opportunity to do the same. Reconnaissance aircraft, such as the U2, unmanned aerial vehicles (UAV) such as the Predator, satellites, and human intelligence form a "system of systems" to collect data and direct air forces to their targets. Precision engagement, together with sophisticated air- and space-based intelligence, surveillance, and reconnaissance systems have revolutionized air power. In summary, given its characteristics, it is very tempting to believe that air power is the instrument par excellence for coercion.

In order to test the propositions of the air power school, it is useful to have a closer look at the Gulf War and Operation Allied Force. On February 24, 1991, US ground troops, supported by British, French, and Arab forces, moved from northern Saudi Arabia to liberate Kuwait. As there were no diplomatic efforts to convince Saddam Hussein to leave Kuwait, the Gulf War is a classic example of coercion. The coalition forces achieved their objectives quickly and with surprisingly few coalition casualties. Most observers concluded that air power neutralized the Iraqi military before the ground war began. During the period of six weeks now known as the air campaign, tons of bombs were dropped on Iraqi targets. For the first time in history, the Americans used smart bombs and cruise missiles that were fired from 1,000 kilometers away at multiple targets.

The air power doctrine applied was parallel warfare. Its conceptual basis was developed by Colonel Warden (chapter 3). He sought to weaken or incapacitate the adversary by integrating centers of gravity into a comprehensive view of the enemy as a system. New techniques for target acquisition, precision weapons, and stealthy aircraft would allow simultaneous attacks on multiple centers of gravity, thus creating system-wide effects. Warden replaced the traditional approach of occupying a country and subsequently toppling its leadership to achieve other strategic objectives by a more subtle method. Weapons systems would be employed in such a manner that they would contribute to the desired effects, that is, the collapse of a regime.

Warden developed a plan based on a five-ring system, with centers of gravity in each ring (table 4.1). The goal was to bring the Iraqi system under rapid parallel attack by simultaneously destroying the centers of gravity in each ring. Thus it was hoped that Iraq as a system would collapse, so that the Iraqi leadership would not be able to sustain the war effort, would withdraw its forces from Kuwait, and would cease to be a threat to regional stability.

Although most of the targets should be attacked simultaneously, some have priority during the initial strikes. In order to achieve air dominance or air superiority, the adversary's air defense assets, air force and command, control, and communications will have priority. As coalition forces cannot operate freely in the enemy's air space, initial attacks are likely to be carried out with stand-off missiles and stealthy aircraft. Parallel warfare exploits three dimensions: time, space, and the levels of war. Time is important because during the first hours or days of the operation massive strikes take place. Space is important because the entire depth and breadth of the theater of operations is subject to attack. Finally, the levels of war are important because strategic targets like leadership facilities, through to the tactical level like fielded forces will be attacked. Parallel warfare aims to achieve rapid dominance, to allow for a quick and decisive victory. The victory is no longer defined in terms of destroying the enemy, but in terms of dominating the adversary's influence on strategic events. In summary, parallel warfare is about weakening, not destroying, the adversary. Operations are aimed at controlling the adversary's vital functions, so that he is no longer able to fight effectively. This is a major departure from the past, where the military simply tried to impede the means of the enemy to conduct war or the will of the people to continue the war. Therefore, the focus is no longer annihilation through outright destruction or attrition or, in other words, exhausting the enemy before he exhausts you. Instead, the new approach is focused on the adversary's political and military organization that allows him to control his power base.

Table 4.1 Warden's Five Ring System

Leadership	Key production	Infrastructure	Population	Fielded forces
Saddam Hussein's government	Electricity	Railroad bridges	Military elites	Strategic air defense
National communications	Retail petroleum		Foreign workers	Strategic offensive systems (air and missile)
Internal security forces	Weapons of mass destruction		Baathists middle class	

However, Iraq as a system did not collapse as a result of the parallel attacks on all centers of gravity. Saddam's regime not only survived the Gulf War but also the numerous strikes in the years to follow. Indeed, it did not even weaken his regime significantly.

Did air power play a decisive role during the Gulf War? Conventional wisdom is that Iraqi forces were rendered ineffective because air power disrupted their command, control and communications, cut off their supplies and reinforcements, and prevented them from maneuvering. Finally, air power destroyed enough equipment and killed enough troops so that they were not able to resist coalition forces effectively when the ground war began.

The US Army argued that the Gulf War reflected the dynamic joint and combined nature of the operational offensive and simultaneous operations in depth. It was joint and combined because Operation Desert Storm started when allied air and naval forces began the destruction of key Iraqi strategic, operational, and tactical targets. Subsequently, the VII Corps and the XVIII Airborne Corps were moved into Iraq. As air interdiction and operational deception operations continued, allied ground forces were set to execute the decisive action against the enemy.

Others also challenged the claim that air power neutralized the Iraqi forces before the ground war began. Daryl G. Press maintained, that although air power played an important role, its role has been exaggerated and misunderstood.[43] Press argued that air power was not decisive and that it did not neutralize the Iraqi ground forces. The air campaign did not even play a necessary, enabling role that made the ground war easier. He

43 Daryl G. Press, "The Myth of Air Power in the Persian Gulf War", *International Security*, vol. 26, no. 2 (Fall 2002), pp. 5-44.

concluded that air power did not neutralize the Iraqi army by destroying its ability to maneuver or even its morale. Iraqi forces were not in disarray. Iraq's heavy divisions were functioning, organized military units until they were destroyed by coalition ground forces. Air power failed to neutralize these divisions because destroying large, static, defensive forces from the air is inherently difficult. These forces require fewer supplies than units conducting offensive or defensive operations. Consequently, cutting off supplies has only a limited effect. Moreover, static forces are very difficult to find, because they emit little heat, so that infrared sensors cannot find them. Neither do they use their radio transmitters, which could reveal their location. Finally, destroying command and control facilities does not necessarily make offensive action impossible if commanders are executing "mission orders."

The media concluded that Iraqi forces were simply overpowered by coalition forces, which were technically more advanced, more powerful, had a superior doctrine and gained a victory ideally suited to US and British military strength. Regarding the role of air forces, he concluded that it fulfilled its traditional missions: air forces gained air superiority, flew reconnaissance missions, were involved in joint coordination of the actions of coalition air and ground forces, conducted strategic attacks deep in Iraq, and degraded and disrupted Iraqi's military.

In summary, because its interests in the Gulf region were at stake, the US used massive and overwhelming force. Furthermore, the US leadership was willing to take risks and to take casualties. The coercive strategy consisted of three elements: weakening or incapacitation, denial, and control. Incapacitation was not successful. Saddam did not lose the support of the majority of the population. He did not lose control over his power base, the Baathists, or the Republican Guard. Air attacks on Iraqi ground forces were not themselves sufficient for a "decisive defeat." They were critical in enabling the ground campaign. This is a sharp break with the past. Air power no longer simply supported ground operations, but preceded and sometimes replaced them.

The principles of parallel warfare were also applied during Operation Allied Force, the 1999 war on Kosovo. In the years preceding the war on Kosovo, NATO nations embarked on a strategy of coercive diplomacy to urge President Milosevic to stop atrocities against the ethnic Albanians in Serbia's province of Kosovo and grant them a degree of autonomy. When the atrocities continued, NATO's credibility was at stake, so that there was no other option but to adopt a strategy of coercion. Diplomacy was sidelined; force was used.

In comparison to the Gulf War, target categories and centers of gravity were almost the same. Instead of attacking Saddam's power base, the Baathists and his Republican Guard, Slobodan Milosevic's socialist party and the forces of the interior ministry were attacked. The same concept of targeting could be applied because both countries had authoritarian regimes with clearly definable power bases and with strong industrial bases. Consequently, both countries were considered vulnerable to attacks against the foundations of the regimes.

As has been argued before, in 1999 NATO military planners wrongly predicted that the air campaign would last only a couple of days. The miscalculation had its roots in Operation Deliberate Force. In 1995, NATO successfully coerced the Bosnian Serbs after the shelling of a Sarajevo marketplace, killing some 40 people. Operation Deliberate Force consisted of almost 300 aircraft from 8 NATO countries, flying more than 3,500 sorties in the space of two weeks. The aim of the air campaign was to shift the balance in favor of the Bosnian Croats, to stop the Bosnian offensive against them, and to coerce the Serbs to accept a peace deal. Operation Deliberate Force succeeded in changing the balance of power in Bosnia and Herzegovina and laid the foundation for the Dayton Peace Accords, signed on December 14, 1995.

By mid-May, the air campaign, which started on March 24, had achieved very little. Milosevic's troops were not on the verge of collapse. Instead, it was feared that the coalition would break up because voices against the war in Germany, Greece, and Italy were becoming stronger. More importantly, Milosevic was able to increase the human tragedy by causing large floods of refugees, thus depriving NATO from achieving its key objective of deterring the Serb leadership from continuing and escalating attacks on Kosovo.

NATO's first goal was to achieve air dominance or air superiority. Initial strikes were aimed at Serb air defenses, airfields, and command and control facilities. During the whole of the campaign, NATO did not achieve complete air superiority because Serb air forces embarked on an asymmetric countercoercion strategy of partial passivity. They hid their aircraft and anti-aircraft missiles in hardened underground shelters. By activating their air defense radar systems occasionally during the air campaign, NATO could not be sure that the threat to its bombers and fighters had been effectively removed. In an attempt to limit the risks for pilots, NATO decided not to drop ordnance from less than 15,000 feet, thus severely reducing the tempo of the air campaign.

The objective of the strategic air campaign was to cut off Serb regular forces from the Kosovo Theater of Operations and to provoke discontent among the population. The main targets were barracks, staging areas, railroads, roads, bridges, command, control, communications, and refineries. These targets were constantly attacked, but the results were limited.

First, this had little impact on the morale of the Serbs. On the contrary, Milosevic became more popular and was supported by the majority of the population. By mid-May, NATO decided to step up the strategic air campaign. This resulted in raids on central Belgrade, and the destruction of power plants and power transmitter installations. NATO spokesman Jamie Shea told the press that the Serb population would suffer "some inconveniences." Despite NATO's rhetoric that the Serb population was becoming demoralized, there was little evidence that Milosevic was losing support. The NATO air campaign did undermine the morale of Serbia's top leadership. Some discontented top generals had to be placed under house arrest and there was a clear danger that Milosevic would lose political control. But there was never a rebellion against the regime.

Second, after the war, it turned out that NATO had greatly overestimated the effectiveness of the attacks. The pieces of destroyed tanks, artillery pieces, and armored vehicles numbered tens rather than the hundreds claimed by NATO. Serb forces used decoys extensively. Because they dropped their bombs from above 15,000 feet, NATO pilots could not distinguish the decoys from real tanks and bridges. Thus Serb forces prevented NATO from achieving the objective to damage Serbia's capacity to wage war in the future.

More importantly, after the cease-fire, Serb forces, which had withdrawn from Kosovo, were far from demoralized. They withdrew in an orderly fashion, taking with them most of their undamaged material.

Serb regular forces were mainly static forces, which could not be found by NATO air forces. Moreover, heavy equipment was stored in urban areas, for example, near hospitals, schools, and churches, so that their destruction would cause unacceptable levels of collateral damage.

As has been argued before, the atrocities were executed by lightly armed, highly mobile irregular forces led by local warlords and those of the interior ministry (MUP). Both the warlords and the MUP operated in small groups that were extremely difficult to find by NATO aircraft during the tactical air campaign. General Clark, NATO's supreme commander, described targeting fielded forces as his number one priority, dedicating approximately 30% of its sorties to attack Serb forces.

Military coercion with air power alone did not produce the desired result. Consequently, at the end of May 1999, the US and its NATO allies tried to find a diplomatic solution, thereby shifting to a strategy of coercive diplomacy. By mid-May, the Russians started to play a more prominent role by putting pressure on the Serb leadership. By the end of May, Finnish president Martti Athisaari, together with former Russian Prime Minister Viktor Chernomyrdin were tasked to broker a peace deal. For Milosevic, the deal turned out to be more favorable than the Rambouillet draft accords in February. Thus, Milosevic could claim the deal as a victory. Among other things, the Rambouillet accords were unacceptable because a plebiscite was to decide on the future status of the Serb province. The new peace deals recognized Kosovo as a province of Serbia and left open the possibility of a continued Serb political struggle for Kosovo. In addition, the new peace deal put the UN in charge. The UN would become the overarching political authority in Kosovo. In the Rambouillet draft accord, NATO was to play this role. This was unacceptable to Milosevic, who saw NATO as an occupying force.

In conclusion, air power was important, but air power alone did not produce the desired results.[44] Operation Allied Force started as military coercion but turned out to be a textbook case of coercive diplomacy, with air power in support of diplomacy. The difference with the Gulf War was the interests at stake. In the Balkans, floods of refugees could undermine the stability of neighboring countries. The striving for a greater Albania or a greater Kosovo by the nationalistic Kosovo Liberation Army could also have severe consequences for the stability of the region. Spillover of the conflict was quite likely, but this did not threaten the vital interests of the US, nor most of its European allies. For that reason, the coalition was not willing to take risks and accept large numbers of casualties, which could have been the result of the deployment of ground forces. Consequently, NATO embarked on a strategy of denial and limited attrition. During the Gulf War, a strategy of denial and control produced the desired results. In Kosovo, diplomacy, backed up by denial and attrition, led to the end of the war. The result was not a clear victory for NATO but an uneasy compromise, codified in UN resolutions.

Finally, the implicit strategy of decapitation did not work because Milosevic did not lose the support of the population and did not lose control over the Socialist Party or the armed forces.

44 Also: I.H. Daalder and M.E. O'Hanlon, *Winning Ugly: NATO's War to Save Kosovo* (Washington, D.C.: The Brookings Institution, 2000), and B.S. Lambeth, *NATO's Air War for Kosovo* (Santa Monica: RAND, 1999).

Lessons learned: the development of joint doctrine

The Goldwater-Nichols Act of 1986 had made the Chairman of the Joint Chiefs of Staff singularly responsible for joint doctrine and the joint employment of the armed forces. In order to carry out his responsibilities, the Chairman reorganized the joint staff and brought the responsibilities for joint plans, doctrine, training, exercise, and interoperability together under a single operations plans and interoperability directorate, J-7. This development encouraged the services to overcome their differences and to emphasize joint operations instead. In addition, during the Desert Storm Aftermath Conference, Commanding General of TRADOC, General Tommy Franks, argued that "Doctrine must be flexible enough to prepare for all levels of war and all types of missions around the world." Both the requirement for joint operations and Franks' views initiated the revision of FM100-5 (1986). Consequently, the lessons learned from the Gulf War and some of the lessons learned from UNOSOM I and II were incorporated into the new FM 100-5 Operations of 1993. The new FM 100-5 started the development of a new doctrine for the US Army, one that put emphasis on a wide spectrum of operations and acknowledged that the US Army's purpose is to win the nation's wars by fighting as part of a joint force.

The TRADOC Pamphlet 525-5, published in 1994, took thinking a step further with the concept of Full Dimensional Operations for Force XXI. With the disappearance of the Soviet Union and the Warsaw Pact, the military was left with multiple threats, requiring a vast array of operations. No longer did the military need to prepare for a strategic attack over one or more axes. Instead, it had to deal with local or regional crises that could affect national interests and regional balances of power, or cause large-scale humanitarian suffering. In addition to defending interests, armed forces were deployed to bring or maintain the peace or disaster relief Somalia has considerable impact on doctrinal thinking. On the one hand, UNOSOM demonstrated that military force was a prerequisite for humanitarian relief. On the other hand, UNOSOM demonstrated that military force, if applied unwisely, could lead to disaster. In Somalia, the US military was confronted with irregular militias and warlords applying unconventional war tactics, for which it had no solution. Experience during the early 1990s convinced the US military that small-scale operations, asymmetrical response, low intensity warfare, military operations in mountainous, and urban terrain would be the key characteristics of the future operational environment. Moreover, it would not always be possible to distinguish between friend and foe. Finally, the military would have to work together with Governmental and

Non-Governmental Organizations and Private Volunteer Organizations, so that civil-military cooperation would become more important. The change in the operational environment would clearly require a different mind-set.

Consequently, the US army had to produce a successor to the AirLand Battle doctrine, one that was based on full spectrum operations, requiring a force that meets the needs in war, armed conflict, and peace. Lessons learned, together with the what were called the Louisiana Maneuvers (1993-1996), the Army War Fighting Experiences (1994-1998) and the Force XXI Process (ever since 1998) drove the US Army's process of transformation. The Louisiana Maneuvers involved a series of historical analyses, interviews, computer simulations, battle labs, and exercises to get a better understanding of the future battlefield. As a result, in 1993, senior military leaders decided that the future battlefield should be digitalized so as to achieve better situational awareness and to reduce the time frame for observation, orientation, decision, and action. In order to increase power projection, the expeditionary character of the US army should be strengthened. An asset tracking system would improve logistics for expeditionary warfare.

After completing the Louisiana Maneuvers and the Army War Fighting Experiences, it was decided which elements would be further developed. Initially, heavy mechanized brigades were used for the experiments. Ultimately, specialized units such as the 10th Mountain division and the 82nd Airborne division were used for combined and joint operations. The Army War Fighting Experiences clearly identified the need for new doctrine and new material. The result of the Louisiana Maneuvers and the Army War Fighting Experiences led to a revision of FM100-5 (1993) and the Force XXI process. The latter envisioned the transformation from a threat-based force structure to a capabilities-based force structure. No longer did a specific threat dictate the force posture; instead, the new force posture was driven by capabilities requirement for specific scenarios. These requirements were defined, for example, by the results of war games and battle labs.

In the meantime, the J-7 Joint Doctrine Division produced more than a hundred joint publications (JP), including JP 3.0 Operations, which was a keystone manual for the development or service doctrine. The successor to FM 100-5 (1993), FM 3.0, was fully in line with the new keystone manual. It no longer took a peer competitor into account. Asymmetric responses were now emphasized: "Adversaries will develop war fighting doctrine that takes perceived US strengths and vulnerabilities into account. They will try to prevent projection of US forces and control the nature and the tempo of US actions through asymmetric operations and adaptive forces. They will try to counter US air operations and neutralize US technological advantages, such as precision strike capabilities. Adversaries will adapt to more nonlinear, simultaneous operations…," and "They will use complex terrain, urban environments, and force dispersal methods – similar to those used by the North Vietnamese, Iraqis, and Serbs – to offset US military advantages. These methods increase targeting difficulties and may result in US forces wasting precision weapons on relatively unimportant targets."[45] In addition, the manual expected the adversary to possess at least some advanced weaponry, ranging from a computer connected to the Internet to weapons of mass destruction.

Technology was still considered a force multiplier. The quality of decision making would depend heavily on advanced methods for intelligence gathering and strategic reconnaissance. In addition, battle commands would benefit from modern microprocessors and telecommunications to collect, process, store, display, and disseminate information faster and with greater precision. Battlefield lethality would increase due to changes in target acquisition, armament, and delivery means.

Air power was considered invaluable in creating the conditions for success before and during land operations. But air power was described in its traditional role as an integral and essential part of each phase of the operation. Interestingly, much emphasis was put on Special Operations Forces, which provide "flexible, rapidly deployable capabilities across the range of military operations."[46] Finally, multinational operations were emphasized.

On the whole, the doctrine was less explicit than both active defense and AirLand Battle. This is explained by the nature of the operational environment. According to the manual, operations may include periods of extremely fluid, nonlinear operations, alternating with linear operations.[47] Operations could become more complex because of nuclear, biological and chemical (NBC) threats, unconventional threats such as terrorist acts, displaced persons, and urban areas. In fact, linear battles could be quite similar to the old AirLand Battle or active defense doctrines. Maneuver warfare, attrition, and deep strike could all be practices in linear battles. Consequently, the most innovative part of the manual was that on nonlinear operations. This requires techniques of maneuver such as infiltration or undetected movement through or into an area occupied by enemy forces, and penetration in which the attacker seeks to rupture enemy defenses on a narrow front to disrupt the defensive system.

45 FM 3.0, pp. 1-28, 29.

46 FM 3.0, pp. 2-25.

47 FM 3.0, pp. 6-54.

In summary, the new operations manual was both more general and specific than FM 100-5. On the one hand, due to the nature of future combat, operations could only be defined in general terms. AirLand Battle was clearly aimed at a peer competitor; FM 3.0 had no particular opponent in mind. The new manual was less descriptive. Instead it reinvented "the art of war," requiring military commanders that understand the nature of warfare and are able to apply the fundamentals of military operations in a flexible way. On the other hand, it was more specific, because it put more emphasis on new tasks such as counterterror and homeland defense. Nevertheless, as the US Army was a legacy force – like other NATO armies – it would take until 2020 before a true full-spectrum force could be created. In 2001, the 4th Infantry Division was the first, fully digitalized experimental US Army unit that became operational.

Achieving full-spectrum dominance would be the key challenge for the armed forces of the US and its allies. Consequently, the US Army was developing the "Objective Force"; a force built around a future combat system, a family of vehicles that will weigh 16 to 20 tons and will be so small that they can be transported within the C-130 air lifter. The objective is to deploy a brigade anywhere around the world within 96 hours, a division within 120 hours, and 5 divisions within 30 days.[48] The US Navy and US Marine Corps were the first to use new concepts to restructure their units. As will be seen, new and innovative concepts became dominant in the whole transformation process.

A principle motivation for transforming the armed forces is to take advantage of America's lead in military technology, doctrine, and weapons systems. According to Joint Vision 2020, published in 2000, full-spectrum dominance would be achieved through the application of dominant maneuver, precision engagement, focused logistics, and full-dimensional protection. Attaining this goal requires the infusion of new technology and modernization and replacement of equipment, as well as new doctrines, organizations, and training methods. The RMA is clearly at the heart of this approach because, "information superiority [is] the key enabler of the transformation of the operational capabilities of the joint force and the evolution of command and control." Thus, Joint Vision 2020 is evolutionary, rather than revolutionary. It elaborates on Joint Vision 2010 (1996), which already had a profound impact on the development of both doctrine (FM 3.0) and capabilities. Consistent with the RMA, Joint Vision 2010 identified

48 H. Binnendijk (ed.), *Transforming America's Military* (Washington, D.C.: National Defense University, 2002), p. 112.

technological innovation as a vital element in the transformation of joint force. Indeed, the document argued that throughout the industrial age, the US has relied upon its capacity for technological innovation. But it also recognized that it is important to capture the importance of organizational and conceptual innovation as well.

Most importantly, for the coming decades, the strategic environment is unlikely to change. The focus is no longer on a peer competitor but rather on smaller-scale contingencies resulting in war, and situations residing between peace and war, such as peacekeeping and peace enforcing. Potential adversaries are expected to adapt as US capabilities evolve. Consequently, planners should take asymmetric approaches and the development of niche capabilities into account. Asymmetric approaches could include long-range ballistic missiles, weapons of mass destruction, terror, and nonlinear tactical concepts.

New capabilities for full spectrum dominance

NATO developed a similar approach to doctrine as the US Allied Joint Publication-01(B). AJP-01(B) was NATO's "keystone" manual for the planning, execution, and support of Allied joint operations. NATO adopted a similar hierarchy of manuals covering all aspects of warfare. The 2002 version of AJP-01(B) required ratification by all members before it could be forwarded to the Alliance's Military Committee for consideration and promulgation. Although for political reasons it was less outspoken, the new NATO doctrine was similar in approach compared with the American joint doctrine.

Consequently, it came as no surprise that the US and "Europe" quickly agreed on the capabilities needed for the new way of warfare. During the 1999 NATO Washington summit, the heads of state and government adopted an ambitious program for defense improvements, the Defense Capabilities Initiative (DCI). The initiative was aimed at improving European capabilities to enhance interoperability and provide the Europeans with expeditionary capabilities "across the full spectrum of Alliance missions in the present and foreseeable security environment with a special focus on improving interoperability." The following areas of improvement were identified:

- deploy ability and mobility;
- sustainability and logistics;
- effective engagement;
- survivability of forces and infrastructure;
- command and control and information systems.

Most of the areas were also mentioned in an audit of assets and capabilities for European Crisis Management Operations by the Western European Union (WEU). The audit concluded that Europeans, in principle, have the available force levels and resources needed to prepare and implement military operations over the whole range of envisioned tasks. Nevertheless, the audit identified a number of gaps and deficiencies, so that considerable efforts are needed to strengthen European capabilities.

Unfortunately, history repeated itself. Like AD-70, both initiatives led nowhere. Regarding the DCI, 58 areas for short-term and long-term improvements were identified. The numbers were simply too big to remedy. Moreover, the continuously shrinking defense budgets of most European allies made it clear that defense was certainly not a top priority. During a NATO summit in 2002, the Prague Capabilities Commitment resulted in a more limited capacity package aimed at improving European capabilities. This new commitment was deemed necessary because the objectives of the DCI had proven to be unattainable.

The history of initiatives taken to remedy deficiencies point to a persistent capabilities gap, one that increasingly undermines the possibilities for US-European operations. In response to the September 11 attacks, the US increased its defense budget by $40 billion, which equaled the combined defense budgets of Germany and Italy. In addition, the US spent roughly $26,000 per soldier on research and development. In comparison, the EU member states spent approximately $4,000. Due to the gap in defense spending, the technology gap was growing and interoperability was decreasing. In contrast to the US, European governments were not willing to spend more money on their defenses, so that the interoperability gap increased. The transatlantic differences in political culture, which emerged after the end of the Cold War, led to important differences in strategic culture as well. These differences help to explain to Europeans why the US has constantly but unsuccessfully tried to persuade its European allies to improve their defenses through ambitious programs. As a matter of fact, Europeans merely paid lip service to improvements.

This also explains why the EU effort to create a European Rapid Reaction Force, which could make use of "separable but not separate" collective NATO assets, was moving slowly. During the "Capabilities Improvement Conference" in November 2001, the European Union's member states identified 144 deficiencies, many of which could also be found in the DCI. Initially, the EU aimed at an operational force by 2003. But due to the large number of deficiencies, the force would not be fully operational before 2012.

Consequently, the EU had very limited capabilities for expeditionary warfare, that is, capabilities to conduct high-tempo, large-scale conventional and unconventional combat operations in distant parts of the world. Only the British and the French could deploy forces rapidly. On the whole, Europeans relied too much on dumb bombs, while precision-guided munitions and stand-off weaponry would reduce both collateral damage and the risks for air crews. Europe had relatively few combat-ready divisions, and other deployable sea-based air power, naval forces, and marines available. For that reason, Europe lacked escalation dominance, which was a prerequisite for successful combat operations.

Two strategic cultures

So, a considerable transatlantic divergence in strategic culture has become visible between modern America and postmodern Europe during the last decades. First, there are transatlantic differences in threat perception. With the exception of the Civil War, no war ever took place on America's soil. Enemies cannot confront the United States head-on because of its geographical position and because they are no match for its army, navy, air force, and marines. Therefore, attackers are likely to exploit the inherent weaknesses and vulnerabilities of America's open, liberal, democratic, and industrialized society through asymmetrical forms of warfare. Terrorism and missile attacks are the most likely challenges for the US and its interests abroad.[49] The fear of the proliferation of missiles armed with weapons of mass destruction, and the threat of catastrophic terrorism, has led to a feeling of vulnerability, as a result of which, the freedom to act in foreign policy would be limited and the hegemonic position would be encroached upon.

In contrast, throughout its history, Europe has experienced numerous and disastrous wars. These were an essential element of a continuous process of nation-building. Europeans have learned to live with a complex security situation. Apart from all this, Europeans are also familiar with terrorism, and it is considered to be the only threat to European societies. Over the last few decades, Europeans have endured many incidents of terrorism, from the IRA in Northern Ireland to the Baader-Meinhof Group in Germany, and from the Red Brigades in Italy to the ETA in Spain. European

49 A.K. Cronin, "Rethinking Sovereignty: American Strategy in the Age of Terrorism", *Survival*, vol. 44, no. 2, Summer 2002, p. 124.

governments are familiar with rogue states as well. The Libyan missile fired at Lampedusa in 1986 was the first direct attack on NATO territory, but it did not result in a European call for missile defenses. In Europe, the security risks of weapons of mass destruction and missiles are just not perceived as great enough to justify the spending of taxpayers' money. Many European policymakers consider the American NMD as a disproportionate measure against a distant threat.

In contrast to most European powers, the US needs an enemy upon which to focus its foreign and security policy. The US has a problem-solving, materialistic culture, and without an enemy there is no problem to solve. American history is full of examples of its unwillingness and inability to organize its policy well until there is a specific threat. Watershed events in American history such as the 1942 attack on Pearl Harbor, the 1950 North Korean invasion of South Korea, the blockade of Berlin, the 1962 Cuban missile crisis, and the September 11 attacks have had a catalyzing effect on American society, which mobilized political will to act decisively. European policymakers, probably with the exception of the British, underestimate the effects of these events since they tend to interpret American action as "unilateralist."

Second, there are transatlantic differences about how security could best be provided. European governments do not underestimate the threats of wars, terrorism, and rogue states, they simply try to *manage* complex security situations, whereas Americans seek military victory. European security management aimed at preventing wars has traditionally been done through engagement, that is, multilateralism and treaties. Europeans put more emphasis on intent; the US stresses capability. Europe emphasizes economics whilst the US emphasizes political and military issues. As a result, Europeans and Americans differ fundamentally in their methods of dealing with contemporary security threats. Europeans put emphasis on "soft security," that is, diplomacy, incentives such as economic aid and peace support operations. Americans emphasize "hard security," that is, limited wars of intervention to defend interests and promote regional security.

The transatlantic distribution of power is another explanation for this. Europeans like international organizations, international law, and agreed-upon norms because they created a postmodern system based on multilateralism and cooperative security; the US likes unilateralism because it is the only remaining superpower. Consequently, European governments seek relative security whereas Americans seek absolute security.

In conclusion, given the European Union's strategic culture, it comes as no surprise that most European leaders see the use of the instruments of military power as an unattractive proposition. Europeans prefer diplomatic and economic measures to coerce others, in combination with inducements to influence an opponent's behavior. Germany gave 50 billion DM to the Soviet Union to encourage its withdrawal of troops from the German Democratic Republic. Europeans focus on conflict prevention and peace building. After all, military interventions can only be very poorly aligned with international law that is so valued by the Europeans. Since interventions often take place in sovereign countries, these countries are usually not enthusiastic about external interference in their internal affairs. In the case of an intervention that has not been mandated by the Security Council, this is perceived as an illegitimate intervention in the eyes of public international law. Furthermore, from an ethical perspective, it is more attractive to be concerned with the efficacy of non-military action.

The EU's vision on security was summarized in its 2003 Security Strategy. Dealing with security risks, it is argued, requires a mixture of instruments: "Proliferation may be contained through export controls and attacked through political, economic, and other pressures, while the underlying political causes are also tackled. Dealing with terrorism may require a mixture of intelligence, police, judicial, military, and other means. In failed states, military instruments may be needed to restore order, humanitarian means to tackle the immediate crisis. Regional conflicts need political solutions but military assets and effective policing may be needed in the post-conflict phase."[50] The strategy emphasizes multilateralism as well: "Our security and prosperity increasingly depend on an effective multilateral system. We are committed to upholding and developing International Law. The fundamental framework for international relations is the United Nations Charter."

Conclusion

The history of active defense, AirLand Battle, FOFA, and full-spectrum dominance demonstrates how the contemporary American military thinks about warfare. First, the focus was on "peer competitors," with comparable military endowments. But, at the same time, there is a tendency to ignore the adversary. In this respect, FM 3.0 is a departure from the past.

50 European Union, *A Secure Europe in a Better World: European Security Strategy* (Brussels, December 12, 2003).

Second, technology is assumed to be the key to success. New technologies increase lethality through better accuracy and intelligence, so that quick and decisive victories without too many losses can be achieved. Third, maneuver warfare is a key element of modern doctrine, which focuses on an armor-dominated battlefield. Fourth, deep strike, preferably with stand-off weaponry and air power, is closely linked to the attrition school of thought. Deep strike is aimed at denying reinforcements from joining the front battle and enable forward-deployed forces to gain victories. Fifth, tactical nuclear weapons are considered a form of firepower, which should be integrated into the conventional battle. Finally, much emphasis is put on achieving interoperability for coalition warfare with allies.

Due to its flexibility, range, speed, and the ability for precision strike, air power is gaining importance in modern warfare. Precision strike, however, does not necessarily make it the coercive instrument par excellence. Precision strike contrasts with the brute force strategy of attrition by terror bombardments in the tradition of Douhet, who believed that the strategic bombing of cities would bring the enemy to his knees. There are few, if any, historical examples in support of this expectation. But reduced collateral damage decreases the hardships of war. For that reason, coercion with precision strike is unlikely to produce the desired results either.

The real innovations are with land force doctrine. After the Gulf War, the US Army said farewell to AirLand Battle. After a period of doctrinal confusion, in 1996, the Joint Chiefs of Staff produced their Joint Vision 2020, which provided input for the 2000 FM 3.0, the army's keystone manual for operations. This manual tried to come to grips with the new security challenges. It was less descriptive than its predecessors; it provided a conceptual framework for linear and nonlinear operations against unknown adversaries. In a way, the manual rediscovered strategy, because the "art of war" was again placed at the center of strategic thinking.

Finally, there are important differences between the US and Europe. Although NATO doctrine was developed in a comparable way, thinking about its actual use started to diverge.

5 Premodern Challenges and the Modern and Postmodern World

In the previous chapter I argued that the liberal democracies' armed forces were trained and equipped for traditional interstate wars in Europe. The main preoccupation was relatively static defenses with large units, that is, divisions and army corps. I concluded that modern armed forces need full-spectrum capabilities to carry out their missions successfully. The key question therefore is what this spectrum looks like. This chapter offers a closer look at the security challenges which shape capabilities and define how coercive strategies should be executed with military means. I will argue that global war is unlikely, and that the number of interstate wars will remain very limited. Most likely, the armed forces of liberal democracies will be deployed in distant parts of the world. President Clinton argued in April 1999 that the West finds itself engaged in "a great battle between the forces of integration and the forces of disintegration; [between] the forces of globalism and the forces of tribalism."[1] A clash was emerging between the premodern world and the modern and postmodern worlds. Consequently, the protection of interests and the defense of values require modern and postmodern states to deal with rogue states and complex contingencies, international terrorism, and criminals in failed or weak states.

The Stockholm International Peace Research Institute (SIPRI) defines a major armed conflict as "prolonged combat between the military forces of two or more governments, or of one government and at least one organized group, incurring the battle-related deaths of at least 1,000 people during the entire conflict and in which the incompatibility concerns government and/or territory." In 1997 there were 19 such conflicts.[2] According to SIPRI, this was the lowest post-Cold War figure, that is, considerably lower than those for 1989, the first year covered in their statistics, when there were 32 conflicts at 36 locations. During the first half of the 1990s, Europe was the only region with a trend toward increased conflict. In 1993 and 1994, the number rose to five. Conflicts took place in four different European regions: Azerbaijan (the government versus the republic of Nagorno-Karabakh and

1 Quoted in A.J. Bacevich, "Policing Utopia", *The National Interest*, Summer 1999.

2 M. Erikson, M. Sollenberg and P. Wallensteen, "Major armed conflicts, 1990-2002", *SIPRI Yearbook 2003* (Oxford: Oxford University Press 2003), pp. 109-114.

Armenia); Bosnia and Herzegovina; Georgia (the government versus the republic of Abkhazia); and the United Kingdom (Northern Ireland). After 1997, the number of conflicts in Europe decreased sharply, whilst in 1998 and 1999 the number of conflicts elsewhere in the world was again on the level of 1989. Due to the Arab Revolutions which started in December 2010, the number of conflicts in Europe's neighborhood rose again. Nevertheless, during the first decade of the new century the trend was a constant and word wide decline in the number of conflicts.

Trends explained

No major power has erupted since the end of World War II. Indeed, interstate conflict is a rare phenomenon. Not only has global war become obsolete, but interstate wars have also become rare. The bi-polar order, which existed until 1989, and the pacifying effect of international regimes help explain why the vast majority – more than 90% – of interstate wars were fought in developing countries. These conflicts have resulted from the preoccupation of states for defending, maintaining, or extending interests and power. But attempts to form new or larger states through border changes or the occupation of neighboring states have become extremely rare. Usually, borders are no longer subject to disputes. Generally speaking, in their relations with other states, leaders tend to stay reasonably well within the norms and standards agreed by the international institutions.[3] The globalization of international relations, increasing economic interdependence, and the emergence of global institutions such as the UN, serves to explain this phenomenon. It also explains why the state as an institution has become relatively weaker so that its ability to wage war has decreased. Moreover, for most leaders, becoming a pariah in the international community is not an attractive proposition. Another explanation for the decline in number of intrastate wars is the peace keeping mission after the end of the Cold War. These operations reduced the chances of the renewed civil wars by 80%.[4]

More than 90% of conflicts were waged within states. The causes of those conflicts varied:[5] The majority of conflicts were of an ethno-nationalist

3 A. Hander Chayes and A. Chayes, "Regime architecture: elements and principles", in J.E. Nolan (ed.), *Global Engagement and Security in the 21st Century* (Washington, D.C.: Brookings Institute, 1994), p. 69.

4 J. Mueler, "War Has Almost Ceased to Exist: An Assessment", *Political Science Quarterly* 124, no. 2 (Summer 2009), p. 307.

5 C.P. Shearer, *Ethno-Nationalismus in Welt System* (Munster: Agenda Verlag), p. 25.

(44.1%), anti-regime (19.9%) or tribal (13.7%) nature. The remaining conflicts were gang wars, genocide, and decolonization wars.

Sometimes the distinction between interstate and intrastate wars was hard to make if foreign powers are involved in intrastate conflicts. One example of such a trans-national conflict is Congo, the former Zaire. After the collapse of the Mobutu government, troops from Angola, Rwanda, Zimbabwe, Uganda, and Zimbabwe supported various factions in the civil war, some of which tried to gain control over Congo's vast resources, including oil, diamonds, gold, copper, and cobalt.

The end of the Cold War can explain both the increase and the decrease in the number of conflicts after 1989. In Europe, the increase is explained by the collapse of the Warsaw Pact and the Soviet Union. In the Balkans and in the republics of the former Soviet Union, political entrepreneurs played nationalistic or religious cards to mobilize parts of the electorate. In some cases, such as in Yugoslavia, the result was civil war.

Elsewhere, the decrease can be explained by the fact that during the Cold War, both the Soviet Union and the United States fought many proxy wars, but withdrew their support to friendly regimes and opposition groups during the 1980s. Due to the cutback of foreign support, wars came to an end. Moreover, in Africa and South America during the first half of the early 1990s, democratization was in vogue, producing new regimes and hopes for a better future.

During the late 1990s, the number of conflicts outside Europe rose to the same level as in 1989. The effects of the end of the Cold War also explain this increase. As has been argued in chapter 2, there is evidence that in the transitional phase of democratization, countries become more aggressive and war prone. In addition, existing regimes became challenged by internal groups and individuals trying to fill the power vacuum as a result of the end of the Cold War and the collapse of the Soviet Union. During the Cold War, many regimes stayed in power through repression made possible with the help of one of the two military superpowers. The superpowers helped repressive regimes to ensure that the other side did not maintain control. They also helped repressive regimes to avoid local conflict from escalating into a regional war and a direct confrontation between the Soviet Union and the US.

In Africa, during the first half of the 1990s, wars had come to a temporary halt because the superpowers no longer supported local factions in the struggle for power. The many proxy wars fought by the Americans and Soviets for ideological reasons came to an end, but with the withdrawal of the superpowers, weak governments and even political vacuums emerged. After a few years, dissatisfied or greedy factions took up the fight. No longer supported by outside powers, some of them tried to acquire funds through control over scarce resources, drug trafficking, and other forms of organized crime.

In Sierra Leone, they tried to gain control over the diamond industry. In Somalia, local factions were able to regain their traditional control over large parts of the country. Since the end of the Cold War, more than 50 states have undergone political transition. Such states are, by definition, politically unstable. Ruthless leaders seeking political power and more likely personal wealth aggravate the situation. Usually, their struggle is for control over government or territory and commodities.

There is also a strong correlation between development and peace. The World Bank's Paul Collier found that beyond an income of $2,700 per capita a year democracies are less prone to violence than are autocracies. Collier argues that most political violence happens in countries where income is far below that threshold. In those cases, democracy is associated with a greater risk of bloodshed.[6]

In Asia, after the Cold War, the pacifying influence of the Kremlin disappeared. The Russians lost control over their southern republics. Some republics, including Chechnya, revolted. In other places, extremist Muslims gained in strength.

The constant global decline in the number of conflicts since the end of the 1990s can be explained by the emergence of regimes or international organizations such as the UN and an ever-increasing set of international laws and norms. Colonial wars and wars of conquest were thus delegitimized. The French scholar Bruno Tertrais explained the declining number of civil wars by the decolonization process and the end of the Cold War which fueled intrastate wars financially and ideologically. About one-fifth of this decline can be attributed to the end of the Cold War. Tertrais also points at the fact that most "national questions" have been solved through the creation of new independent states.[7] One should add that, in Europe, the process of the breaking up of states such as Czechoslovakia and Russia was relatively painless because of the pacifying impact of international institutions such as the Organization for Security and Cooperation in Europe (OSCE).

6 Paul Collier explains his thesis that democracy tends to increase political violence in the poorest countries in *Wars, Guns and Votes: Democracy in Dangerous Places* (New York: Harper/HarperCollins Publishers, 2009).

7 B. Tertrais, "The Demise of Ares: The End of War as We Know It?" *The Washington Quarterly*, Summer 2012, p. 11.

To use military power successfully, knowledge of the characteristics of the conflicts mentioned is required. Generally speaking, interstate wars are conventional wars with linear operations fought by regular or standing forces, while intrastate conflicts are unconventional wars with nonlinear operations fought by irregular forces, including guerrillas, gangs, and terrorists. Each type of conflict requires armed forces possessing different characteristics and different doctrines. As has been argued before, a fundamental problem for Western armed forces is that they seem to be prepared for the wrong kind of war. The key question therefore is: for which types of conflicts should armed forces prepare? The following sections discuss the security risks of the future: interstate wars, intrastate conflicts, non-state actors, and antisystemic terror.

Interstate conflicts

Due to the geopolitical changes of the 1990s and the emergence of the United States as the dominant power, global war has become unlikely. As long as the United States remained the sole superpower, it could not be challenged by another great power. As long as liberal democracies remain allied to the United States, this holds true for them as well.

By the end of the first decade of the 21st century, Western supremacy was challenged by emerging economies. Already in 2001, Goldman Sachs coined the term BRIC, referring to the emerging economies of Brazil, Russia, India, and China. Later South Africa was added. But as a matter of fact, Fareed Zakaria's "rise of the rest" was only about one country: China. In 2011, China overtook Japan as the world's second-largest economy, and in 2013 China eclipsed the United States as the world's biggest trading nation. Only China has maintained high growth levels over the previous decade. Growth figures of the other BRICs have dropped.

The key issue is that China used its economic power to increase its political and military power. China's assertiveness was supported by double-digit growth of its defense budget. For that reason China's energy and raw material needs are sometimes seen with apprehension. Would China be willing to fight for the unrestricted access of scarce resources? Indeed, there are frictions with Brunei, Malaysia, Vietnam, and the Philippines about fishing and exploration rights in the South China Sea, most notably around the Spratly Islands, the Parcels, and the Scarborough Shoal. China considers the whole area as part of its historical territory. Frictions with Japan about some uninhabited islands, called Senkaku by Japan and Diaoyutai by China, escalated in 2010. Japan acquired the Senkaku Islands in 1895 after defeating China in the First Sino-Japanese War. But after the discovery of oil in 1968, the ownership of the islands was disputed by China. In September 2010, a Chinese trawler tried to shake off a Japan Coast Guard. After a collision, the captain and others were arrested by the Japan Coast Guard's patrol ship for interfering with official duties. Due to nationalistic reactions on both sides the conflict quickly escalated. In Japan people who put the territorial dispute into question were accused for being unpatriotic. In China nationalism increased anti-Japanese feelings. As a result, Beijing curtailed the export of rare earth minerals to Japan and restricted the number of Japan-bound Chinese tourists.

In sum, by 2010 international relations were on the brink of a paradigm shift. America's dominance was increasingly challenged by China, which embarked on an increasingly assertive foreign policy. But it was too early to conclude that interstate conflict or even major power conflict was on the rise.

Intrastate wars and complex contingencies

Contemporary conflicts are best defined as complex contingencies, which "combine internal conflicts with large-scale displacements of people, mass famine, and fragile or failing economic, political, and social institutions". Complex contingencies usually occur in failed states. The key issue is that weak governance prevents proactive policies for dealing with the challenges ahead.

Years of conflict and persecution, often fueled by the motives of political entrepreneurs, could cause a breakdown of government and chronic insecurity. Violent eruptions usually follow from the deliberate actions of determined leaders in response to corruption, discrimination, economic failure, poor administration, discrimination, repression and poor economic conditions. With an interest in protracted internal strife, political entrepreneurs, terrorists, and criminals are unlikely to help improve domestic stability, and continue oppression and human rights abuses. Of the victims in internal conflicts, 84% are civilians, and most of these are children and women.

Fragile states are more vulnerable to natural disasters, and climate change can worsen the situation. Oxfam International found that each year, some 250 million people are affected by natural disasters; 98% of them spring from climate-related disasters such as droughts and floods. By 2015, this could grow by more than 50% to an average of 375 million people affected by climate-related disasters each year. An estimated 46 countries will face a "high risk of violent conflict."[8] These staggering figures indicate that the vulnerability of fragile states will increase in the near future. Highlighting the relationship between climate change and insecurity, retired generals argued in 2007 that "climate change acts as a threat multiplier for instability in some of the most volatile regions of the world. Projected climate change will seriously exacerbate already marginal living standards in many Asian, African, and Middle Eastern nations, causing widespread political instability and an increased likelihood of failed states".[9] Furthermore, Oxfam observed that "economic and environmental conditions in already fragile areas will further erode as food production declines, diseases increase, clean water becomes increasingly scarce, and large populations move in search of resources. Weakened and failing governments, with an already narrow margin for survival, foster the conditions for internal conflicts, extremism, and movement toward increased authoritarianism and radical ideologies."

Paul Collier and Anke Hoeffler found that countries whose wealth is largely dependent on the exploration of natural resources and agriculture are prone to internal conflict.[10] From this vantage, conflict is explained by greed and grievances. Greed fueled conflict in the coltan-rich east of the Democratic Republic of Congo. Grievances played a role in Nigeria, where local groups want access to the oil wealth. Indeed, scarce resources play an important role in local conflicts. As most commodities become increasingly scarce, thereby driving up prices, the likelihood of resource conflicts will increase.

Climate change, internal and regional conflict, and human rights violations are the most likely causes for the protracted refugee situations in which two-thirds of the world's refugees are already trapped. In 2007, UNHCR estimated that 26 million people were internally displaced. Domestic refugee situations, defined by UNHCR as "one in which refugees find themselves in a long-lasting intractable state of limbo," cause tensions with the local population, thus undermining stability and economic recovery. Another 16 million sought refuge in other countries. As a metric to define a protracted refugee situation, UNHCR considers 25,000 refugees in exile for five years. Internationally, such situations generate instability in the wider region as refugee camps can become sanctuaries for criminals, insurgents,

8 Oxfam International, *The Right to Survive: The Humanitarian Challenge for the 21st Century* (Oxford: Oxfam International, 2009), p. 4.

9 General E. Sulivan et al. *National Security and the Threat of Climate Change* (Alexandria, Virginia: the NCA Corporation, 2007), p. 6.

10 P. Collier and A. Hoeffner, *Greed and Grievance in Civil War.* Working Paper WPS 2000-18 (Washington, D.C.: World Bank).

and terrorists. Today, the African continent has the worst refugee crisis, especially in the Central African Republic and Chad.

Gil Loescher and James Milner studied the relationship between chronic refugee flows, regional and interstate conflict and economic underdevelopment. They argued that recognizing this relationship is a first step in formulating responses.[11] Loescher and Milner found that direct threats to the host state are posed by the spillover of conflict. The presence of "refugee warriors" represents by far the strongest link between refugees and conflict. Some refugees support insurgencies in their home countries or use the camps for illicit activities, including smuggling, prostitution, and arms trade. Stability is further weakened when refugees compete with the local population for jobs and social services. Generally, the local population is likely to consider refugees as aliens, causing trouble and forming a threat to local security.

Complex contingencies tend to unfold in less-developed parts of the world and very rarely do they involve regular armies on both sides, though often regulars on one side fight guerrillas, terrorists, and civilians on the other.[12] There is some evidence that low-intensity war will replace high-intensity interstate warfare almost completely, because opponents are likely to fight only asymmetrical wars.[13]

These conflicts are misleadingly called "low-intensity" wars. "Low intensity" suggests a low level of violence and limited numbers of casualties. But even in low-intensity wars, thousands, sometimes millions, could die. During the 20th century, some 250 wars were fought, causing approximately 110 million deaths. In the period since 1945, some 200 wars have taken place, with around 45 million people being killed, most of them in low-intensity wars. "Low intensity" refers to the arms and tactics used in the conflict. These wars are unconventional wars fought against an irregular opponent, who uses non-linear techniques such as guerrilla and terrorism. Indeed, most of the fighting involves low-tech weaponry; artillery, and the use of light arms. A more important characteristic of these conflicts is the blurred distinction between war and violent, large-scale crime. The combatants are usually young males, even children. In Cambodia and Sierra Leone, five-year-old children were used as soldiers. The targets of the fighters are usually segments of the population that belong to another ethnic or religious

11 G. Loescher and J. Milner, *Protracted Refugee Situations: Domestic and International Security Implications* (Londen: IISS, Adelphi Paper 375, 2005), p. 7.

12 M. Van Creveld, *The Transformation of War* (New York, The Free Press), p. 20.

13 The Interdisciplinary Research Program on Causes of Human Rights Violations (PIOOM) at Leiden University, the Netherlands, produces a yearly *World Conflict and Human Rights Map;* the Oxford University Press publishes the *SIPRI Yearbooks.*

group. So, the traditional view of a war as a clash between two hierarchically structured organizations of soldiers does not apply to these conflicts.

Non-state actors and the use of black holes

Especially worrisome is the rise of non-state actors with military capabilities comparable to those of small states. Thus, to protect their interests and to provide humanitarian assistance, liberal democracies will have to deal with rogue states and powerful non-state actors, mostly terrorists, gangs, and separatists. In failed and weak states, governments, dissatisfied groups, and multinational corporations establish their own armed forces to protect their interests against other dissatisfied groups, gangs, criminals, and government-related forces. But gangs and organized criminals, especially drugs-related and terrorist organizations, build up their own armies as well.

Building up an armed force is relatively easy. Modern military equipment is lethal and readily available. In some African states, an AK-47 Kalashnikov costs less than $100.[14] Shoulder-fired surface-to-air missiles can be bought on the black market and can be very effective in bringing down commercial aircrafts. In Mombasa, on November 28, 2002, terrorists used a man-portable air defense system to target an Arkia Airlines Boeing 757-300 carrying 261 passengers, mostly Israeli. The attack failed, probably because the aircraft flew too low (152 m) for the Strela 2M surface-to-air missile, with a minimum engagement range of 800 meters.[15]

The difference between military and civil technologies has become blurred. The Global Positioning System increases precision of weapons at little cost. Non-state actors can easily develop chemical, biological, and radiological weapons.

A complicating factor is that, especially during the first half of the 1990s, Russian weapons and know-how fueled local conflicts outside the Russian Federation. In the Russian armed forces, crime was flourishing and poor social and economic conditions led to the collapse of values, and nihilism.[16] The soldiers were badly nourished, badly housed, and badly paid, if paid at all. Crimes include premeditated murder, grievous bodily harm, embez-

14 http://www.smallarmssurvey.org/fileadmin/docs/A-Yearbook/2007/en/Small-Arms-Survey-2007-Chapter-08-summary-EN.pdf.

15 D.A. Kuhn, "Mombassa Attacks Highlight Increasing NAPADS threat", *Jane's Intelligence Review,* February 2003, pp. 26-31.

16 T.R.W. Waters, *Crime in the Russian Military* (Sandhurst: Conflict Studies Research Centre, United Kingdom, November 1996).

zlement, theft, drugs trafficking, rape, and hooliganism. The incidence of weapons and ammunition theft is alarming. After the collapse of the Soviet Union, it was reported that in the first quarter of 1992, in one military district alone, the following weapons were stolen: 27 T-72 tanks, over 100 armored personnel carriers, 1,330 cars and armored vehicles, 3,851 guns and mortars, 180,000 mines, and 1,118 railway wagons containing 20 tons of ammunition each. In 1992 and 1993, more than 22,000 units of weapons were stolen, and 1,183 attacks were made on military installations. More than half of the firearms on the Russian black market originated from army supplies.[17] Russian weaponry found its way to terrorists, guerrilla fighters, and unfriendly regimes, thus fueling armed conflicts around the world.

The same happened during the Libyan Revolution of 2011. Numerous guns and surface-to-air missiles fell in the hands of criminals and extremists in the region, including al-Qaeda in the Islamic Maghreb (AQIM) which has "close relations" with the branches in Yemen and Pakistan. In an interview in the *Washington Post* in September 2012, Ismail Salabi, the commander of Rafallah al-Sahati, a powerful Islamist militia in Benghazi, said that: "missiles, used by fighters to 'hit airplanes' and known to the US intelligence community as MANPADS (man-portable air-defense systems), were stolen along with 2,000 semiautomatic rifles and ammunition, as the militia withdrew from its base amid a firefight."[18] The influx of Libyan weapons fueled the Mali crisis of 2012 when Tuareg rebels, AQUIM, and other fighting groups challenged the government.

Some rogue states use insurgents and terrorists to fight other states. Iran is an example. First, Iran targets Western interests in the region. US Attorney General Janet Reno stated in late 1999 that the US had information that Iran was behind the 1996 bombing of the US Air Force Khobar Towers residence in Dhahran, Saudi Arabia. Second, Iran's top priority is Israel. Teheran is believed to train, finance, and equip terrorist organizations such as Hamas and Hezbollah.

More worrying, however, are the "black holes," or ungoverned territories, that exist in a number of failed and weak states. Criminal organizations use these areas either as hubs for the dispersal of drugs, weapons, dirty money,

17 Waters, *Crime in the Russian Military*, p. 7.

18 *Washington Post*, "Libya militia leader: Heat-seeking missiles, other weapons stolen during fire fight", September 25, 2012.

and illegal immigrants, or for other criminal practices such as cultivating drugs and illegally exploiting forests, and commodities such as diamonds.

Terrorist organizations could also be involved in these practices in order to raise funds for operations. In addition, they use black holes as sanctuaries and for training purposes. Actually, al-Qaeda "owned" Afghanistan, although most of its training camps were located in the eastern provinces along the mountainous border with Pakistan. Osama bin Laden paid the Taliban regime approximately 120 million dollars a year to allow him to use the country as a safe haven.

These black holes are pools of recruits and other supporters of terrorists and criminal organizations as well. The local populations, if not forced to cooperate, sometimes would receive payment for their services.

The Fergana valley is a good example. In this valley, in the border region of Uzbekistan, Tajikistan, and Kyrgyzstan, al-Qaeda leader Osama bin Laden extended logistical support and guerrilla training to the Islamic Movement of Uzbekistan, whose leaders maintained close ties with the Taliban in Afghanistan. Afghans used the valley as a transit point for the transfer of weapons and fighters, as well as a transshipment point for drugs produced in Afghanistan.[19]

Rogue states and black holes in failed and weak states constitute the greatest challenge for liberal democracies, especially if linked to anti-systemic terrorism and the proliferation of weapons of mass destruction and their means of delivery.

Religious anti-systemic terrorism

In their study *Political Terrorism*, Alex Schmid and Berto Jongman identified 109 different definitions of terrorism.[20] In general, terrorism can be defined as the intentional use of, or threat to use, violence against civilians and civilian targets, in order to attain political aims.

Traditionally, terrorists used well-known techniques such as hostage taking, murder, blackmail, and terror aimed at specific segments of the population to achieve specific, limited political objectives such as the release of prisoners. Their operations could be deadly, but were relatively low scale.

19 R. Takeyh and N. Gvosdev, "Do Terrorist Networks Need a Home?" *The Washington Quarterly*, Summer 2002, p. 99.

20 A.P. Schmidt and A.I. Jongman, *Political Terrorism* (Amsterdam: SWIDOC and Transaction Books, 1988), p. 5.

Nonetheless, a few well-armed terrorists could seriously disrupt public order, since violence against the population will result in fear and chaos. Liberal democracies have always been extremely vulnerable to terrorism.

Since the targets are civilians, terrorism is distinguished from other types of political violence, such as guerrilla warfare. The latter is defined as a form of warfare against a state by which the strategically weak side assumes the tactical offensive in selected forms, times, and places. The 9/11 attacks carried out by al-Qaeda blurred the traditional distinction between terrorism and war. War is usually associated with combating state actors who pose a threat to international peace and security; terrorism is usually associated with deadly, but small-scale, actions and limited objectives.

However, the new threat cannot be considered a tactical or local challenge, requiring cooperation between the national intelligence services and the police. The new threat is a strategic or international challenge, which requires international cooperation between intelligence services, armed forces, and the traditional law enforcement authorities. Combating terrorists could involve interventions in failed and weak states, especially black holes, used by terrorists as sanctuaries. Here, terrorists could use small armies to protect their interests. In Afghanistan, Bin Laden used the 1,500 troops of the multinational Arabic "55th Brigade" to protect his training camps and other bases, and to keep elements of the Taliban in check. Terrorist organizations could possess the military capabilities of small states and turn nonmilitary means – such as passenger airliners – into weapons of mass destruction to achieve strategic objectives.

The new threat is sometimes called "catastrophic terrorism"[21] because its intention is to kill people on a large scale. As terrorist groups such as al-Qaeda also targeted symbols of Western "decadence," power, and religion, such as American military bases, embassies,and even synagogues, this definition does not explain the specific nature of the threat.

This kind of terrorism is of a cultural and religious nature and aimed at removing alien influences from the Islamic world. Therefore, some authors name the new threat cultural or religious terrorism, which is not an accurate description, either.[22] Thus, 9/11 and the destruction of two giant Buddha statues in Bamiyan (Afghanistan) by the Taliban in February 2001, and

21 This term was used by A. Carter, J. Deutch and P. Zelikow, "Catastrophic terrorism", *Foreign Affairs,* November-December 1998, pp. 80-94.

22 S. Shay, "Cultural Terrorism and the Clash of Civilizations", ICT Papers on Terrorism (The International Policy Institute for Counter Terrorism, The Interdisciplinary Center, Herzliya, Israel, 2002), pp. 69-96.

the attacks on numerous tombs of Muslims saints in Libya in 2011 and in Mali by extremists in 2012 and 2013 fell in the same category. What really distinguishes the events of 9/11 from other terrorist acts is that the Islamic terrorists fought a war against infidels both at home and abroad. Thus, this kind of terrorism is religious anti-systemic terrorism, defined as the unconventional, but worldwide large-scale use by non-state actors or state-sponsored actors against civilian and government targets, with the aim of changing the (international) system and establishing a caliphate. The most important examples of this form of terrorism are listed in the box below.

- World Trade Center bombing (February 26, 1993). Six people were killed and over a thousand injured when a truck bomb exploded in the basement of the World Trade Center in New York.
- Landmarks plot (1993). The FBI disrupted a plan to blow up landmarks in the New York City area, including the Lincoln and Holland Tunnels, the George Washington Bridge, the United Nations, and the New York FBI Office.
- Manila Airlines plot (January 1995). The Philippine police uncovered a plot to blow up twelve aircraft on their way to the United States. Some of the perpetrators had also discussed the possibility of flying a plane into the headquarters of the CIA.
- Khobar Towers bombing June 25, 1996). Terrorists blew up the towers in Dhahran (Saudi Arabia), killing 19 US military personnel and wounding hundreds more.
- East Africa Embassy bombings (August 7, 1998). In the attacks on the American embassies in Nairobi and Dar es Salaam, twelve Americans and 200 Kenyans and Tanzanians were killed, and over 4,000 were wounded.
- Millennium plot (December 13, 1999). A plot to conduct an attack on the Los Angeles International Airport was thwarted.
- USS Cole bombing (October 12, 2000). Terrorists conducted an attack on the American naval warship in the port of Aden, Yemen. Seventeen sailors were killed, 39 were injured.
- Christmas Market plot (December 2000). Terrorists tried to attack the Christmas market in Strasbourg (France).
- US Embassy plot, Paris (September 2001). A Frenchman with an Algerian background was arrested who had been instructed by one of Osama bin Laden's lieutenants to bomb the American embassy in Paris.
- World Trade Center and Pentagon bombings (September 11, 2001). Terrorists crashed passenger planes into the Twin Towers and the Pentagon, killing 2,973 and injuring thousands more.

During the three years following 9/11, hundreds of terrorist attacks were carried out, and dozens of major plots were thwarted. Some of the more spectacular examples are:

- US Embassy and drinking water plot, Rome (February 2002). Italian police arrested four Moroccans in possession of a cyanide-based substance. They were suspected of plotting to poison the water supply of Rome in conjunction with an attack on the American Embassy.
- NATO warship plot, Straits of Gibraltar (June 2002). Moroccan authorities broke up an al-Qaeda cell that was planning to attack US and British warships.
- Discotheque bombing, Bali (October 12, 2002). 202 were killed in Bali (Indonesia), mostly Australian tourists.
- Mombasa bombings (November 2002). Sixteen died in an attack on a hotel full of Israeli tourists. The attack was followed by an attempt to shoot down an aircraft that took off from the Mombasa Airport (Kenya).
- Riyadh bombings (May 12, 2003). 25 were killed and 194 injured during attacks on three living quarters of Westerners in Riyadh (Saudi Arabia).
- Hotel bombings, Casablanca (May 16, 2003). 41 were killed and 100 wounded during three attacks on hotels and clubs in Casablanca (Morocco).
- Istanbul bombings (November 15 and 20, 2003). Truck bombings targeted two synagogues, the British consulate, and the local headquarters of the London based HSBC Bank, leaving 61 dead and more than 600 injured.
- Marriott Hotel bombing, Jakarta (August 5, 2003). Ten people were killed and 74 were injured during the bombing of an hotel in Jakarta (Indonesia).
- Train bombings, Madrid (March 11 2004). 191 people were killed and 1,463 were injured during a train bombing in Madrid (Spain).
- Financial buildings plot (mid-2004). Arrests in Pakistan, the United Kingdom and the US thwarted a plot to bomb financial institutions in the US including the New York Stock Exchange and the Citigroup buildings in Manhattan, the Prudential Financial in Newark, and the IMF and World Bank in Washington. Those arrested in the United Kingdom were also charged with conspiring to use "radioactive materials, toxic gases, chemicals, and explosives".
- Train bombing, Mumbai (July 11, 2006). A series of seven bomb blasts took place over a period of eleven minutes on the Suburban Railway in Mumbai. 209 were killed and over 700 were injured.
- Qahtaniya bombings, Iraq (August 14, 2007). Four suicide vehicle bombers carried out the deadliest attack during the Iraq war. Nearly 800 members of northern Iraq's Yazidi sect were killed.

- Casablanca bombings (March and April 2007). Seven suicide bombers killed one and injured four.
- Toulouse and Montauban shooting (March 20, 2012). An Algerian gunman on a motorcycle attacked French soldiers and Jewish citizens. Seven were killed, five were injured.

Religious anti-systemic terrorism is associated with the late Osama bin Laden's al-Qaeda network. Bin Laden's goal was to unite all Muslims and to establish a government that follows the rule of the caliphs, the ancient religious rulers. Bin Laden stated that because the caliphate could only be established with force, the overthrow of all Muslim governments is necessary. In his view, these governments are corrupt and under influence of the "Judeo-Crusader Alliance," an alliance of Jews and Christians, embodied by Israel and the United States and supported by liberal democracies in general. In Bin Laden's view, this unholy alliance occupied the land of Islam's holy places (Mecca, Medina, and Jerusalem) and is trying to crush Islam. To end this influence, the destruction of Israel and the United States is a prerequisite for reform of the Muslim societies. Consequently, in August 1996, Bin Laden issued a "Declaration of War" against the US. In his March 1997 interview with CNN's Peter Arnett, Bin Laden said that he would only target US soldiers. But he hardened his line in his February 1998 fatwa, when he called for attacks on Americans wherever they were to be found.

Other al-Qaeda-inspired groups and franchises in the Arabic peninsula, the horn of Africa, the Maghreb and countries such as Afghanistan, Pakistan, the Philippines and Indonesia might also have similar aims. In general, Muslim extremism considers the war against the West a clash of civilizations. They hate everything represented by the decadent western civilization: commerce, most notably its banking system, sexual freedom, artistic freedom, secularism, democracy, religious tolerance, scientific pursuits, and pluralism. They reject everything that makes Western civilization "modern," and strive for a pure, simple and uncorrupted world, one that is based on religious principles, self-denial, tied to the soil, and obedient to authority, especially God. Thus, the West and the Islamic world seem to be diametrically opposite civilizations.[23]

23 For example: T. Ali, *The Clash of Fundamentalisms: Crusades, Jihads and Modernity* (London and New York: Verso, 2002); B.R. Barber, *Jihad vs. McWorld: Terrorism's Challenge to Democracy* (New York: Ballantine Books, 1995 and 2001); B. Lewis, *What Went Wrong? The Clash Between Islam and Modernity in the Middle East* (New York: Harper Collins, 2002); B. Lewis, *The Crisis of Islam: Holy War and Unholy Terror* (London: Weidenfeld and Nicholson, 2003); A. Rashid, *Jihad: The Rise of Militant Islam in Central Asia* (New Haven and London: Yale Univerity Press, 2002).

In *Jihad vs. McWorld*, Benjamin Barber argues that there is a collision going on between the forces of Islamic disintegrable tribalism and reactionary fundamentalism ("Jihad") and the forces of integrative modernism and aggressive economic and cultural globalism ("McWorld"). In contrast to Samuel Huntington, Barber does not consider this a "clash of civilizations," but a "dialectic expression of tensions built into a single global civilization as it emerges against the backdrop of traditional ethnic and religious divisions, many of which are actually created by McWorld and its infotainment industries and technological innovations."[24] The premodern world, using the technologies of the modern and postmodern worlds to fight McWorld, seeks to overcome sovereignty and make its impact global. Indeed, in order to achieve their objectives, Bin Laden and other Muslim extremists are using the things they are supposed to hate: the media, the global financial system, modern technology, and the Internet.

This particular form of terrorism has its roots in the idea that Islam is the solution to the political and socioeconomic problems that became manifest in the 1970s. As a result of increasing oil revenues, rapid but uneven modernization, urbanization, and economic liberalization took place, leading to social tensions in large parts of the Muslim world, especially the Middle East. Youngsters in the fast-growing cities felt betrayed by their rulers, who failed to use the oil revenues to create a civil society based on Islamic values, but used them for their own purposes instead. They also accused their leaders of becoming the puppets of Western companies and governments.

The resurgence of fundamentalist Islam is both a product of this development and attempts by Muslims to deal with this development by rejecting Western culture and influence, committing to Islam as the guide to living in the modern world. Muslim extremism is closely linked to this resurgence. Fundamentalism is mainstream and not extremist at all. Extremism is only one aspect of the resurgence that began in the 1970s when Islamic symbols, beliefs, practices, and institutions won support throughout the Islamic world. As a product of modernity, the core constituency of Islamic resurgence consists of middle-class students and intellectuals. Indeed, the militants who carried out the September 11 attacks were well-educated, middle-class males.

The extremist variant of fundamentalism presents the West with a major challenge. First, both for the West and for the Muslim extremists, vital interests are at stake. For the West it is about protecting interests in oil- and commodity-rich regions and trade routes; for the extremists it is about

24 Barber, *Jihad vs. McWorld*, p. xvi.

protecting the Islamic nation and its values against Western imperialists. Second, both see the struggle in ideological or religious terms. There is a striking similarity between Muslim fundamentalism and neo-conservatism of the kind mentioned in chapter 2. Both are guided by strong beliefs about values and the desired world order. Both believe that they are trying to destroy each other's society. Third, as the Islamic resurgence is fundamentally anti-Western, building and maintaining coalition with Islamic states is not easy. This gave both a military and a moral advantage to the radicals. The coalition with Islamic states that was built in the aftermath of the September 11 attacks was basically anti-Bin Laden, not pro-Western. As Bin Laden sought to establish a new caliphate under a political-religious leader, he posed a challenge for most regimes in the Islamic world as well. Most regimes and large parts of the population shared the anti-Western ideas of Bin Laden and other ideologues. Many Muslims, in Bin Laden's words, will consider a military campaign as a "Zionist crusader alliance," which is carried out by Western forces. As a consequence, the coalition remained fragile and was willing to give only passive support at best.

Fourth, a number of events led to the idea that Jews and Christians can be expelled from the Islamic world, providing a powerful incentive for the extremists to continue the struggle. The Iranian revolution, the Soviet defeat in Afghanistan, together with the breakup of the Soviet Union in 1991 led to the belief that Islam is so powerful that new states could be created and the infidels expelled from the Muslim world. The Iranian revolution by the Shiite Muslims revived ties with Shiites elsewhere. Shiites in Lebanon began to carry out suicide bombings to expel US and other foreign forces that had entered the country after the 1982 Israeli invasion.

It is of crucial importance that, in the eyes of the extremists, the West did little to protect their interests. In 1979, the Americans did not act when the Shah was replaced by Ayatollah Khomeini, who founded a fundamentalist Islamist republic. In 1983, the Americans withdrew their forces from Lebanon after marines had been killed. In 1993, Bin Laden successfully helped warlord Aideed combat the US during the humanitarian intervention in Somalia.

Following the attacks on the Khobar Towers, the United States relocated from the capital of Saudi Arabia to Prince Sultan Air Force base in the desert. In August 1998, al-Qaeda attacked the US embassies in Kenya and Tanzania, killing almost 300 people, including 12 Americans and wounding thousands. The Americans responded to the attacks on the American East Africa embassies with Operation Infinite Reach, aimed at killing Osama bin Laden, who was the main suspect. Operation Infinite Reach ended in being a retaliation with cruise missiles on targets in Sudan and Afghanistan.[25] In Sudan, the attack was directed against the Shifa chemical complex in Northeast Khartoum, which was believed to be involved in al-Qaeda's production of chemical weapons agents, including the nerve agent VX. In Afghanistan, the attack was directed against the largest training facility in the world, 100 kilometers south of the capital Kabul. Neither attack affected the al-Qaeda network. It later turned out that Operation Infinite Reach was the default option, because it was the only option left after the rejection of other, riskier options, that is, using Special Operations Forces.[26]

Nevertheless, for the first time in history, cruise missiles were used against terrorists. Secretary of Defense Cohen considered Bin Laden a legitimate military target: "To the extent that he or his organization has declared war on the United States or our interests, then he certainly is engaged in an act of war."[27] National Security advisor Samuel Berger justified the attacks by referring to Article 51 of the UN Charter or the right of self-defense. With this, he presented a new interpretation of international law. Berger no longer saw the right of self-defense exclusively in the context of interstate war, but also in the context of aligned threats by terrorists operating from other countries that did not pose a threat to them.

The next attack came in December 2000, when the USS Cole was struck in the harbor of Aden, Yemen. But again, the United States did not retaliate.

Undoubtedly, the first phase of the war against the West, which runs from the early 1990s to September 11, 2001, was won by the Muslim radicals. But also after 9/11 and America's declaration of war on terrorism, extremists were quite successful. Tourism in some parts of the Muslim world was affected, especially after the October 2002 attack on a night club on Bali, killing 202 people, mostly Westerners. In May 2003, a series of attacks was carried out against Western and Jewish interests in Riyadh and Casablanca, killing dozens. As a result, some Western embassies were temporarily closed and their staffs reduced.

It was only after the events of 9/11 that the Americans embarked on Operation Enduring Freedom in Afghanistan, Iraq, the Philippines, the Pankisi Gorge, Trans Sahara, and the Caribbean and South Africa. Nevertheless, the Americans decided to withdraw their forces from Saudi Arabia and redeploy them to Iraq. This move was again applauded by extremists:

25 D.J. Gillet, *US Strike Against Terrorist Forces,* American Forces Press Service, August 20, 1998.

26 National Commission on Terrorist Attacks, *The Military,* Staff Statement no. 6 (2004).

27 Department of Defense news briefing, August 20, 1998.

although the Americans claimed victory, the wars in Afghanistan and Iraq were far from over and American forces had withdrawn from important countries such as Saudi Arabia so that it would be easier to topple the "corrupt" Saudi monarchy.

Biological and chemical threats

The efforts of the international community to ban chemical and biological weapons altogether have not been very effective. Some countries, like North Korea, did not comply with international treaty obligations. Other countries were illegally acquiring weapons of mass destruction and their means of delivery, such as ballistic missiles. The unchecked drain of knowledge, technology, and materials from countries from the former Warsaw Pact, especially Russia, also gave rise to concern, as did the unfavorable side effects of the spread of dual-use technologies that can be used for civil and military purposes.

Both states and non-state actors were able to try to acquire biological and chemical weapons. Fewer than a dozen countries are believed to possess offensive biological weapons programs. As early as in the 1930s and 1940s, Japan carried out top-secret experiments using biological weapons. In October 2011, a report was found in the National Diet Library in Tokyo revealing that during the 1937-1945 second Sino-Japanese War, 25,946 people were infected by biological weapons. Army unit 731 released plague-infected fleas in six operations between 1940 and 1942 in several Chinese provinces.[28] Development of biological weapons is still going on, despite the 1972 Biological and Toxin Weapons Convention (BTWC). In Article III, parties pledge not to undertake the transfer to any recipient whatsoever of biological agents, toxins, weapons, equipment or means of delivery, and never to assist, encourage or induce any state, group of states or international organizations to acquire biological weapons.[29]

164 states ratified the BTWC and thirteen signed it, including Egypt and Syria. Among the 19 non-signatories is Israel. There have been doubts about some of the signatories. Egypt was believed to have been producing biological weapons since 1972, but there has been evidence that it has abandoned

28 *SIPRI Yearbook 2012*, J. Hart, "Allegations of chemical and biological weapons" (Oxford: Oxford University Press), p. 406.

29 *SIPRI Yearbook 1998*, J.P. Zanders and J. Hart, "Chemical and Biological Weapon Developments and Arms Control" (Oxford: Oxford University Press 1998), pp. 470-471.

the efforts. There was evidence that even though Russia had closed down some factories, it was still technically capable of producing these weapons at any time. It was also claimed that Iran had produced biological weapons in small quantities.[30] With respect to Iran, there were allegations that this country developed its biological arsenal with the aid of Russian scientists. There have been some allegations of the use of biological weapons against populations. The Government of Myanmar was under suspicion of using these weapons against the Karen ethnic minority.

A special case was, of course, Iraq. Saddam Hussein denied the existence of biological weapons until August 1995, but subsequently admitted producing 19,000 liters of botulinum, 8,000 liters of anthrax, and 2,000 liters of aflatoxin and clostridum. Iraq also admitted to filling warheads and bombs with biological agents. Saddam Hussein was one of the very few leaders with extensive experience in the use of chemical weapons that are also forbidden.

In 1997, the 1993 Chemical Weapons convention (CWC) came into force. At the same time, after four years of preparation, the Organization for the Prohibition of Chemical Weapons (OPCW) became operational. But countries like North Korea, Iran, and Syria were still believed to possess programs for the development of chemical weapons. During the Syrian civil war both regime and rebel forces used chemical weapons. On 14 September 2013 the US and Russia reached agreement to destroy Syria's chemical weapons arsenal. In December the UN confirmed the use of chemical weapons.[31] In December 1996, the South African Truth and Reconciliation Commission received a report about a top-secret program called Project Jota, which planned to use chemical weapons under the apartheid regime. A chemical attack was carried out in Mozambique, against Frelimo. The report also revealed links between South African chemical weapons experts and the Pentagon and Libya.

The poison gas attack by Iraq on the Kurdish town of Halabja was the largest-scale chemical attack against a civilian population in modern times. The population of 80,000 had sympathized with Iran during the Iran-Iraq war in the 1980s. In March 1988, the town fell into the hands of the Kurdish Patriotic Union of Kurdistan (PUK) amidst heavy resistance to Iraqi security forces. The PUK troops prevented the civilian population from leaving the

30 ACDA, *Adherence to and Compliance with Arms Control Agreements* (Washington: Arms Control and Disarmament Agency), May 30, 1995.

31 U.N. Office for Disarmament Affairs, *Report on the Alleged Use of Chemical Weapons in the Ghouta Area of Damascus on 21 August 2013*, New York, 12 December 2013.

town, hoping that Iraqi armed forces would not attack a densely populated city. On the evening of March 16, the first group of eight aircraft began dropping chemical bombs. The bombing continued all night according to Christine Gosden, who visited Halabja in 1998, and was the first to carry out research into the effects of the attacks. The attacks involved multiple chemical agents, including mustard gas and the nerve agents sarin, tabun, and VX.[32] Protecting and treating the population against such a "cocktail" is impossible. Handbooks for doctors in the Iraqi military show detailed medical knowledge of the effects of chemical weapons; the military used mustard gas in a cocktail for which no antidote exists. During the attacks, an estimated 5,000 people were killed, and another 10,000 injured.

UN Security Council Resolution 687 of April 1991 set out the cease-fire terms for ending the Gulf War. Iraq was obliged to accept the destruction of all its weapons of mass destruction programs and ballistic missiles with a range of over 150 kilometers. In addition, it was obliged to accept the dismantling of all its research and development, and manufacturing facilities and means of delivery. UNSCOM was able to destroy 38,000 chemical weapons, 6,990 tons of chemical weapons agents, 3,000 tons of 45 different precursor chemicals, and hundreds of chemical weapons production equipment items. UNSCOM also discovered that Iraq was able to produce the nerve agent VX, sarin, tabun, and mustard gas on an industrial scale and had actually produced four tons of VX. Finally, UNSCOM discovered a special biological weapons factory that was able to produce 500,000 liters of anthrax and botulinum. By 1999, UNSCOM had not reported evidence that Iraq still retained weapons or material. But Saddam Hussein had also not provided evidence to support its claim that all of Iraq's capabilities had been destroyed. For example, some 4,000 tons of chemical weapons precursor chemicals, 31,000 chemical weapons munitions, and chemical weapons production equipment were unaccounted for.

Despite an extensive investigation led by David Kay, in the period following the months after operation Iraqi Freedom, nothing was found. Investigators found no support for the main fears expressed in Washington and London before the war: that Iraq had a hidden arsenal of old weapons and was building advanced weapons for new ones.[33] With regard to biological warfare, new evidence hinted at the destruction of the program in the summer of 1991. With regard to chemical weapons, it turned out that Iraq

32 C.M. Gosden, Testimony Before a Combined US Senate Panel on Technology, Terrorism, Government and Intelligence, Washington, D.C., April 22, 1998.

33 "Iraq's Arsenal Was Only on Paper", *Washington Post*, January 7, 2004.

had no large, ongoing, centrally controlled program after 1991; its chemical capabilities had probably been entirely destroyed during Operation Desert Storm and Operation Desert Fox, and 13 years of UN inspections.[34] The inability to find weapons of mass destruction led to a bitter debate on the credibility of intelligence and the justification for the war.

There are two significant cases of non-state actors using biological and chemical weapons. The first is the attempt by the Rajneeshees, a religious cult located in Oregon, which sought to win the local elections in 1984. Using their medical clinics, the cult ordered bacterial cultures from a laboratory in Maryland. They then contaminated ten salad bars with a strain of salmonella, causing some 175 people to become ill. The second case is the Aum Shinrikyo attack on the Tokyo subway in 1995. The cult used the nerve agent sarin on March 20, which resulted in 12 deaths and over 5,500 injured. Relatively few people died, because only one chemical agent was used, which was rapidly identified, and due to the quick reaction of the Tokyo emergency services and hospitals. The Tokyo police found 11 plastic pouches on different trains on the underground lines. They were scheduled to arrive at the same time at the Kasumigaseki station in the heart of the federal government district between 08:09 and 08:13. The pouches were punctured with umbrellas but the terrorists were able to puncture only a small portion of the pouches. Aum Shinrikyo's chemical expert, Masami Tsuchiya, confessed that the cult had produced 30 kg of sarin over a period of two years. It was also found that the cult had experimented with other chemical agents, such as VX and tabun.

After the Tokyo attack, more incidents occurred. On April 19, 1995, some 570 people were treated after tear gas had been released near Yokohama train station. In the same month, other people were injured in Yokohama and Maebashi by a relatively harmless gas. A more serious incident was one involving two bags being set ablaze in the Tokyo underground on May 5, 1995. The bags were intended to release hydrogen cyanide gas.

Chemical weapons threats were also occurring outside Japan. In April 1995, an unidentified terrorist threatened to attack Disneyland in California; in June 1995, right-wing terrorists in Chile threatened to release sarin in the Santiago underground; and in July of the same year, German authorities announced that neo-Nazis were experimenting with toxic chemicals.[35] In

34 Statement by David Kay on the Interim Progress Repost on the Activities of the Iraq Survey Group before the House Permanent Select Committee on Intelligence, the House Committee on Appropriations, Subcommittee on Defense and the Senate Select Committee on Intelligence, Washington, D.C., October 2, 2003.

35 *SIPRI Yearbook 1996*, T. Stock, M. Haug and P. Radler, "Chemical and biological weapons developments and arms control" (Oxford: Oxford University Press, 1996), p. 705.

March 2001, terrorists attempted to release sarin in the European Union's parliament in Strasbourg, in an attempt to kill the 625 parliamentarians in the building. Later that year, in May and September, anthrax spores were dispersed through the mail in the US, causing panic among the population. The first significant act of bioterrorism in the US took place in the fall of 2001, when four or five letters containing anthrax were mailed via the US postal system. In total, 18 people contracted anthrax in five states.

Documents recovered from al-Qaeda bases in Kabul in 2001 and 2002 contained evidence that the network was trying to develop biological and chemical weapons and would be prepared to use them. Apart from the attempt to poison the drinking water system in Rome mentioned above, in December 2002, French officials arrested four suspects in possession of chemicals that may have been intended for use in an attack. In January 2003, authorities arrested Islamic militants who may have been planning to poison the food supply of a British military base using ricin. In April 2004, American and British intelligence agents foiled a chemical bomb plot. The plotters were thought to be sympathetic to the aims of al-Qaeda and intended to target civilians with osmium tetroxide. On January 19, 2009, a British newspaper reported an outbreak of bubonic plague at a training camp of Al-Qaeda in the Isamic Mahgreb (AQIM) in the Tizi Ouzou province in Algeria, killing at least forty militiamen.[36] A day later, a senior US intelligence official source said that the incident was unrelated to bubonic plague, but was an accident involving either a biological or chemical agent.[37]

In conclusion, chemical and biological weapons are not only used by regimes, but also by terrorist groups. The killing of thousands of people might no longer be the result of major war but could be done by governments of small states and small but well-organized terrorist groups. Especially biological weapons are relatively easy and cheap to produce, while the effects are beyond imagination. Even very small quantities of biological agents can be lethal. 10,000 to 20,000 spores of anthrax, "something smaller than a speck of dust," are lethal.[38] Nevertheless, mass killings could only occur if the circumstances are right and nothing goes wrong when using these weapons. Experience so far has demonstrated that terrorists have great difficulties using these weapons effectively. For this reason, in the hands of terrorists these weapons are primarily weapons of mass *disruption*.

36 Alex West, "Deadliest Weapon So Far... The Plague", *The Sun*, January 19, 2009.

37 Eli Lake, "Al Qaeda Bungles Arms Experiment", *Washington Times*, January 20, 2009. p. 1.

38 Department of Defense press conference, November 14, 1997.

Nuclear and radiological weapons

The proliferation of nuclear weapons causes fewer problems than the spread of chemical and biological weapons. In 1963, President John F. Kennedy predicted that by 1970 "there may be ten nuclear powers instead of four, and by 1975, fifteen or twenty."[39] Kennedy was wrong in his forecast. It was only as recently as 1998 that India and Pakistan joined the nuclear club, which was by then composed of the five permanent members of the UN Security Council and Israel. The nuclear status of North Korea, Libya, and Iran has been a source of concern for many years.

Nuclear non-proliferation and nuclear arms control have been relatively successful. The permanent five have been fully aware of the grave consequences of employing nuclear weapons, and consequently saw these weapons as political weapons to deter opponents. Treaties prevent the spread of nuclear weapons. The Non-Proliferation Treaty (NPT) was signed in 1968, and came into force in 1970. During the NPT Review Conference in 1995, states agreed that the treaty would have an indefinite duration. The treaty prohibits the transfer of nuclear weapons or other nuclear explosive devices or of control over them by nuclear weapons states to any recipient. The treaty also prohibits the receipt by non-nuclear weapons states from any transfer – as well as the manufacture or other acquisition by those states – of nuclear weapons. The non-nuclear weapons states concluded safeguard agreements with the International Atomic Energy Agency (IAEA) with a view to preventing the diversion of nuclear materials from peaceful use to nuclear weapons. The NPT was adopted by an overwhelming majority of states; notable non-signatories were India, Pakistan, and Israel.

Most states are also in favor of the Comprehensive Nuclear Test-Ban Treaty (CTBT), which was adopted by an overwhelming vote of the UN General Assembly on September 10, 1996. It marked the end of four decades of negotiations on a nuclear test ban. However, ratification was difficult. The major obstacle is the list of dozens of states with nuclear programs, which must sign the treaty before it can come into force. Of those on this list, India, Pakistan, and North Korea had not signed the treaty.

The most likely explanation for the limited number of nuclear weapons states is that the research, development, and manufacturing of nuclear weapons programs are costly and complex, although the technology is almost 70 years old. Other weapons of mass destruction, such as biological and chemical weapons, are as effective and can easily be developed for a

39 R. Reeves, *President Kennedy: Profile of Power* (New York: Simon and Schuster, 1993), p. 477.

fraction of the cost. States usually acquire nuclear weapons to underscore their status as a global or regional power. It is only in very few cases that states develop nuclear weapons because they believe they face an existential threat: India, Iran, Israel, North Korea, and Pakistan. These states claim they need weapons of mass destruction as a deterrent against hostile neighbors. Israel has an ongoing nuclear program and owns approximately 100 nuclear weapons. Israel's nuclear arsenal is believed to have deterred the use of chemical warheads on Saddam Hussein's Scuds when attacking Tel Aviv during the 1991 Gulf War. India and Pakistan have fought three wars since the Asian subcontinent gained independence in 1947. Hindu India and Muslim Pakistan came dangerously close to a fourth, possibly nuclear, confrontation over Kashmir in 1990. In May 1998, India conducted a series of nuclear tests at the Pokaran testing site, about 500 kilometers southwest of the capital. Indian tests, the nation's first since 1974, came one month after the test fire of a ballistic missile with a range of 1,500 kilometers by Pakistan, but defense minister George Fernandez identified another neighbor, China, as the principle military threat to India, which had humiliated India during the 1962 border war.[40] Since then, India has had nuclear aspirations. But it was only after the Bharatiya Janata Party (BJP) won the March 1998 elections that the new Hindu nationalist and anti-Muslim government made the decision to test five nuclear devices. Two weeks later, on May 28, Pakistan conducted five nuclear tests in response to the same number by India. The tests came as a shock. Most world leaders had hoped that after the French and Chinese tests in 1996 and the subsequent approval by the UN of the Comprehensive Test Ban Treaty on September 11, the nuclear arms race had come to a halt. But especially the tensions between both countries over Kashmir, where Muslim militants seek to break away from Indian rule, aroused fears that this part of the world might be the eyewitness of the first inter-state nuclear war.

In the same region, other states have, or have had, nuclear programs as well. After the defection in 1995 of Hussain Kamel, Saddam Hussein's son-in-law and former head of the Iraqi military industries, Iraq admitted to having had a crash program for the development of nuclear weapons. Hussein's nuclear program has been destroyed by UNSCOM, but Iraq was assumed to have retained the capabilities to restart such a program. Months after Operation Iraqi Freedom, however, no evidence was found to support this claim.

40 "India's Atomic Tests Revive Old Fears", *International Herald Tribune,* May 12, 1998.

American and Israeli policymakers are convinced that Iran is actively pursuing a policy to acquire nuclear weapons, probably with Russian assistance. On January 20, 1992, a task force of the US House Republican Research Committee concluded that there was a "98% certainty that Iran already had all of the components required for two or three operational nuclear weapons made with parts purchased in the ex-Soviet Muslim republics." A modified Chinese M-II missile, the Zalzal 300, is believed to be the delivery vehicle for these weapons. In 1998, the *Jerusalem Post* wrote that Iranian government documents proved that, in the early 1990s, Iran received up to four nuclear warheads from the former Soviet republic of Kazakhstan, and that Russian experts were maintaining them. The Russian underworld could have helped Iran to acquire these weapons.[41] In 2003, after Operation Iraqi Freedom, America again focused its attention on Iran's nuclear weapons program. This move was not unexpected because in his 2002 State of the Union Address, President Bush stated that Iran belongs to the "axis of evil" that actively tries to acquire weapons of mass destruction, especially nuclear weapons, including their means of delivery. A report by the International Atomic Energy Agency (IAEA) said that there was no evidence thus far that Iran had sought to build nuclear weapons. However, Iran had manufactured small amounts of enriched uranium and plutonium as part of a nuclear program that operated in secret for 18 years. In February 2004, inspectors of the IAEA discovered blueprints for an unknown Iranian program to enrich uranium, despite earlier promises to disclose its nuclear activities.

The nuclear programs of Iran and North Korea are sources of ongoing frictions with the international community. The nuclear program of Iran was launched in the 1950s. Iran received technical support from the West until the 1979 Iranian Revolution toppled the Shah. After the revolution, Ayatollah Khomeini stopped a secret nuclear program on religious grounds, but during the Iraq-Iran War, the program restarted and was expanded after the Ayatollah's death in 1989. In 2011, the Bushehr I reactor was opened. The key issue is that the international community was very suspicious of Iran's nuclear ambitions. The IAEA revealed time and again details about Iran's nuclear program. Iran first denied and later admitted the allegations, but the status of its nuclear program remains in dispute. Moreover, Iran is a party to the NPT but was found to be in non-compliance with the Safeguards Agreement.

North Korea became a party to the NPT in 1985. But on January 10, 2003, it announced that it was withdrawing from the Treaty and no longer accepted

41 *Jerusalem Post*, October 4, 1998.

the binding force of its Safeguards Agreement with the IAEA. On October 9, 2006, the North Korean government announced that it had successfully conducted its first nuclear test. In April, IAEA Director General Mohamed ElBaradei agreed that North Korea had become a "fully fledged nuclear power." This was confirmed by another test on May 25, 2009. The third nuclear test took place on February 11, 2013. North Korea's nuclear program has led to UN sanctions and isolation of one of the last remaining Stalinist states. In 2010, war almost broke out when North Korea shelled a South Korean island and torpedoed a South Korean warship. As a result of the sanctions imposed after the third nuclear test, North Korea mobilized its artillery and missile forces and escalated its war rhetoric, bringing the two Koreas again to the brink of war.

In early 2004, the IAEA announced that Libya had been producing small amounts of plutonium and had been accumulating large stores of illicit uranium-processing equipment for 20 years. Libya also surrendered a 1960s nuclear weapons design that it acquired in late 2001 or early 2002.[42]

Early in 2004, a nuclear network run by the "father of Pakistan's atomic bomb," Abdul Qadeer Kahn, was broken up. Kahn led a trading network that sent bomb-making designs, equipment, and partly enriched uranium to at least Iran, North Korea, and Libya.[43]

In December 2003, Libyan leader Muammar Gadhafi agreed to give up his weapons of mass destruction and his nuclear weapons program.[44] Libya is probably the only example of a country giving up its nuclear ambitions under the threat of military force. Gadhafi's former Foreign Minister, Abdel Rahman Shalgham, argued Gadhafi gave up his WMDs and nuclear weapons program when US President George W. Bush told Gadhafi in 2001 that: "Either you get rid of your weapons of mass destruction or [the United States] will personally destroy them and destroy everything with no discussion."[45] The US intervention in Iraq also contributed to Gadhafi's decision to give up its WMD program. Days before the invasion of Iraq, his envoy contacted US President George W. Bush, Russian President Vladimir Putin, and British Prime Minister Tony Blair about his willingness to dismantle Libya's nuclear

42 "Libya Made Plutonium, Nuclear Watchdog Says", *Washington Post,* February 21,2004.

43 "A Tale of Nuclear Proliferation: 'How Pakistani Built his Network'", *The New York Times,* February 12, 2004.

44 Judith Miller, "Gadhafi's Leap of Faith", *The Wall Street Journal,* May 17, 2006.

45 Norman Cigar, "Libya's Nuclear Disarmament: Lessons and Implications for Nuclear Proliferation", *Marine Corps University,* January 2012, p. 2.

program. Subsequently, Libyan officials provided details on the chemical, biological, and nuclear activities.

The end of the Cold War increased the risk that nuclear weapons would fall into the hands of terrorists. Prices of Russian nuclear weapons were found in the papers of Shoko Asahara, the blind Japanese leader of the Aum Shinrikyo sect who received the death penalty in 2004. The sect also tried to build weapons, which involved buying land in Australia from which to extract uranium. Despite their assets of more than one billion dollars, and access to a huge pool of scientific and technical knowledge, they shifted their attention to chemical and biological weapons. This indicates that for non-state actors, developing nuclear weapons is probably impossible.

Al-Qaeda was assumed to be interested in acquiring nuclear weapons ever since 1993. In February 1999, Bin Laden stated that in doing so he was carrying out a religious duty. There is some evidence that al-Qaeda tried to buy nuclear weapons on the black market. They may have succeeded in doing so, because there are reports that he acquired some nuclear weapons from the former Soviet arsenals. The issue of security of Russian weapons of mass destruction, know-how, technologies, and components has been discussed earlier. For example, there have been reports about suitcase-sized nuclear bombs having disappeared from the former KGB arsenals. In an interview with the CBS news magazine *60 Minutes* at the beginning of September 1997, former Russian national security advisor Aleksandr Lebed said that the Russian military had lost track of more than 100 suitcase-sized nuclear bombs. Duma member Alexey Yablokov wrote that the statement of Lebed had real credibility.[46] Yablokov wrote that suitcase bombs were created in the 1970s on orders from the KGB to perform terrorist acts. These nuclear devices were not assigned to the Ministry of Defense and correspondingly were not taken into account in the negotiations on nuclear arms reductions. Assuming that these weapons exist, some of them could have fallen into the hands of terrorists.

Nevertheless, the most likely nuclear threat is the dispersion of highly radioactive materials by conventional explosives; radiological or "dirty" bombs. In 2001, Jose Padilla, alias Abdullah al Mujahir, was arrested at O'Hare Airport in Chicago. He was accused of trying to assemble and detonate a dirty bomb, probably in an apartment building in Chicago. Fears that a dirty bomb might explode on New Year's Eve led to the cancellation of more than a dozen transatlantic commercial flights and an extensive

46 *Novaya Gazeta,* September 9, 1997.

search in Washington, D.C., New York, Las Vegas, Los Angeles, and Baltimore in December 2003.

Radiological weapons are unlikely to inflict massive casualties or mass destruction. Nevertheless, they could turn large parts of Western cities into no-go areas. Consequently, just as chemical and biological weapons, these weapons are primarily weapons of mass disruption.

Another likely threat is attacks on nuclear facilities. After the 9/11 attacks, the head of the IAEA said it was far more likely that terrorists would start to target nuclear facilities, nuclear and radioactive sources worldwide. For that reason, France put air defenses around its major nuclear facility at La Hague.

Missile proliferation

In 1988, William Webster, then director of the CIA, predicted that 15 to 20 third world countries were likely to be building their own ballistic missiles in the year 2000.[47] This claim was wrong, although for more than two decades, proliferation of missiles capable of delivering weapons of mass destruction undermined stability in regions where Western powers have considerable economic and strategic interests, particularly in Southwest Asia and the Middle East. Regimes armed with those missiles could deter Western involvement in those areas, especially when they possess missiles capable of reaching their homelands. Consequently, in the 1980s, missile proliferation became an item on the agenda of the Western powers. It became the basis on which Washington gained the support to control missile transfers as well.

In the early 1980s, the Soviet Union sold the 300 kilometer-range Scud surface-to-surface missile to states in Europe and the Middle East, in particular Iran and Iraq. The latter produced a double-range version of the missile, called the Al-Hussain. The Soviet-designed 500 kilometer-range SS-23 was sold to Bulgaria, Czechoslovakia, and East Germany.

Consequently, President Ronald Reagan began secret discussions with Canada, France, West Germany, Italy, Japan, and the United Kingdom on measures to counter missile proliferation. Reagan was particularly concerned that states involved in missile programs would also be able to produce nuclear weapons, or had an interest in doing so. This fear was certainly justified. Iraq, Iran, Israel, Pakistan, India, North Korea, and South

47 A. Karp, *Ballistic Missile Proliferation: The Politics and Technics* (Oxford: Oxford University Press, 1996), p. 20.

Africa had nuclear programs and saw missiles as the principle means of delivery.

In April 1987, Washington and its six economic partners announced the Missile Technology Control Regime (MTCR) to limit the spread of nuclear-capable missiles.[48] Through the MTCR, the United States sought to control the spread of missiles with a 500-kilogram payload and a range of at least 300 kilometers. The MTCR has become an increasingly effective body for controlling missile proliferation. Prompted by the Gulf War, the MTCR participants took the initiative to extend the MTCR guide lines to all missiles capable of carrying weapons of mass destruction. In 1991, the payload restriction was reduced so that the regime now covered all missiles with a range of over 150 kilometers. Today, most potential suppliers of missile technology adhere to the restriction. The only exceptions are North Korea and some Arab countries with ballistic missile capabilities. In addition, the threat of interstate warfare abated during the 1980s and 1990s, so that the need for these systems abated as well.

Nevertheless, in 1998, India tested its first Agni intermediate range ballistic missile (1,500-2,000 km). Israel worked on the Jericho system, and South Africa was developing the Arniston intermediate-range ballistic missile with the assistance of Israel. With India and Israel, North Korea was and still is the only regional power working independently on a missile program. Work started in the early 1970s, and was accelerated during the 1980s when Scud technologies became available. By 1987, Scud copies were sold to Iran, and by 1992 extended range Scud copies were sold to Iran and Syria. In 1999, the Rodong, with a range of 1,300 kilometers, became operational. Consequently, the US started to upgrade its missile defenses in South Korea, while Japan started plans to deploy new advanced interceptor missiles. It was feared that Japan would be a prime target, because it was still hated for its colonial rule of Korea between 1910 and 1945.

China provided technical assistance to Pakistan in the development of the Hatf I and II. The first tests took place in 1989. In 1988, China sold 2,650 kilometer-range missiles to Saudi Arabia. By the late 1980s, Argentina, Egypt, and Iraq were collaborating on the medium-range Condor II system, which was brought to a halt in 1990.

The Gulf War underscored the need to counter missile proliferation. During that war, Iraq launched 88 missiles against Saudi Arabia, Israel, and

48 A.A. Pikayev, L.S. Spector, E.V. Kirichenko, R. Gibson, *Russia, the US and the Missile Technology Control Regime* (London: IISS, Adelphi Paper 317, 1998), p. 10.

Bahrain. Ballistic missiles played an important role in Saddam Hussein's attempts to force Israel into the war. The Iraqi leader apparently calculated that Israel would retaliate, thus triggering a full-scale Arabic war in which most Arabic states would side with Iraq. Scud attacks on Tel Aviv began on January 17, 1991 and caused great alarm. It was feared that Saddam might attack Israel with missiles armed with chemical warheads. As this was not the case, and as Patriot missile defenses appeared to have some effect, the fear eased. In 1998, British intelligence believed that Iraq still had up to ten Scud missiles hidden away that were capable of carrying weapons of mass destruction. If Saddam Hussein had used chemical warheads, he might have succeeded in forcing Israel into the war.

The Gulf War experience demonstrated that ballistic missiles can have disproportionate effects, although their use itself may not be decisive. Ballistic missiles are useful under specific circumstances. First, air defenses raise the costs of attacks with manned aircraft. For countries facing adversaries with heavy air defenses, ballistic missiles might be a cost-effective solution. Second, as air defenses are only partially effective, ballistic missiles demonstrate the vulnerability of the population. Thus the use of only a few missiles can have a significant political effect. Depending on the situation, ballistic missiles can either deter a government from intervention in a conflict, or force them into the war. During the Gulf War, missile proliferation became the symbol of the anarchy prevailing in international relations. Ballistic missiles have a psychological effect on the population. They are unmanned and a symbol of terror.

During the first decade of the 21st century, Iran and North Korea caused the most concern. Both countries developed medium- and long-range missiles and threatened their enemies. Early in 2013, North Korean leader Kim Jong-Un threatened the US with strikes on bases in Guam, Hawaii, and mainland America in response to new sanctions. In March 2013, North Korea put its missile units on standby again to attack US military bases in South Korea and the Pacific, after the United States flew two nuclear-capable stealth bombers over the Korean peninsula.

Largely in response to the growing ballistic missile threat, NATO's leaders decided to develop a ballistic missile defense (BMD) The first phase of an initial capability to protect Alliance forces against ballistic missile threats was acquired in 2010. NATO's work on BMD started in the early 1990s. The initial focus was on protecting deployed troops. In 2002, the system was to include the protection of population centers and territory. A report for the US Congress concluded in 2012 that Iran probably is no longer on track to having intercontinental missiles as soon as 2015.[49] Sanctions and the lack of foreign assistance, that is, from North Korea, slowed down the program.[50] Medium-range missiles include the Shahab-3 which is based on the North Korean Nodong missile. It has a range of about 900 kilometers. A modified version of the Shahab-3, the Ghadr-1, began flight tests in 2004. It theoretically extends Iran's reach to about 1,600 kilometers. The Sajjil-2 is a domestically produced missile with a range of about 2,200 kilometers, which began test flights in 2009. According to Brigadier General Abdollah Araghi, a Revolutionary Guard commander, this allows Iran to "target any place that threatens Iran."

By 1984, North Korea was building its own Scuds, the Hwasong-5 and Hwasong-6, as well as a medium-range missile, the Nodong. In 2006, North Korea tested a Taepodong-2 missile with an estimated range of 6,500 kilometers. Missiles with related technology were tested in 2009 and 2012, but all launches ended in failure. On December 12, 2012, North Korea made another, apparently successful launch of a three stage missile.

A rapidly emerging concern is the spread of cruise missiles. The main concerns are anti-ship missiles that pose a threat to the intervention forces of the United States. China is reported as having procured SS-N-22 Sunburn anti-ship cruise missiles from Russia, which might deter US intervention on behalf of Taiwan. Moreover, China sold anti-ship missiles to Iran, thus creating risks for American intervention forces in the Gulf. Representative James Lightfoot told the House Committee on Appropriations that "For those of you who are unfamiliar with the Sunburn-class missile (...) our navy has no defense against such a missile."[51] Sophisticated but cheap guidance systems dramatically enhanced the accuracy of cruise missiles during the 1990s. Advanced cruise missiles are hard to counter. Anti-missile missiles, point defenses, and passive measures such as jamming, are partially effective. Moreover, improving the speed of cruise missiles such as the Sunburn missile can reduce the effectiveness of some defensive systems.

In 2009 the debate on the vulnerability of ships gained a new impetus with the recognition of anti-access/area-denial (A2/AD) challenges for the US in the Asia-Pacific region. Due to military-technological improvements, China was able to carry out "asymmetrical threats" to counter American superiority. By

49 Steven A. Hildreth, *Iran's Ballistic Missile and Space Launch Programs* (Washington, D.C.: Congressional Research Service), December 6, 2012, p. 4.

50 Jim Wolf, "Iran's long-range missiles said to lag US intelligence fears" (Reuters), http://www.reuters.com/article/2012/12/07/us-iran-usa-missile-idUSBRE8B61C920121207.

51 *SIPRI Yearbook 1998*, E. Arnett, "Military Research and Development" (Oxford: Oxford University Press, 1998), p. 282.

developing the DF-21D, the world's first anti-ship ballistic missile, China could circumvent America's traditional military strengths during a crisis. Effective access denial would imperil US interests and weaken US commitments to its allies. As a response to a Chinese official arguing that the South China Sea was a "core interest" of Chinese sovereignty, the Obama Administration stated in 2010 that freedom of maritime navigation in the region is a US national interest. In 2012, US Joint Chiefs Chairman Martin Dempsey presented the Joint Operational Access Concept, or JOAC, outlining the A2/AD concept. To overcome the A2/AD challenge "future joint forces will leverage cross-domain synergy – the complementary vice being merely additive employment of capabilities in different domains such that each enhances the effectiveness and compensates for the vulnerabilities of the others – to establish superiority in some combination of domains that will provide the freedom of action required by the mission." Cross-domain synergy refers to joint air-sea operations, or the AirSea Battle doctrine, which was inspired by the AirLand Battle doctrine mentioned earlier. The new doctrine required the military to "conduct operations to gain access, (...) seize the initiative by deploying and operating on multiple, independent lines of operations, (...) exploit advantages in one or more domains to disrupt or destroy enemy anti-access/area-denial capabilities in others, disrupt enemy reconnaissance and surveillance efforts while protecting friendly efforts, create pockets or corridors of local domain superiority to penetrate the enemy's defenses (...), attack enemy anti-access/area-denial defenses in depth (...), maximize surprise through deception, stealth, and ambiguity to complicate enemy targeting, and protect space and cyber assets while attacking the enemy's cyber and space capabilities."[52]

Conclusion

Nowadays, most wars will be intrastate wars waged in an unconventional manner. Irregular militias, warlords, rebels, and terrorists dominate the new environment. They cause humanitarian disasters, the destabilization of countries and regions, and they pose a threat to Western interests. Military operations are likely to be carried out:

- in complex emergencies, usually internal conflicts in weak or failed states with large-scale displacements of people, mass famine, and fragile or failing economic, political, and social institutions;

52 *Joint Operational Access Concept* (JOAC), version 1.0 (DOD, Washington, D.C.) January 17, 2012, p. iii.

- against non-state actors who could use "black holes" in weak or failed states. These ungoverned territories are used as safe havens, hubs, or for criminal practices;
- against rogue states, believed to support international terrorism or affect Western interests in a region;
- against emerging states seeking unlawful access to scarce resources, oil and gas deposits and fishing grounds.

Both governments and terrorists could acquire weapons of mass destruction and their means of delivery. In February 2004, President Bush argued that the proliferation of weapons of mass destruction posed the most serious danger to world peace: "Chemical, biological, and nuclear weapons in the hands of terrorism or outlaw regimes could bring catastrophic harm to America and the international community."[53] Consequently, he proposed new steps to help combat the development and spread of these weapons. Measures included improvement and modernization of non-proliferation laws; restricting the sale and transport of nuclear technologies and equipment; the closing of loopholes in the non-proliferation regime; and new efforts to secure and destroy nuclear weapons and materials.

Indeed, the spread of weapons of mass destruction could undermine the prospects of successful interventions. Weapons of mass destruction could deter coercers. Moreover, religious anti-systemic terrorism could make use of these weapons to inflict mass destruction, massive casualties, and fear, or transform large parts of Western cities into no-go areas.

The consequences of the emerging security situation of doctrine and force posture will be dealt with in the next chapter.

53 The White House, *Fact Sheet: Strengthening International Efforts against WMD Proliferation*, Washington, D.C., February 11, 2004.

6 Dealing with Complex Security Challenges

In chapter 3, I argued that coercive strategies can only be effective if the coercer is willing to use force. And if force is used, it must be done effectively. Due to Western superiority in combat power, adversaries have no other choice than to use the "great equalizer" to thwart this superiority: unconventional and asymmetrical strategies of countercoercion. If this is done in a smart way, this can even nullify the West's might. In the previous chapter I concluded that the armed forces of liberal democracies could be deployed in distant parts of the world. They must not only be prepared to fight conventional wars against regular forces, but also unconventional operations against the opponents' irregular armed forces and terrorists.

In conventional wars, armies take and hold ground, air forces conduct strategic bombing operations and support ground forces, and navies support land forces with land attack missiles by conducting offshore attacks and cutting off lines of supply. Gaining air superiority is a prerequisite for success, and air power plays a key role in paving the way for land forces.

In unconventional warfare it is only through the physical *control* of an area or *isolation* of the opponent that military objectives can be met. Special operations forces and specialized forces, such as air maneuver units, play a key role. Air superiority is no problem because the opponent is unlikely to possess aircraft, although he may have a limited number of MANPADS (man-portable air-defense systems). But the actual role of air forces is limited to close air support and interdiction. I consider unconventional warfare primarily a political struggle and a method of achieving asymmetry. At the strategic level, the opponent using asymmetrical tactics exploits the fears of the civilians, thereby undermining the government, compromising its alliances, and affecting its economy. To achieve this, the opponent uses unconventional warfare techniques at the tactical level to change the course of action in order to prevent the opponent from achieving political objectives. The tactics of unconventional warfare include guerrilla, hit-and-run attacks, sabotage, terrorism, and psychological warfare. Usually, rebels, terrorists, and criminals with small, but well-organized forces or militias will adopt these tactics.

This chapter is mainly devoted to unconventional warfare, traditionally a much neglected part of Western military thinking. Neglecting this form of warfare is dangerous, because most conflicts will be fought in an unconventional manner. The concluding paragraphs deal with the concept of network-enabled warfare, which holds the promise that Western military forces could conduct conventional and unconventional warfare in a similar way.[1]

Western preoccupations

The neglect of unconventional warfare comes as no surprise if one takes the history of Western military thought into account (see chapter 4). In unconventional operations, small units are used. Technology plays a supporting role at best. In unconventional warfare, the tactical and technical levels of warfare are extremely important. In fact, this kind of warfare does not lend itself to the usual categorizations of the strategic, operational, tactical, and technical levels of war. In conventional warfare, the strategic level gives the overall direction; the operational level is concerned with armies and army corps fighting campaigns; the tactical level is concerned with divisions and brigades fighting battles; the technical level deals with small units and the effects of weapon systems.

In unconventional warfare, two levels are most important: the strategic level for overall direction and the technical level for the actual war fighting. The strategic level could also deal with political and diplomatic actions. The operational and tactical levels oversee the operation in the target area and could play a supporting role, for example, to provide air support for soldiers on the ground. Most importantly, the operational level will oversee the hearts and minds campaign, including psychological operations, carried out at the tactical level. Thus, in conventional warfare, doctrine deals with the interaction between the various levels of war. In unconventional warfare, the different levels fight different "battles." The different roles of the levels in conventional and unconventional warfare make it extremely difficult for commanders to conduct both types of operations simultaneously.

In unconventional warfare, skills are important factors for success.[2] Because the skills of Western forces are traditionally limited to a small spectrum of the total arena, the chances of success are small when facing

1 Joint Publication 3.0, pp. IV-8. JP 3.0 makes a distinction between linear and nonlinear operations. Linearity is referred to as the conduct of operations along clearly defined Forward Lines of Own Troops (FLOT), whilst nonlinear operations tend to be conducted from selected bases of operations, both ashore and afloat, but without clearly defined lines of operations.

2 J. Arquilla, *Dubious Battles: Aggression, Defeat and the International System* (Washington, D.C.: Crane Russak, 1992).

irregular forces. This demands capabilities in the field of counterguerilla warfare, which Western powers on the whole are not trained for.

As has been pointed out before, conventional warfare in open terrain is the preferred form of combat for modern Western military forces. Insurgents and terrorists will avoid open terrain. Instead, they will try to confront the adversary in cities or mountains. This creates a fundamental problem for Western political and military leaders. History suggests that it is extremely difficult for modern forces to use their technological advantages in "complex terrain." Mountains are no-go areas for tanks and armored vehicles. They can only be used to block roads and to provide fire support. The actual fighting requires small units that carry out search-and-destroy missions. Troops hunt down the adversary and neutralize them in hand-to-hand combat. They can call in air power, but in practice there is a shortage of lucrative targets, because air power is unlikely to find and destroy small bands of fighters.

The disastrous performance of US troops during the Vietnam War (1965-1973) contributed to the neglect of unconventional warfare. As a result, a second disaster in Somalia (1994) followed. Obsession with conventional wars is equally strong in other armies. Soviet forces performed disastrously in Afghanistan (1979-1989).

In the US, only the marines were interested in unconventional warfare. During the "Banana War" period of 1915-1934, marines were sent to South American countries, including Haiti and the Dominican Republic, to restore order. Experience with these operations was used for their counterinsurgency doctrine. This doctrine was published in the *Small Wars Manual,* published in 1940 and reprinted in 1987 when the US again became involved in internal struggles in South America. The army never produced a similar doctrine. FM 100-5 (1983) maintained that the AirLand Battle doctrine for conventional warfare applied equally to low-intensity warfare, including peace support operations, disaster relief, counterguerrilla warfare, and counterterrorist operations. The same assumptions were made by field manuals on counterguerrilla operations, special forces operations, and low-intensity operations. By 1990, Field Manuals no longer mentioned low-intensity operations. Instead, the preferred terminology had become Operations Other Than War (OOTW). In 1994 FM 100-20 *Military Operations Other Than War,* replaced *Military Operations in Low-Intensity Conflict.* But in practice, none of these manuals dealt with unconventional warfare.

The rejection of unconventional military operations was demonstrated during Operation Allied Force. In 1999, the "ground option" was constantly being debated. Using ground forces against the Serbs in Kosovo would require a military offensive through the mountainous border region with Albania. In the Pentagon, the Chairman of the Joint Chiefs of Staff, General Hugh Shelton, rejected this option because the risks involved would result in too many casualties. Given the relatively limited interests at stake, this was considered intolerable. Former Russian Prime Minister and Kosovo-negotiator Viktor Chernomyrdin later said that Slobodan Milosevic had hoped that NATO would indeed launch a ground offensive, so that he would be able to practice partisan tactics and inflict great numbers of casualties to NATO forces.[3] NATO, however, believed that the threat of a ground war contributed to Milosevic's decision to accept a peace deal. But Chernomyrdin's observation is consistent with the logic of unconventional warfare. As a result of the wars in Afghanistan and Iraq, unconventional warfare emerged as a new priority for the US Army. The 2003 version of the field manual *Operations,* discussed in chapter 4, contained a chapter on stability and support operations. It described the basic tenets of counterinsurgency operations. The manual stressed that counterinsurgency is essentially a political task aimed at neutralizing the adversary. While there was no indication that the Army embraced the concept with enthusiasm, the ongoing struggle with insurgents in Afghanistan and Iraq forced its leadership to adopt an interim counterinsurgency manual.[4]

Nevertheless, counterinsurgency operations should be avoided if possible. The solution is to fight wars by proxy. Proxy wars have been fought frequently. Local fighters usually have a greater understanding of both the terrain and the adversary. Moreover, they are usually highly motivated, because they have an existential cause to fight for. In Mindanao, in the Philippines, the US Special Operations Forces conducted joint operations with the Filipinos against the Abu Nidal Group, which was supposed to have close links with al-Qaeda. Some 600 Special Operations Forces formed a joint team with the armed forces of the Philippines.

At the same time, local fighters could be unreliable, because they could consider outside powers as a means to achieve their own goals. This happened during Operation Allied Force, when the Kosovo Liberation Army (KLA) considered NATO as its own air force. The KLA was convinced that NATO would support its cause, that is, an independent Kosovo. If there is a mismatch between expectations and reality, local fighters may turn against the intervener. For these reasons, Western armed forces may have no other choice but to fight unconventional wars themselves.

3 Private communication with Viktor Chernomyrdin.

4 FMI 3-07-22 Counterinsurgency Operations (October 2004).

Savage warfare

Actually, there is nothing new about unconventional warfare. In 1898, in *Lockhart's Advance Through Tirah,* Captain L.J. Shadwell wrote about "savage warfare," also known as colonial or non-European warfare "that differed from that of civilized people."[5] Many areas in the world have not changed much since Shadwell's time: "A frontier tribesman can live for days on the grain he carries with him, and other savages on a few dates; consequently, no necessity exists for them to cover a line of communications. So nimble of foot, too, are they in their grass shoes, and so conversant with every goat-track in their mountains that they can retreat in any direction. This extraordinary mobility enables them to attack from any direction quite unexpectedly, and to disperse and disappear as rapidly as they came. For this reason, the rear of a European force is as much exposed to attack as its front or flanks."

For example, in Afghanistan, the biggest change was that army boots and Nikes replaced the grass shoes. Local fighters of the Taliban and al-Qaeda possessed limited numbers of advanced weaponry, such as Stinger anti-aircraft missiles, which were acquired during the 1980s when the US considered the Taliban to be freedom fighters who needed support in their struggle against the Soviet occupation. The basic weapons platform is the pick-up truck, which carries fighters armed with guns; in mountainous regions, horses and mules are still the most important mode of transportation. In *Foreign Affairs,* US Secretary of Defense Donald Rumsfeld gave a clear picture of the "new" kind of war American soldiers had to fight in Afghanistan. Soldiers, Rumsfeld wrote:

> ... sported beards and traditional scarves and rode horses trained to run into machine-gun fire. They used pack mules to transport equipment across some of the roughest terrain in the world, riding at night, in darkness, near minefields and along narrow mountain trails with drops so sheer that, as one soldier put it: "it took me a week to ease the death-grip on my horse." Many had never been on a horse's back before.[6]

The lesson of Afghanistan is: "not that the US Army should start stockpiling saddles. Rather, it is that preparing for the future will require new ways of

5 L.J. Shadwell, "Savage Warfare", in L. Freedman (ed.) *War* (Oxford: Oxford University Press, 1994), pp. 318-319.

6 D.H. Rumsfeld, "Transforming the Military", *Foreign Affairs,* May-June 2002, p. 20.

thinking and the development of forces and capabilities that can adapt quickly to new challenges and unexpected circumstances."

Nevertheless, most Western armed forces still consider irregular or non-conventional warfare "savage warfare" for which there is no preparation. Historically the British and the Dutch, in particular, fought unconventional wars quite successfully in their colonies. With the loss of Indonesia in the 1950s, the Dutch lost not only all their experience in waging this kind of war, but also their mental preparedness for such action. In 2001, in drafting a new field manual on counterinsurgency warfare, the Dutch army staff utilized the old manuals that General Johannes van Heutsz had used in the early twentieth century when he was combating insurgents and terrorists in what is now known as the Republic of Indonesia. Van Heutsz also reorganized his conventional ground forces to confront the insurgents, creating small units of a dozen men to carry out search-and-destroy operations. This military action led to an episode the Dutch have no desire to repeat. Today, that army's counterinsurgency operations could be perceived as war crimes. No distinction was made between combatants and non-combatants. The Dutch burned down entire villages in order to eliminate fighters' bases. From a conceptual point of view, two methods of counterinsurgency warfare can be distinguished here. Search-and-destroy operations are a form of maneuver warfare; burning down villages is attrition or brute force.

Unsurprisingly, during the stabilization phase following Operation Enduring Freedom, American forces applied similar techniques in Afghanistan. A Human Rights Watch report concluded that US forces have used excessive or indiscriminate force when conducting arrests in residential areas in Afghanistan, which violated international humanitarian law. The report also stated that the Americans fought against an opponent that showed little willingness to abide by international humanitarian law or humanitarian standards: "they have carried out abductions and attacks against civilians and humanitarian aid workers and detonated bombs in bazaars and other civilian areas."[7] Indeed, the report confirmed that unconventional warfare could easily escalate into "savage warfare" in which both parties use methods that cannot be classified as "civilized."

In addition to Van Heutsz's manuals, in drafting the new manual, the Dutch army staff used the British counterinsurgency manual, which is still the most detailed for this type of warfare. Of the former colonial powers, only the British have not given up their military skills; at the same time,

7 Human Rights Watch, *"Enduring Freedom: Abuses by U.S. Forces in Afghanistan"*, March 2004, p. 1.

British politicians and the military have maintained the mental preparedness needed to carry out "counterinsurgency operations." Especially, the counterinsurgencies in the Dhofar province in Oman (1965-1975) and Northern Ireland (since 1969) have given the British firsthand experience. In Dhofar, strategic interests were at stake because Oman's leaders could control the vital oil route of the Strait of Hormuz. The Dhofar campaign was a classical, rural counterinsurgency campaign, while that in Northern Ireland was a mix of rural and urban terrorism.

As will be seen, unconventional war fighting requires combat skills and a basic understanding of the dynamics of the conflict, as well as the application of non-military means to win the hearts and minds of the local population. In unconventional operations, understanding the strategic consequences of tactical actions is crucial.

Revolutionary warfare

The problems of confronting irregular troops with regular forces are well-documented. Western forces have an impressive record of failure, but non-Western forces make similar mistakes. The Egyptian performance during the 1962-1967 counterinsurgency operations in North Yemen is a less well-known example.[8] Egypt was invited to protect the newly established revolutionary government against the opponents of the revolution. The environment in Yemen was well-suited for guerrilla warfare. Mountains made movement difficult. Mechanized warfare was impossible and large formations could easily become divided and separated. A lack of understanding of Yemen's society led to the conclusion that the war was being fought by organized groups and that the army would be able to use conventional tactics. In addition, they had no maps of the country. The initial purpose of the intervention was to safeguard the republic and to consolidate the new regime's control over the country. The expectation was that this task was to be completed within three months. Egypt's President Gamel Abdel Nasser believed that a successful operation in North Yemen would allow the revolution to spread to Saudi Arabia. Finally, Egypt wanted to expel the British from Aden. In October and November 1962, the Egyptian and Republican forces tried to control all of North Yemen and to keep lines of communication open throughout the country. In an attempt to stop Saudi

8 D.M. Witty, "A Regular Army in Counterinsurgency Operations: Egypt in North Yemen 1962-1967", *The Journal of Military History* 65 (April 2001), pp. 401-440.

support for the Royalists, the Egyptians bombed Royalist safe havens, the Saudi border towns of Najran and Jizan. However, the air raids had little effect. On October 10, the Royalists took a number of towns in eastern Yemen and advanced towards Sana. In response, an Egyptian armored battalion left Sana to recapture the eastern towns. On October 22, Egyptian paratroopers were dropped east of Sirawah. The objective was to carry out a joint operation with the armored battalion to trap the Royalist troops. Due to the absence of maps, the paratroopers got lost in the mountains. Tribesmen killed almost one-third of them. Royal forces ambushed the battalion. The same happened to another Egyptian force, leaving the remaining paratroopers isolated. These and other setbacks made the Egyptians realize that a quick victory would be impossible. Consequently, they developed a new long-range strategy. They withdrew into a triangle formed by the cities of Sana, Hodeilah, and Taiz. After that, the Egyptians prepared for a proxy war by training Republican forces, so that they could defend the country. Only a small group of Egyptian advisors would remain. This strategy was also destined to lead nowhere. The Republican forces were incompetent, leaving the Egyptians to fight the war themselves until 1966. From February 16 to March 7, 1963, they carried out a nationwide Ramadan Offensive. The operation was quite successful. After three weeks and a series of well-planned and well-executed surprise attacks, the Egyptians regained control over the roads, cities, and towns in more than half of the country. During the rest of 1963, the Egyptians merely consolidated the gains. Royalist forces, however, continued to ambush Egypt's forces and bring in supplies from Saudi Arabia. Despite the fact that Egypt had 63,000 troops in Yemen, they were unable to physically control the countryside. The Egyptians embarked on an attrition strategy, wasting large amounts of ammunition in fighting guerrillas. This strategy was also unsuccessful. They were unable to distinguish between friends and foes. The opponent fought in small groups and dispersed, leaving few if any targets for the air force. Royalist forces poisoned wells and the rugged terrain made movement slow. The tribes were the biggest problem because they were disloyal to the republic. The Egyptians followed a carrot and stick policy. On the one hand, they tried to destroy their fighters; on the other hand they tried to bribe them. But the tribes also accepted money from the Royalists. Thus, buying the loyalty of the tribes was also unsuccessful. Finally, problems of morale arose. Due to the losses, the long service, and the hardships the families faced in Egypt, soldiers began to question why they were fighting other Muslims. Frustrated by the absence of success, the Egyptians embarked on a strategy of attrition. They destroyed the agricultural lands, wells, and houses of the tribes supporting the Royalists. By late 1966 and early 1967, many areas had been left deserted. In addition, they tried to eliminate the Imam and his family. This had the opposite effect and caused many tribes to support the Royalists.

The example mentioned above is a classic example of unconventional warfare that is hard to deal with. The British counterinsurgency manual, mentioned earlier, defines insurgencies as the actions of a minority group within a state, forcing political change by means of a mixture of subversion, propaganda, and military pressure. Insurgents will manifest themselves against governments that are unable to meet the security demands of the population or a privileged group. Unconventional warfare requires the application of special techniques. As combating insurgents, gangs, militias, and terrorists requires similar techniques, the British counterinsurgency manual had a broader application than its title suggests.

Traditionally, unconventional warfare is synonymous with counterinsurgency operations, aimed at destroying revolutionary movements. Mao Tse-tung provided the first coherent theory of revolutionary struggle using a mix of unconventional and conventional warfare techniques. He had a clear idea of the strengths and weaknesses of unconventional warfare. Therefore, his ideas are still important in understanding this kind of warfare. Mao wrote two books about the subject: *Guerrilla Warfare* (1937) and *Strategic Problems in the Anti-Japanese Guerrilla War* (1938) in which he maintained that the struggle is primarily political, rather than military. First, Mao outlined a seven-step strategy that any revolutionary strategy must follow:

1 arousing and organizing the people;
2 achieving internal unification politically;
3 establishing bases;
4 equipping forces;
5 recovering national strength;
6 destroying the enemy's national strength; and
7 regaining lost territories.

Subsequently, he outlined his famous three stages of insurgency: "The first stage is one of the enemy's strategic offensive and our strategic defensive. The second stage is one of the enemy's strategic defensive and our preparation of the counteroffensive. The third stage is one of our strategic counteroffensive and the enemy's strategic retreat."

The first stage would require guerrilla warfare, supplemented by "mobile warfare" or the deployment of forces over an extended, shifting, and indefinite front. This would require a high degree of mobility, and is characterized by swift attack and withdrawal. Mao predicted that the end of this phase would divide the territory into three areas: the enemy's bases, the guerrilla's bases, and contested areas. The duration of the second phase would depend on the correlation of forces and the international situation. The third phase would require a type of conventional warfare. Indeed, not many examples exist of irregular forces gaining victory when using unconventional warfare techniques. Actually, Mao never contended that a guerrilla force alone could win the war. According to him, guerrilla warfare was the only type of war that an oppressed people could use to fight an opponent superior in numbers. He believed that victory could be obtained by regular troops after guerrilla forces had altered the relative strengths. During the Vietnam War, guerrilla warfare changed the balance of power between the US and the Viet Cong. The prolonged nature of phase two destroyed the political will and the popular support for the war in the US. The end result was phase three, in which the Viet Cong successfully transitioned into a conventional fighting force. Mao's concept guided the Vietnamese through 30 years of conflict, though it was not necessarily used as a "handbook." Mao's ideas also guided Jonas Savimbi in his struggle for an independent Angola.

Nepali rebels of the United People's Front considered themselves Maoists and used his concepts in their fight against the monarchy. In the early 1990s, the insurgent army grew rapidly in the Tamang and Harbung communities in the western part of the country. The first and second phases of the struggle were concluded with the rebels in control of large parts of the countryside. After a number of successes, the rebels transformed part of their guerrillas into a full-time uniformed military force with a vertical control structure and military ranks. A logistical party and an intelligence group supported this force. A commissar group maintained the ideological integrity of the battalion. This signaled the third phase of the struggle. By the end of 2002, the rebels were ready to move into the final stage of the protracted war, the strategic offensive, with some 3,000-4,000 regular troops and some 10,000-15,000 men and women organized in local militias. The rebels used stolen, captured, home-made, and hunting rifles and pistols, but lacked modern weaponry such as machine guns. On paper, the Nepalese armed forces were stronger and better equipped. But they had for decades been deployed around Nepal as a garrison. For that reason, they lacked combat experience, motivation, logistics, and an effective counterinsurgency strategy based on sound intelligence. The Royal Nepalese Army (RNA) limited itself to the protection of critical installations. When the battle with the government had reached a strategic stalemate in 2001, the Maoists and the government held peace talks. The talks were unsuccessful and the Maoist resumed the insurgency. However, the rebels were unable to penetrate and capture the larger villages and towns, where the police and the RNA were more popular. Moreover, they exhausted public support due to the great number of insurgent casualties and the duration of the struggle.

Nevertheless, the insurgents won the war. In April 2006, the major political parties and the Maoists organized nationwide protests forcing the King to give up powers. The King reinstated Parliament which was dissolved in 1999. Both the Maoists and the new government declared cease-fires and started peace talks. What followed were painful and complex negotiations leading to the interim constitution of 2007 that turned Nepal into a republic led by a multiparty coalition which included the Maoists. Until 2009, there was significant political violence. But by 2012, the situation was stabilized so that the parliament could set up a Truth and Reconciliation Commission to investigate wartime killings, torture, and forced disappearances during the insurgency. The case of Nepal illustrates that a stalemate is a prerequisite for peace negotiations and that stable peace can only be the won during a political process.

The British counterinsurgency manual described Mao's strategy as "protracted popular war." This strategy was developed to gain control over rural areas where government control is weak or absent. It assumes that the cause will attract an ever-increasing number of supporters. Insurgents will establish base areas, build parallel political and military structures, and gradually expand the area of influence. The strategy involves a mix of terrorism, guerrilla tactics, and political activity. The political activity, aimed at the poor, is the most important. Good works are used to get the support of the willing part of the population. Terror and intimidation are used to "gain support" of the unwilling part of the population. The local population is used for recruitment, logistics, and shelter. In its initial stages, rural insurgencies rely on small bands of men. Usually they carry out small-scale operations in remote areas, such as ambushes, sabotage, terror, and assassinations. As the movement becomes successful, its objectives will be more ambitious, so that larger forces will be needed. The transformation of irregular guerrilla forces into a regular army would be necessary to gain victory.

However, Mao's strategy is only one of many. The British manual wrote that in achieving their aims, insurgents could also use the following strategies:

- *Conspiratorial strategy.* This strategy is designed for an urban environment. Small cells of leaders try to generate uprisings by means of armed action, and attempt to get media coverage. The strategy aims to seize key points and decapitate the governing regime.

- *Military strategy.* In this strategy, political action is secondary to military action. The assumption is that the population will choose the winning side. The strategy focuses on discrediting the government's security forces. Initially, the insurgents are likely to apply guerrilla warfare techniques with small, mobile forces. As the movement is more successful and more men are available, conventional warfare techniques may be applied. In Mao's view, the military strategy is the third and final phase of the struggle.
- *Urban insurgency.* This strategy involves applying organized crime and terror in a systematic manner. Insurgents try to disrupt city life through terror, ethnic cleansing, assassination of public figures, establishing no-go areas, and mounting attacks on public services. The aim is to undermine the credibility and the morale of authorities. For that reason, demonstrations can also be engineered. Insurgents will seek media coverage to generate panic. Violence is the catalyst for political change, for example, by forcing a repressive military response that in turn will alienate the masses and move them to revolt. In contrast to the popular war, the insurgent cannot use the population for recruitment and logistics, but he will use the population as shelter. Here again, media coverage is crucial.
- *Isolated terrorism.* This strategy seeks to undermine society and government through assassinations, kidnappings, hijackings, sabotage, bombings, raids, and attacks on public facilities. This form of terrorism is considered a local or tactical challenge, which should be handled by the internal security forces, the police, and the intelligence communities.

Religious anti-systemic terrorism is not dealt with in the British manual. Al-Qaeda is pursuing a form of revolutionary warfare as well. It carries out acts of isolated terrorism, albeit on a grand scale, and conducts military strategies to create and defend sanctuaries.

To be successful, the leader of an insurgency must be charismatic. Revolutionary leaders will try to exploit a just cause based on nationalistic, ethnic, and religious motives. These motives could generate support among the population. Osama bin Laden was an obvious example of a charismatic leader. As a terrorist "Chief Executive Officer," he used modern management techniques, issued orders, defined goals and, most importantly, provided the ideological motivation. Other, non-revolutionary leaders may promote private interests, such as the desire for power of control over territories for criminal practices. Whatever their objective, they have to motivate the people to fight for their cause.

The insurgents' tactics are well known. *Constructive activities* involve the formation of cadres for training, the creation and development of areas for subversive activities, the organization of alternative police and military units to take over the internal and external security tasks, and the creation of an administrative machinery to take over the bureaucracy. But insurgents will also seek extensive media coverage. First, they could make use of radio and TV stations and Internet sites to promote their cause. Osama bin Laden made extensive use of the media by sending videotapes to Al Jazeera, the Arabic version of CNN. Second, they could win the hearts of the population. In some cases, insurgents have become popular because they provided a rudimentary welfare system, including health care and education. In the Islamic world, fundamentalist groups develop a social and cultural infrastructure to build an Islamic civil society and fill a vacuum that their countries' governments have neglected. During the 1990s in Egypt, Jordan, the Palestinian territories, Afghanistan, and Pakistan, radical movements provided health care, education, and welfare for the poor. Radical movements such as Hamas and al-Qaeda use nongovernmental organizations extensively for these purposes. After the 1992 earthquake in Cairo, these organizations were on the streets within hours, whereas the Egyptian government's relief efforts lagged behind. Bin Laden was popular because of his "good works" in the Islamic world, especially in Pakistan and Afghanistan. Koranic study centers have become the single most important source for recruiting new members for the radical movements. These types of campaigns have successfully undermined the legitimacy of governments, and gained the support of the local civilian population.

Destructive activities are usually aimed at undermining the political elite's authority and power base, including the internal security forces, police, and armed forces. By creating an atmosphere of insecurity, the population loses faith in the authorities. Intimidation, sabotage, terror, information warfare, and guerrilla warfare are the most likely tactics. Insurgents will try to balance their political aims and the means of achieving them. If the means and ends mismatch, insurgents may lose popular support.

As an insurgency is principally a political struggle, a military solution alone will usually not suffice. Political, economic, social, and military measures should be complementary and mutually reinforcing. Civil authorities, internal security forces and the police and other law enforcement authorities, intelligence services, and the military should work closely together. In some cases the deployment of troops is needed to buy time for a political solution; in other cases there is no other choice but to impose a military solution.

As a consequence, since an insurgency is primarily a political struggle, a military victory may not be necessary. Success may be defined as "not losing" or making the situation manageable. In all cases the coercer should be clear with regard to the legitimacy of the operation. The coercer should also choose sides and secure a firm base essential to the survival and functioning of the government and state it is supporting.

Planning an operation

The planning of a counterinsurgency operation requires first an analysis of the type of conflict, its implications, and the method to stop, neutralize, or reverse actions of the opponent. To achieve the desired end state, clear political objectives must be defined. During the campaign, political authorities will keep overall responsibility, while delegating implementation to military authorities. The sole way to rein in rebels, terrorists, and gangs is to separate them from their bases, either physically or politically. This is done by denying them information, logistics, recruits, safe havens, and popular support through physical separation and hearts and minds campaigns aimed at winning the support of the local populace. The latter is important, because the strategic center of gravity is the support of the mass of the population. Consequently, in contrast to conventional warfare, unconventional warfare seeks to avoid attacking the center of gravity. Military victories will therefore never be spectacular. Rather, victory will be achieved by a sequence of small successes.

A typical counterinsurgency campaign consists of the following elements:

- protection of the local, neutral, and sympathetic parts of the population against irregular troops;
- elimination of the support system of the insurgent, including the prevention of external support from other organizations and countries. The aim is cut off the insurgents from food supplies, recruits, and information, and to separate them from the population;
- hearts and minds activities to gain the support of the population;
- physical and psychological isolation of the armed resistance;
- elimination of the resistance's intelligence network;
- force protection and protection of NGOs to increase freedom of action;
- well-coordinated command structure and a continuous flow of intelligence;
- direct action against the insurgents, to eliminate them physically, if necessary with selective and proportionate use of force.

There are two techniques for direct action to physically control an area:

Attrition or brute force

Straightforward attrition is based on absolute repression and destruction of the adversary. Firepower is the key to success. Mobility is primarily used to maneuver firepower into favorable positions. Relentless bombings and attacks with heavy weapons systems such as tanks and artillery and the systematic destruction of buildings by bulldozing or demolition are common techniques. In urban warfare this comes close to the medieval siege of walled cities. The advantage is that it can be done with limited friendly losses; the disadvantage is the level of destruction. Saddam Hussein used chemical weapons against the Kurds; in 2002, Israeli forces destroyed parts of Jenin in an attempt to stop suicide attacks on Israel's soil; in 2004, the Americans destroyed Fallujah in an attempt to crush the Iraqi insurgency. Unsurprisingly, in these cases, leaders were accused of barbarism and war crimes. For that reason, attrition is an inappropriate strategy for liberal democracies. Moreover, the record of success for a strategy based on attrition is generally poor. Nevertheless, armies trained and organized for conventional warfare may be tempted to use attrition if they are unable to gain victory. But insurgents will be delighted when the adversary embarks on an attrition strategy. The indiscriminate use of firepower will barely affect them, while causing widespread suffering among the civilian population. As a consequence, the population will most likely turn against the intervener and be in favor of the rebel's cause. Sometimes an attrition strategy works. For instance, during the Malayan Campaign (1948-1960) British forces used their superior firepower to drive Chin Peng's communists into remote parts of the country, where they were hunted down.

Maneuver

A counterinsurgency campaign is maneuver warfare in its most basic form. Direct action to gain control over an area involves cutting off logistics (isolation), cordon operations, and search-and-destroy operations. A well-tried approach in combating insurgents is the "inside out" method of expanding secured areas. The aim is to consolidate areas. First, a bridgehead inside the area is established. Second, friendly and local loyal forces will secure the surrounding area to release regular mobile troops to secure the next area. Securing adjacent areas can be done with specialized troops, such as air mobile and air maneuverable troops and Special Operations Forces.

Combating insurgents usually requires deploying small patrols into the terrain that the insurgent sees as its own. Surprise, tempo, and simultaneity are used to overwhelm the adversary, bringing about a collapse of will and ultimately helping to create conditions for a political solution. Nevertheless, force should be applied in a selective and controlled manner. Limiting collateral damage is extremely important in order to spare the lives of non-combatants. Typical operations are *search and destroy*, and *cordon and search*. Both operations are difficult to execute. First, the search part is usually a lengthy affair. Second, cordon operations are difficult because closing a cordon quickly and effectively is nearly impossible. Maneuver warfare theory assumes that shattering the adversary's moral and physical cohesion is more effective rather than achieving his destruction. Consequently, the strategy should focus on people and ideas, instead of on a military victory. Importantly, the British counterinsurgency manual argues that some elements of conventional war fighting wisdom may become irrelevant and that these operations will be governed by tight political control. Usually, minimal use of force works best, because intense media coverage could undermine the effectiveness of the operations in the case of excessive force. Media coverage could also undermine support for the operation if there is a widespread feeling that international law is not being obeyed.

Operations in urban areas pose the greatest challenge for modern armed forces. First, urban warfare can be extraordinarily destructive, especially if a strategy of attrition is applied. During the Second World War battle for Stalingrad, divisions lost 50% of their strength in less than two weeks. In October 1993, the Americans were unable to contain Aideed forces in Mogadishu. Second, throughout the world, but particularly in Europe, urban and industrial areas continue to grow in number and size. More than half the population of the world today lives in cities; 70% will be living in urban areas in 25 years' time. The biggest cities already have populations in excess of 20 million. Consequently, most political and social unrest is likely to occur in urban areas. Moreover, adversaries will position their forces in cities to fight on the most advantageous ground possible. As Ralph Peters put it: "The future of warfare lies in the streets, high-rise buildings, industrial parks, and the sprawl of houses, shacks, and shelters that form the broken cities of the world."[9]

Urban warfare has an important vertical dimension. Modern Western armed forces are not well-equipped for warfare in cities, with their multi-story buildings and sewers. Technological advantage is typically associated with

9 R. Peters, *Fighting for the Future: Will America Triumph* (Mechanicsburg, PA: Stackpole Books, 1999), p. 43.

long-range firepower, mass and mobility, not with the vertical dimension of urban warfare. The greater the cover and the shorter the ranges, the less utility is gained from long-range weapons systems. Tanks have limitations because their armaments cannot be elevated sufficiently to engage targets on upper floors of high buildings or to engage targets at ground level at close range. Moreover, tanks are vulnerable to attacks from above. Consequently, in cities, tanks need protection from dismounted infantry. In turn, tanks provide heavy direct fire against enemy buildings and strong points in support of the infantry. Tanks will also be used to breach walls and fortifications. The close nature of the fighting also limits the use of artillery. Artillery can be used against enemy artillery and mortars or it can destroy enemy reserves. Helicopters will be used in support of ground forces. First, their sensors will be useful for reconnaissance tasks. Second, helicopters can be used for assault tasks.

Fighting in cities requires small groups of dismounted soldiers engaging in hand-to-hand combat. The British army conducts military operations utilizing the concept of "combined arms groupings." The groupings are elements of combat and combat support arms. They are organized on all levels to undertake specific tasks. Moreover, the grouping will depend on the mission and the threat, while the environment will dictate the type of forces. Protection of individual soldiers is extremely important. Patrols in sewers could result in fatal illness. They need simple items such as eye protection because of the splintering effects of fire fights.

The rifle and the machine gun are the most common weapons in urban warfare. Grenade launchers can be used to enter buildings. Anti-tank weapons are effective against armor when fired from upper stories, the flanks, or the rear. Armored fighting vehicles can be used in support of dismounted forces inside a city. Use of these vehicles allows them to maximize their protection, mobility, range of the weapons systems, and firepower. Armored vehicles can also be used to breach walls, destroy enemy positions, resupply friendly forces, and evacuate casualties.

Close air support with fixed-wing aircraft in an urban environment is challenging. Targets are difficult to locate and identify, and enemy and friendly forces will be intermingled. Furthermore, aircraft are vulnerable to shoulder-fired surface-to-air missiles and rocket-propelled grenades. Aircraft, both fixed-wing and rotary wing, will be useful for surveillance and reconnaissance, communication and liaison tasks, the insertion of special forces and troop lift, psychological operations (dropping leaflets, airborne radio, and TV stations), close air support, and interdiction.

Naval support may be needed for coastal patrols to arrest, sink, or deter insurgent supplies or raiding vessels. Minesweepers may be necessary for coastal patrols. Finally, depending on the theater of operations, amphibious forces could be used.

In short, manned arms fight conventional warfare; armed men wage unconventional warfare. Indeed, in contrast to conventional warfare, unconventional warfare is extremely manpower-intensive.

Communications differ too. Fighting a counterinsurgency requires individual soldiers to communicate with their superiors. This is because tactical actions could have a strategic impact. Due to the large number of non-combatants, the wrong people might be shot. Consequently, in some cases, superiors should decide whether individuals must be neutralized.

In fact, warfare in cities requires combat skills more than doctrine, because military operations in built-up areas and mountains tend to develop into a series of low-level tactical engagements. This kind of maneuver warfare will turn into a battle of attrition if the momentum is lost. If such a situation develops, the operation is likely to be very costly in terms of casualties and logistics.

The high population density poses extreme challenges for commanders. Fighting in urban environments places many restrictions on the operational commanders, as they are responsible for protecting civilians and their property. Indeed, one of the most notable differences with open terrain is the great number of non-combatants. Thus, limiting collateral damage is crucial. But at the same time, limiting collateral damage is extremely difficult, because urban warfare usually requires cordon operations, followed by systematic house-to-house search-and-destroy operations. One way of dealing with the problem of collateral damage is the use of non-lethal weapons (NLW). However, effective NLWs are not yet available. Also, the use of precision weaponry can reduce collateral damage.

Small-scale urban operations could involve traditional *policing operations* to prevent the outbreak of violence. Raids can have different goals, for example, evacuating nationals, rescuing hostages, or seizing key facilities such as airfields. The key to success is surprise and overwhelming force. The insertion and extraction of forces is the hardest part in these operations. Good intelligence is the key to success.

Instead of conducting a direct assault on a city, the attacker could first establish a loose cordon around the city and control the surrounding countryside. This was the first phase of the siege of Baghdad in 2003. The Americans blocked all avenues, controlled the airfields in and around the capital, controlled sources of power, water, and food, and carried out air strikes against leadership targets in the city. This technique was also applied after the withdrawal from Fallujah, Iraq, in March 2004. The aim was to regroup and wait for more favorable circumstances.

But to take the city, units have to go in. According to the US Army Field Manual on Urban Operations, there are three different tactical concepts for larger-scale urban operations.

1 *Urban penetration.* This tactic is designed to quickly maneuver to the objective area and establish control in a dispersed and noncontiguous area. Penetration requires sufficient mobility to move quickly to the area. Subsequently, the penetrating force should conduct an offensive operation to seize the objective, and isolate and protect it from the adversary and non-combatants. This method was used by the Americans during the second phase of the siege of Baghdad in April 2003.
2 *Urban thrust.* This tactic is focused on achieving an assault against the adversary on a narrow axis of attack. As this attack is occurring, the axis of advance is defended in order to hold the flank against potential enemy attacks. The urban thrust can be conducted on multiple axes simultaneously. In addition, the commander will conduct periodic shifts in the axis of the attack in order to confuse the adversary. The overall intent of the tactic is to avoid linear assault, while confusing the adversary, forcing his flanks, isolating his forces, and deceiving him as to the real objective for the assaulting force.
3 *Urban swamp.* This is similar to the tactic used by police forces responding to an emergency, that requires backup. The concept requires numerous small teams operating in a dispersed, non-contiguous fashion. As units patrol the area, they have to be prepared to quickly reinforce neighboring teams. The key to this tactic is speed and flexibility. This was the technique used by US forces after the siege of Baghdad. It was also the technique they used in Fallujah before withdrawing from the city.

Of crucial importance is the hearts and minds campaign, which could include aid to win the support of the population, and psychological operations and information operations. After all, the objective is to separate fighters from their base. This effort using several approaches, including humanitarian aid and propaganda, must be made along with the diplomatic measures and military operations. From 1985 until 2000, Israel carried out a counterinsurgency campaign in Southern Lebanon, while at the same time it provided aid to the Lebanese population, including projects to rebuild the infrastructure and programs to provide health care. In Afghanistan, during Operation Enduring Freedom, food was used for the first time as a weapon. C-17 air lifters dropped tens of thousands of packets of food and medical supplies in Afghanistan in

2001. Each package contained the message that it was a gift from the people of the United States of America. In addition to food rations, US aircraft dropped leaflets and small transistor radios to enable Afghans to receive Washington's message. It was part of a dual strategy of destroying the government and a hearts and minds campaign to gain the support of the population.

Special forces and intelligence

Special Operations Forces (SOF) are indispensable for counterinsurgency operations. A severe restriction is that Western nations do not have these forces in sufficient numbers. A distinction should be made between Special Operations Forces, which are used for overt and covert action, and specialized forces, which carry out specialized overt operations.

The most famous of all Special Operations Forces, Great Britain's Special Air Service (SAS), conceived by Captain David Stirling, has existed since 1941. Most Special Operation Forces – such as Australia's Special Air Service Regiment; the Netherlands' Bijzondere Bijstands Eenheid (BBE); France's joint Commandement des Operation Special (COS) units; Germany's Grenzschutzgruppe (GSG) 9; Israel's Sayeret Matkall Unit 269; and the US Army 1st Special Forces Operational Detachment, Delta Force, and Naval Special Warfare Development Group – were established in the 1970s as a direct response to terrorist incidents. Special Operations Forces specialize in clandestinely rescuing hostages. The Special Operations Forces' military tasks focus on infiltration into enemy territory to carry out sabotage, as well as search-and-destroy and rescue missions, forward air control, and liaising with command local forces. Finally, they could prepare the ground for specialized forces. Western militaries have a limited number of Special Operations Forces. In addition, specialized forces that carry out overt actions are needed. Air maneuverable forces are key assets. They could be used for seizing airports, protecting key locations, conducting cordon operations, and consolidating areas. For example, on October 19, 2001, four MC-130 Combat Talon air transporters dropped more than 200 US Army Rangers at a remote desert airstrip near Kandahar, Afghanistan. The operation, code named Operation Rhino, was to seize the airstrip as a staging area for Special Operations Forces and marines. The operation was successful. The Rangers shot several Taliban fighters, collected documents, and prepared the ground for the Marines, who would arrive a month later.

Good intelligence is vital in any phase of counterinsurgency operation. Intelligence will allow commanders to conduct operations with precision and limited collateral damage. This is important for gaining the support of the local population and keeping the political and public support at home. Human Intelligence (HUMINT) is probably the most important method of intelligence-gathering. HUMINT requires the use of highly-trained, well-equipped agents, informants, surveillance, and reports from police and army patrols. HUMINT is the most controversial, but at the same time a very effective, form of intelligence. However, the status of the West's HUMINT is similar to Special Operations Forces. For data collection, the West relies primarily on satellite imagery, signals intelligence, and electronic intelligence. Satellite imagery guides both Special Operations Forces and HUMINT to targets. Although satellite imagery acquires important strategic information, Special Operations Forces and HUMINT are the best way to obtain tactical information on the ground, especially because terrorists groups make only limited use of cellular phones and satellite communications. After US cruise missiles attacked his training camps in August 1998, Bin Laden no longer used his satellite telephone, which made him easy to detect. Instead, he issued "mission orders," instructing his lieutenants orally, in writing, or on videotape that television stations broadcast widely. Consequently, there is no other choice but to infiltrate the networks of insurgents and terrorists. In the case of al-Qaeda this was an enormous task, because it had its bases and cells in 50 to 60 countries. Without HUMINT, Special Operations Forces, and specialized forces capabilities that can effectively address unexpected threats and unconventional warfare – the only option the West's opponents have – the US and its allies will find the campaign on terrorism almost impossible. In its most basic form, unconventional warfare uses one side's comparative advantage against its enemy's relative weakness. Successful unconventional warfare exploits vulnerabilities – which are easy to determine – by using weapons and tactics in ways that are unplanned or unexpected. As has been argued in chapter 5, the main observable weakness of the West is the desire to reduce collateral damage and limit body bags by emphasizing technological solutions, the need to maintain coalitions, and the need to adhere to the international rule of law. Moreover, Western societies are economically and socially vulnerable.

The Chechen wars

Case studies reveal the strengths and weaknesses of particular counterinsurgency operations. During the Chechnya Wars (1992-1996, and 1999-2009) the Russians responded to the insurgent's techniques of asymmetrical warfare and terrorist attacks with brute force and maneuver warfare. The lack of success caused widespread suffering of civilians and protests, both inside and outside Russia.

On December 10, 1994, Russian President Boris Yeltsin ordered the Russian armed forces to end the insurgency of Chechen rebels. Yeltsin's objective was clear: keep Chechnya as part of Russia. This objective should be achieved by removing the Chechen President Dzhokhar Dudayev and capturing Grozny. The fact that the Chechens never accepted Russian rule wholeheartedly and the desire to gain control over the oil and gas industry motivated Chechen separatism.

The Russians made the classic mistake of trying to combat irregular forces with conventional warfare doctrine, emphasizing the massing of forces and carpet bombings from the air. This was a classic brute force strategy of attrition. The Russians were organized in a hierarchical fashion. They maneuvered in a linear, sequential manner in order to seize control over territory, including the capital Grozny. The Chechens fought back with small mobile teams of light, well-equipped fighters. They fought in a non-linear fashion based on mission orders, enabling them to "swarm" advancing Russian columns from all directions. The organization of the Chechen forces depended on the clan structure. Chechen unit cohesion benefited greatly from the fact that fighters were almost always serving in combat with their kinsmen. A Chechen clan could supply up to 600 fighters. This group was broken down into units of 150, which were further divided into squads of about twenty and ensured that a clan would always have a team in action. Moreover, the groups commuted from their homes to the battlefield. As a consequence, they could exchange information so those fighters kept an overview.[10]

In the first battle for Grozny, the Russians took the city with a conventional massed armed force with infantry and close air support. In the opening month of the war, the Russians suffered severe losses: 225 armored vehicles, or more than 10% of all armored vehicles used during the campaign. The loss of armored vehicles was due to inappropriate tactics, underestimation of the rebels and a lack of preparation. The biggest mistake was that the Russians tried to enter the city with armored vehicles. Consequently, they were easy targets for Chechen anti-tank teams.

10 John Arquilla and Theodore Karasik, "Chechnya: A Glimpse of Future Conflict?" *Studies in Conflict & Terrorism*, 22, 1999, p. 210.

After this humiliating defeat, the Russians shifted to a military strategy of maneuver warfare. They brought in more infantry and began systematic block-by-block and house-to-house search-and-destroy operations. Armored vehicles were now used in close support of infantry, which was organized in small task forces. This tactic worked. In April 1995, the war moved to the rural and mountainous regions in the south and the east of Chechnya. Some fighting also occurred in and around the villages on the border of Ingushetia. In mountainous areas, the Russians applied the same tactics they had used during the war against the Nazis in the Caucasus and during the Afghan war of the 1980s. The Russians used small, mobile forces, but tactical mobility was the weak spot. For tactical mobility, helicopters were used, which were quite vulnerable to Chechen surface-to-air missiles. In addition, pick-up trucks and cars provided the Chechen with great mobility. This allowed them to maneuver quickly so that Russian forces became vulnerable to snipers, rocket-propelled grenades and hit-and-run operations as soon as they were on the ground. Consequently, the Russians were not able to gain control over the mountainous areas.

The rebels practiced the traditional tactics of insurgents. First, they used a swarming type of doctrine, for small, well-connected forces that were constantly moving. The radio was used for command and control purposes. Thus they were quite invulnerable to the Russians and innovative tactics helped to engage an adversary superior in numbers. Second, in the battle for Grozny, they used rocket-propelled grenades against armor in an innovative way by coordinating massed firings from rooftops and windows. Corrupt Russian traders supplied most of the weapons systems. Third, they used snipers, which were very hard to deal with. As these snipers pinned down Russian forces, they caused considerable delay. Fourth, Chechen rebels routinely dressed in Russian uniforms so that they could strike behind enemy lines. Fifth, Chechnya's leader Dudayev used video cameras and transmitted his own tapes to override Russian television programming. In addition, the rebels had their own websites. In trying to influence public opinion outside Chechnya, they organized mass protests of women, tried to get the support of non-governmental organizations, and spread misinformation, for example, about Russian use of weapons of mass destruction. Thus, the Russians lost the information war. Sixth, outside Chechnya, rebels carried out hijackings and assassinations. In January 1996, rebels hijacked a Russian Black Sea ferry, the *Eurasta,* taking 200 passengers hostage. In March 1996, four Chechens hijacked an aircraft with over 100 passengers on board. But the Chechens also made use of nuclear threats. Dudayev repeatedly threatened to launch a nuclear attack against Moscow. In a video message on November 8, 1995, Dudayev showed four containers, which he claimed were filled with Caesium-137. He suggested that four containers had already been placed in four cities throughout the Russian Federation. As a matter of fact, Chechen rebels left caesium-137 wrapped in conventional explosives in Izmailovo Park in Moscow in 1996.

The first Chechen war made clear that small bands of highly-motivated and well-organized fighters can gain a victory over a large force that is not well-prepared and applies wrong doctrines and tactics. Indeed, the Russians took Grozny, but only after considerable losses and the city's destruction. Moreover, they never took control of the mountainous areas of Chechnya, and after a short time the rebels were able to recapture the capital. In other words, the rebels were the overwhelming victors in their first war with Russia.

The second Chechen war started in August 1999 after an incursion of Chechen guerrillas in Dagestan. The Russians again opted for a strategy of attrition with air power, with the aim of destroying rebels who carried out an incursion in Dagestan. Insurgents responded with a series of asymmetrical attacks on apartment buildings and a mall in Moscow and Volgodonsk and the Dagestani town of Buynaksk. More than 300 people were killed. On September 22, Russian land forces were ready to retake Chechnya, but avoided making the same mistakes they made in the first battle for Grozny. Fear for heavy casualties made military commanders reluctant to enter the city with ground forces. Nevertheless, Prime Minister Putin decided to retake the capital. Russian forces moved with ease in the open plains of northern Chechnya, but avoided heavy fighting in the rugged terrain south of the River Terek and in the capital. To minimize the risk of friendly losses, the Russians used artillery, short-range ballistic missiles, and air power against Grozny. During the following months, Russian forces moved slowly forward and seized Gudermes, Chechnya's second largest city, on November 12, 1999, followed by a number of smaller towns and villages. After a siege that lasted until February 2000, Russian forces and pro-Russian Chechens seized the capital. Due to the heavy attacks, most citizens left the city. Consequently, Russian forces could take the capital relatively easily using search-and-destroy operations.

A strategy of attrition was also carried out against the insurgents in the mountains of southern Chechnya. Again the number of civilian casualties mounted. On February 9, 2000, a Russian missile killed 150 civilians in Shali. The attack was a response to insurgents entering the city. The mounting number of civilian casualties caused widespread international protests. The US Secretary of State Madeleine Albright described the events in the republic as "deplorable and ominous."[11] Following the almost complete destruction of Grozny, the United States Holocaust Memorial Museum placed Chechnya on its Genocide Watch List. However, from the Russian point of view, the new strategy was successful. In May Putin established direct rule on Chechnya. But in reality, the military situation appeared to have reached an impasse. Federal forces controlled the cities and towns, but even there they were not immune to attack. Insurgents controlled the rest of Chechnya and continued to inflict heavy casualties on Russian forces for several more years. After the siege of Grozny, large-scale military operations ended. But insurgents regrouped and started a protracted guerrilla, using hit and run tactics, Improvised Explosive Devices (IED), assassinations, and suicide attacks both in Chechnya and Russia. In Grozny, Russian forces retaliated with COIN operations and air strikes. The terrorist attacks, causing widespread fear in Russia, were more difficult to counter. About 200 Russians were killed during train, metro, and aircraft bombings between 2002 and 2004. In addition, hostage takings, the 2002 Moscow theater crisis, and the 2004 Beslan school siege resulted in the deaths of hundreds. Especially the southern wooded part of Chechnya became a place of continuous ambushes and a safe haven from which attacks could be launched against Russian troops and other pro-Russian elements. But by 2009, the rebels ran out of steam and in April 2009 the operation was officially declared ended.

Operation Defensive Shield

Another example of a failed attempt to deal with an insurgency is Operation Defensive Shield. On March 29, 2002, one day after a Palestinian suicide bomber had killed 29 people and wounded dozens in the Israeli coastal resort of Netanya, Israel's Prime Minister Ariel Sharon launched this operation in an attempt to end suicide bombings for good. There would be no more political negotiations. Sharon no longer accepted Yasser Arafat as the legitimate leader of the Palestinians. Instead, the Prime Minister decided that only a military strategy could end the insurgency. The political objectives of the operation, according to Sharon, were to sideline Arafat and to encourage a much more cooperative leadership; to crush Palestinian militant groups and reassert Israel's military primacy in the Palestinian

11 BBC News, "Civilian casualties mount in Chechnya", October 24, 1999, http://news.bbc.co.uk/2/hi/europe/484244.stm.

territories. Thus he tried to turn the intifada into a subtext of the war on terrorism, which was being fought by the US after the September 11 attacks.

As dawn broke, Israel set in motion the largest military operation in two decades. The objective was to reenter major cities, villages, and refugee camps on the West Bank and the Gaza Strip. To man the operation, some 20,000 reservists were called to duty. Operation Defensive Shield started with an incursion into Ramallah, during which the Israeli Defense Forces seized most of the buildings on Arafat's compound. Operations followed in Tulkarm, Qalqilya, Bethlehem, Jenin, and Nablus. By April 3, six of the largest cities on the West Bank were occupied. On April 21, the end of the operation was announced, as the withdrawal from both Nablus and Ramallah was completed.

The strategy was based on a classic cordon operation, followed by search-and-destroy operations in cities and refugee camps. The UN reported: "In each incursion, Israeli troops, tanks, and armored personnel carriers entered the cities and Israeli Defense Forces imposed curfews on their civilian populations. In each case, the incursions were accompanied by the entry of Israeli Defense Forces into nearby villages and refugee camps. The Israeli Defense Forces declared the cities they had entered "special closed military areas," imposing restrictions on, and at times completely barring, the movement of international personnel, including at times humanitarian and medical personnel as well as human rights monitors. In each of these incursions, the Israeli Defense Forces arrested Palestinians whom they believed were involved in armed actions against Israel, including suicide bombings and other terrorist attacks against Israeli civilians.[12] Some 8,500 Palestinians were arrested, almost 500 were killed and some 1,500 were wounded. Operation Defensive Shield affected almost one million people.

What started as a classic form of maneuver warfare, ended up in brute force attrition. Large parts of the centers of Nablus and Jenin were flattened in an attempt to deprive insurgents of their homes and to deter support to those insurgents. The Israeli Defense Forces used tanks, attack helicopters, and bulldozers to carry out this strategy, which was justified as being necessary to destroy the infrastructure of militant groups that had carried out attacks on Israel.

Although Nablus was hit harder, the Jenin case led to international protest. On April 3, 2002, the Israeli Defense Forces entered the city and destroyed some 150 houses and damaged many more. Initially, the Israeli Defense Forces

12 United Nations, Report of the Secretary-General prepared pursuant to General Assembly resolution ES-10/10.

carried out house-to-house searches and destroyed the homes of militants. Following an ambush on April 9 that killed 13 soldiers, Israel decided to destroy parts of the Jenin refugee camp with bulldozers, tanks, and missiles.

The UN estimated the costs of the destruction of property at approximately $27 million. The destruction of the old inner cities of Jenin and Nablus demonstrated again that counterinsurgency operations could not only be very deadly and destructive, but could also come close to war crimes. The results were mixed. First, it only temporarily stopped the suicide bombers. When Sharon was on his way to President George Bush with a new peace proposal, on May 8, the next suicide bombing took place. As a consequence, Sharon aborted his visit to Bush and called for an emergency meeting of his cabinet to discuss a response. Second, Arafat's popularity grew. This reached a new standing among Palestinians and throughout the Arab world. In addition, Arafat could not be prevented from receiving visits from US Secretary of State Colin Powell and Javier Solana, the EU high representative for the Common Foreign and Security Policy (CFSP). It was clear that the outside world still considered Arafat as a legitimate leader.

Operation Cast Lead

Operation Cast Lead was a new episode in the ongoing struggle between Israel and the Palestinian territories. The operation took place during the winter of 2008-2009. On November 4, 2008, Israel launched a search-and-destroy operation with infantry, tanks, and bulldozers into a residential area of Dayr al-Balah in central Gaza. Hamas responded by intensifying its rocket and mortar attacks against civilian targets. When negotiations on a cease-fire led nowhere, Israel decided to carry out a large-scale operation. Israel's objective was to stop Hamas from firing rockets into Israel and weapons smuggling into the Gaza Strip.

In an attempt to prepare the battlefield, Israel launched Operation Cast Lead on December 27, 2008. The operation started with attrition, that is, airstrikes by F-16 fighter jets and AH-64 Apache attack helicopters against the homes of Hamas leaders, weapons storage sites, command and control centers, rocket launchers, headquarters and logistics. The Navy was involved with surface-to-surface missiles. During the first wave of attacks, approximately 230 Palestinians were killed and more than 700 were injured. The Israeli attack was the deadliest single-day death toll of this conflict, which had started 60 years before. Because many children and women died, this day is remembered by Palestinians in Gaza as the Massacre of Black

Saturday. On January 5, Israel started the maneuver phase with ground forces. The Israeli Defense Forces (IDF) moved in the densely populated urban centers of Gaza. Israeli politicians had decided to strike deep into the population centers of Gaza amid concerns of higher casualties on both sides. What followed were two weeks of urban warfare. The conflict ended on January 18 when Israel first declared a unilateral cease-fire, followed by Hamas. The conflict resulted in between 1,166 and 1,417 Palestinian and 13 Israeli deaths. As a result, Israel was accused of excessive violence, war crimes and crimes against humanity.

On April 3, 2009, the UN appointed Richard Goldstone to chair a United Nations Fact Finding Mission on the Gaza Conflict, which would: "investigate all violations of international human rights law and international humanitarian law that might have been committed at any time in the context of the military operations that were conducted in Gaza during the period from 27 December 2008 and 18 January 2009, whether before, during or after."[13] The commission accused both the Israel Defense Forces and Hamas of war crimes and possible crimes against humanity. The commission accused Israel for intimidating the population in Gaza. The commission wrote that the military assault on Gaza was designed to "humiliate and terrorize a civilian population, radically diminish its local economic capacity both to work and to provide for itself, and to force upon it an ever increasing sense of dependency and vulnerability." The "wanton" destruction of food production, water and sewerage facilities was considered a war crime. Thus Israel breached the Fourth Geneva Convention. The commission also accused Israel of using Palestinians as "human shields" and torturing detainees. However, in 2011 Goldstone reconsidered his report's central conclusion, namely that Israel specifically intended to kill innocent Palestinian civilians. The rehabilitation of Israel was also evidenced by *Wiki Leaks*, which revealed that Israel took greater care to avoid civilian casualties than any other armed forces fighting comparable wars.

The report wrote that the Palestinians committed war crimes and crimes against humanity as well, by deliberately launching rockets and firing mortars into Israel against civilian targets. Later, a leader of Hamas acknowledged that most of the Palestinians killed during Operation Cast Lead were Hamas fighters. The number of killed civilians was 500-600, while the number of combatants killed now appears to be approximately 700.

13 The Goldstone Report: http://www2.ohchr.org/english/bodies/hrcouncil/docs/12session/A-HRC-12-48.pdf.

Nevertheless, Operation Cast Lead was a good example of the atrocities of urban warfare. During air strikes, cordon-and-search and search-and-destroy operations in an urban environment the killing of civilians cannot be avoided. Except for unwanted collateral damage caused by the coercer, militias will try to provoke collateral damage. First, the distinction between militia members and innocent civilians is hard to make. Second, insurgents deliberately use the population as shelter and for the purpose of logistical support and intelligence gathering. Finally, they will establish their command posts and weapons storage sites in or near facilities such as hospitals and schools. This will deter the adversary from attacking them and when they do attack, the world will be appalled by the levels of collateral damage.

Afghanistan: Operation Enduring Freedom

Operation Enduring Freedom started on October 7, 2001.[14] The objectives were clear: remove the Taliban from power so that Afghanistan could no longer host al-Qaeda; destroy al-Qaeda elements in Afghanistan; and capture Taliban leader Mullah Mohammed Omar and al-Qaeda leader Osama bin Laden. The Americans carefully studied the Russian failures in Afghanistan and Chechnya, and Israeli mistakes. They concluded that innovative concepts and the use of advanced technology could solve the problem of unconventional warfare. Within two months, a US-facilitated operation removed the Taliban from power, all the major cities had fallen to opposition forces, and al-Qaeda had been forced to leave its training camps. After the first phase of the war, coalition forces had to fight pockets of Taliban and al-Qaeda resistance. Nevertheless, the victory had little precedent. The US supported warlords of the Northern Alliance to fight a proxy war, with US Special Operations Forces, such as the CIA Special Operations Group and the Army Special Forces Detachments, and air power as force multipliers. The arrival of Special Operations Forces in Afghanistan changed the situation rapidly. But the success of the Special Operations Forces was unexpected. British and American special forces for example worked jointly to take Herat in November 2001. It was expected that larger specialized infantry forces, such as the US Army rangers, had to conduct

14 D. Chipman, "Air Power and the Battle for Mazar-e-Sharif", *Air Power History*, Spring 2003, pp. 35-54; A.H. Cordesman, *The Lessons of Afghanistan: War Fighting, Intelligence, Force Transformation, Counterproliferation, and Arms Control* (Washington, D.C., CSIS, June 18, 2002); A. Davis, "How the Afghan War was Won", *Jane's Intelligence Review*, February 2002, pp. 6-13.

a series of heavy operations. Within three weeks, however, the A-teams, as the Special Operations Forces call the units of a dozen selected troops, transformed the Northern Alliance into a capable fighting force.

As it was almost impossible to use bases near landlocked Afghanistan, the US had to rely on long-range bombers, sometimes operating from the US, and carriers in the seas in the south. Special Operations Forces, operating with the United Front, gathered intelligence and provided forward air support to guide precision-guided munitions (PGM) to targets. They called in air power for real-time attacks on Taliban and al-Qaeda fighters. This technical capability was extremely useful. Close air support was not only conducted by helicopters and ground-attack fighters, but by heavy bombers as well. From the start of the war, the US extensively used B-52, B-1, and B-2 strategic bombers to destroy the Taliban's reserves, air defenses, air force, and command and control systems. These bombers were also used during the tactical air campaign for the destruction of fielded forces.

The air campaign began on October 7 with the launch of 50 cruise missiles from British and American ships. The strikes were aimed at Taliban headquarters, airfields, air defenses, and other key targets. On October 9, Secretary of Defense Donald Rumsfeld claimed that US air forces had achieved air superiority. This came as no surprise, because the Taliban's air defenses were extremely weak. By week three, the air forces focused on attacking fielded forces and tanks in support of the ground war.

The war on the ground was fought by Afghan United Front forces, which had survived between 1996 and 2001. These forces were not just a band of guerrilla forces, but a relatively well-organized, conventional fighting force, capable of tying down opposing forces. United Front commander Mohamed Massoud controlled the northeastern part of the country with some 12,000 troops backed by artillery and mortars, 55 tanks and some helicopters bought from Russia in 2001. Massoud also conducted guerrilla warfare behind enemy lines in north and central Afghanistan. Crucial for the victory was also the decision to link up with the forces of other warlords, such as the Uzbek Abdul Rashid Dostam and the Tajik Ustaz Atta Mohammed.

On October 20, some 100 US Army Rangers carried out the first commando raid north of Kandahar, the Taliban's political and religious center, and the next day, the US bombed the forward edge of the battle area north of Kabul for the first time. Special Operations Forces were used for forward air control near the airport, north of Kabul. The attacks, however, remained limited. Consequently, the United Front commanders could do little. The objective of the US was to find a political solution for the post-wartime situation first, in order to avoid a new struggle for power after the overthrow of the Taliban and al-Qaeda. For that reason, the United Front had agreed not to attack Kabul until an interim government had been set up. On October 25, the US and the UN reached an agreement whereby air strikes against the Taliban frontline positions would be forestalled until an agreement had been reached for a transitional authority in Kabul. The diplomatic process, however, had not been very successful so far. As a consequence, there was a clear danger that the tempo of the operation would slow down and the initiative lost. Very soon, United Front warlords made clear that they had no desire to wait. Therefore, between October 17 and 20 they decided to carry out an offensive against Mazar. This offensive had to be aborted due to a successful counterattack by the Taliban.

Despite the lack of diplomatic progress, the Americans stepped up the tempo on October, 30. In the first week of November, the US carried out its most intensive air campaign on Taliban and al-Qaeda defenses south of Mazar-e-Sharif. Here, the US carried out carpet bombings on forward deployed forces.

At the same time, the US and Russia supplied United Front troops. On October 24, Russia reportedly was sending over 100 armored vehicles to the United Front. This paved the way for a second offensive against Mazar, starting on November 4. On November 9, the city fell. According to one observer, three key elements contributed to the victory: the intensity and accuracy of the relentless bombings on Taliban and al-Qaeda positions; the high level of coordination between the attacking forces achieved by the US; and the attacks on the main defensive positions of the Taliban in the outlying districts of Zaare, Ak Kupruk, Keshendeh, and Sholgarah. Once they had fallen, there was no second defensive line.

The fall of the city resulted in a domino-like collapse of Taliban forces, first across the north, then across Afghanistan as a whole. On November 12, Kabul fell; by mid-November, the United Front controlled half of Afghanistan. On December 2, Afghan groups meeting in Bonn reached an agreement on a post-Taliban government to rule the country for six months. Five days later, on December 7, the Taliban abandoned its political and religious center Kandahar, which marked the end of the first phase of the war. After two months, the objective of removing the Taliban from power was achieved.

After the regime change phase, Operation Enduring Freedom focused on the two remaining objectives mentioned above, that is, destroy al-Qaeda elements in Afghanistan and capture the leadership of the Taliban and al-Qaeda. After being removed from power, the Taliban and al-Qaeda, including its leadership, moved into the mountains from where they continued to fight US and coalition forces. In the meantime, US Navy ships had begun stop-

and-search operations in the Arabian Sea on all vessels leaving Pakistan, as part of the search to find elements of al-Qaeda seeking to leave the region.

The most challenging part of the new campaign was the battle of Tora Bora, the al-Qaeda tunnel and cave complexes in eastern Afghanistan. American Special Operations Forces, backed by Delta Force, UK Special Forces entered the area, whilst the US Air Force dropped extraordinarily heavy bombs, including the 15,000 pound BLU-82 slurry bombs ("Daisy Cutters") and fuel air explosives on the cave complexes. In addition, new experimental thermobaric bombs were rushed into production. The difficulty of destroying hardened underground targets also led to a renewed interest in the use of earth-penetrating nuclear weapons to defeat hard and deeply buried targets. A Pentagon report argued that the United States had insufficient means to deal with these targets. Only one earth-penetrating nuclear weapon existed in the US inventory, the B61 Mod II gravity bomb, "but it cannot survive penetration into the many types of terrain in which hardened underground facilities are located." For those reasons, the report urged the development of new nuclear weapons "with a much lower yield than would be required with a surface burst weapon."[15]

Without Special Operations Forces, the first phase of Operation Enduring Freedom could not have been successful. The combination of Special Operations Forces, precision guided ammunition and real-time targeting was an extremely effective force multiplier. The small, highly-trained units were able to accomplish large, strategic missions by exploiting the adversary's weaknesses. Attacks on command and control facilities were very successful. Quite early, commanders lost control over their already ethnically fragmented forces.

Nevertheless, the operation carried considerable risks. First, the operation itself was risky for the Special Operations Forces involved. Second, there was a clear danger that the wrong people might be attacked, or that Special Operations Forces were being misled by faulty intelligence. Attacking the wrong people could further inflame hostility to the Americans, thus undermining the support needed for the operations. The wholesale integration of air and groups operations would have an impact on future doctrine. New methods and protocols allowed air power to respond very quickly to intelligence and to attack all targets more effectively.

Soon after being removed from power the Taliban regrouped and regained strength. Consequently, coalition forces had no other choice but

15 Department of Defense, *Nuclear Posture Review,* submitted to Congress on December 31, 2001, p. 4.

to fight the remaining Taliban and al-Qaeda forces. To eliminate pockets of resistance, US, British and Canadian Special Operations Forces from Operation Enduring Freedom conducted traditional counterinsurgency campaigns in southeastern Afghanistan with search-and-destroy operations, which were far less reliant on air power. Their mission was to hunt for relatively small numbers of al-Qaeda and Taliban who had dispersed to avoid detection. The goal was to apply continuous pressure, so that the fighters could never find any breathing space. A serious problem, however, was that a foe was lacking. For example, during the UK-led secret Operation Snipe in May 2002, Special Operations Forces discovered caves, tunnels, and training camps, but the enemy had already disappeared. In March 2002, the Americans launched Operation Anaconda in the Shahikot Valley in eastern Afghanistan. It was the first battle to involve regular Specialized Forces rather than Special Operations Forces. Two thousand troops of the 101st Airborne Division and the 10th Mountainous Division were given the task of fighting at high altitudes (more than 3,000 meters) against an unknown enemy. The original plan was supposed to be Afghan-led and US-supported, but it ended up becoming US-led and Afghan-supported. The battle of Shahikot became a classic intelligence failure. The American forces commanded by Major-General Franklin L. Hagenbeck thought they would have to fight approximately 150 to 200 al-Qaeda fighters. After several days, the estimate had risen 600 to 700. Most probably, an influx of additional fighters from neighboring Pakistan caused this. In reality the number was higher, given the fact that after a 17-day battle some 500-800 militia members were killed. Al-Qaeda used mortars and rocket-propelled grenades. With mortars they could shoot over hills and ridges. At the start of the week, there were already eight friendly troops dead and more than 40 wounded, the majority of these killed in an ambush while getting out of a helicopter. The battlefield situation turned around when the US air force conducted a series of strikes with fighter jets, bombers, and attack helicopters. In conclusion, the battle once again emphasized the importance of intelligence, because it was believed that the ridge on which the helicopter had landed was uninhabited. Moreover, the number of enemy fighters had been underestimated. Also, the regular US forces were not capable of dealing with the fighters, who knew the terrain and used their weapons systems in a tactically clever way.

In the spring and summer of 2002, the Taliban and other insurgents began to conduct offensive operations against foreign troops and the Afghan government forces. By 2006, the Taliban controlled one-third of Afghanistan; in 2009, two-thirds. In 2006, the north was relatively safe; in 2009, only a few safe pockets in the north existed. As a matter of fact, due to the lack of troops, a conceptually unsound stabilization operation and an underestimation of the dynamics of the Afghan conflict the Taliban could strike back. A crucial mistake was that the Americans diverted their attention to Iraq in 2003 and left Afghanistan to NATO.

Afghanistan: the stabilization phase

In 2004, the NATO-led multinational International Security Assistance Force (ISAF) was established. The objective of the first phase was to stabilize the north. The following years, the west, south and east followed. In 2006, ISAF was 35,000 troops strong. Until 2009, both ISAF and Enduring Freedom made little progress.

The American RAND analyst Seth G. Jones concluded the US should focus "its resources on developing that help improve the capacity of the indigenous government and its security forces to wage counterinsurgency warfare."[16] Jones argued that the analysis of 90 insurgencies since 1945 correlates with the success (and failure) of counterinsurgency efforts:
- capability of indigenous security forces, especially policy;
- local governance; and
- external support for insurgents, including sanctuary.

In Afghanistan there was hardly an indigenous security force. Local governance was absent, and insurgents received external support from Pakistan, which they used as sanctuary as well.

The key insurgent movement which operated in the south and Pashtun areas in the west and the north was the Taliban faction of Mullah Omar. Omar's shura or council was based in Quetta, Pakistan. The Haqqani network, based in North Waziristan, Pakistan, working closely with the Quetta Shura, carried out attacks in Kabul. The third group was Hizb-e-Islami Gulbudding, which was also based in Pakistan. Finally, al-Qaeda provided support and funding from a safe area in Pakistan as well. The insurgency gained momentum when the insurgent groups adopted common strategic objectives: the overthrow of the Karzai Government, the establishment of a Salafist Islamic regime and the expulsion of foreign troops. The insurgents controlled populated areas and used the local population as a source of income and recruitment, logistic and shelter. Terror and intimidation were

16 Seth G. Jones, *Counterinsurgency in Afghanistan* (Rand Corporation: Santa Monica, 2008), pp. xi-xii.

used to "gain support" of the unwilling part of the local population. Initially, the insurgents fought conventionally with platoon or company seized forces, using small arms and rocket-propelled grenades. As the insurgents put too much emphasis on classical maneuver warfare and firepower, they were no match for Western forces. Gradually, the insurgents shifted to asymmetrical tactics, including hit-and-run attacks on isolated outposts and convoys of Afghan security forces. The new tactics also involved operations with groups of 50 men and then breaking up into groups of 5-10 men to evade close combat. The insurgents also turned to assassinations, suicide bombings, and the use of IEDs, which were very difficult to counter. In 2009, ISAF commander General Stanley McChrystal responded to the deteriorating security situation with the decision to improve the quality and quantity of the Afghan National Security Forces ANSF). He also introduced "embedded partnering" of coalition forces. The latter concept tried to combine coalition combat power with Afghan situational awareness. In 2009, the Americans also decided on a troop surge. A classified assessment of the war by General McChrystal revealed that a successful counterinsurgency strategy would require 500,000 troops and five years of fighting.[17] McChrystal only got 30,000 additional troops. ISAF reached a strength of 131,000 by December 2010. In those days its main effort was the Taliban's heartland in Helmand and Kandahar. But the troop surge also meant a six-fold increase in Special Forces operations. Despite the surge, the Taliban could not be defeated. The major success was the killing of Osama bin Laden on May 2, 2011, in a Special Operation conducted by the CIA and US Navy SEALs, in Pakistan.

On June 22, 2011, President Obama announced that 10,000 troops would be withdrawn from Afghanistan by the end of 2011, and that an additional 23,000 troops would leave the country by the summer of 2012. Other NATO countries announced reductions in troop numbers as well. By 2014, all foreign troops would have left Afghanistan. The termination of foreign involvement was explained by the fact that Afghan Security Forces – the Afghan National Policy and the Afghan National Army – would have gained sufficient strength to take over the responsibility for security in the country from NATO. In reality, despite a number of successes, including the removal of the Taliban from power, the destruction of al-Qaeda in Afghanistan, the death of Osama bin Laden, and tactical successes of the troop surge in Kandahar and Helmand, Afghanistan was not turned into a politically stable and secure country. Fears that Afghanistan would be as unstable as

17 Tom Andrews, "Classified McChrystal Report: 500,000 Troops Will Be Required Over Five Years in Afghanistan", *Huffington Post*, September 24, 2009.

Iraq and Libya after Western interventions were therefore justified. Experts recommended American policymakers leave Special Operations Forces to strike at terrorist leaders in Afghanistan and Pakistan.[18] Despite numerous tactical successes, the coalition failed in bringing security and stability because the political battle was lost.

Unified Protector (2011)

The uprisings in Tunisia and Egypt triggered uprisings in Bahrain, Yemen, and Libya. In Libya, the revolt started in the eastern part of the country. In March 2011, the Libyan leader Colonel Muammar Gadhafi stepped up his military campaign against the rebels in the east. On March 17, the Security Council, with China, Russia, Germany, Brazil, and India abstaining, passed Resolution 1973. The Resolution, proposed by France, Lebanon, and the United Kingdom, authorized nations "to protect civilians and civilian populated areas under threat of attack in the Libyan Arab Jamahiriya, including Benghazi, while excluding a foreign occupation force of any form on any part of Libyan territory." The justification of the intervention was that "the widespread and systematic attacks currently taking place in the Libyan Arab Jamahiriya against the civilian population may amount to crimes against humanity." The deteriorating situation in Benghazi triggered an intervention carried out by a coalition led by France and the United Kingdom. It was feared that without the intervention, Gadhafi would have regained control over the entire country in a matter of days. Resolution 1973 established a no-fly zone in Libyan airspace, authorized enforcement measures for the arms embargo established by Resolution 1970, and authorized the use of all means necessary short of foreign occupation to protect civilians against Gadhafi's troops, but ultimately aimed at the regime itself. The operation, codenamed Unified Protector by NATO and Odyssey Dawn by the US, became a matter of fierce dispute between coalition partners and those who abstained during the voting in the UN Security Council. Coalition forces quickly established command of the air over Libya's major cities, destroying large portions of the Libyan air defenses, and attacked pro-Gadhafi forces which posed a threat to civilians. The air operation was almost similar to operation Allied Force, the air operation against Serbian troops in Kosovo. In both Libya and Kosovo, there were no land forces

18 Carter Malkasian and J. Kael Weston, "War Downsized: How to Accomplish More With Less", *Foreign Affairs*, vol. 91, no. 2, May-June 2012, p. 111.

deployed, although there were rumors about special forces for intelligence gathering, forward air control, rescue missions, and fighting with the rebels.

According to the BBC, the first significant involvement of British forces inside Libya was a rescue mission mounted just a couple of weeks after the uprising against Gadhafi broke out: "On 3 March, Royal Air Force C130 aircraft were sent to a desert airstrip at Zilla in the south of the country to rescue expatriate oil workers (...) This airlift of 150 foreigners (...) went smoothly, despite one of the aircraft being hit by ground fire soon after taking off." The BBC also reported the rescue mission was supported by two dozen men from C Squadron of the Special Boat Service (SBS).[19]

The endplay, the battle for Tripoli – codename Operation Mermaid Dawn – started mid-August 2011. A reconstruction of the operation by the British newspaper *The Telegraph* revealed close connections between SOF and rebels. *The Telegraph* reported that "groups of young male volunteers left their homes in Tripoli and travelled to Benghazi to learn the art of insurgent warfare from an international force of covert units composed of the British SAS and MI6 agents and troops from the French, Qatar, and United Arab Emirates special forces."[20]

The British government also supplied body armor, advanced telecommunications equipment, and night-vision goggles. Weapons, ammunition, and communications equipment were smuggled into Tripoli. According to *The Telegraph* the plans for capturing the city were drawn up by rebel commanders, advised by SAS and MI6. By the middle of August, more than 200 volunteers were trained, were infiltrated back into the capital and became sleeper cells. The rebels had recruited Mohammed Eshkal, the head of Mohammed Megrayef Brigade – whose battalions were charged with protecting Tripoli's gates.

Operation Mermaid Dawn started with "shaping attacks" carried out by NATO. The Alliance attacked command and control centers. Five precision-guided Paveway IV bombs were dropped on a secret intelligence base while other aircraft, including predator drones, attacked troop concentrations, tanks and artillery batteries. Ashkal who wanted to take a personal revenge from Gadhafi, led the ground operation. He commanded hundreds of fighters who came to the city as NATO aircraft attacked Gadhafi's forces. His fighters were supported by foreign SOF who supplied them with real time

19 http://www.bbc.co.uk/news/magazine-16573516.

20 http://www.telegraph.co.uk/news/worldnews/africaandindianocean/libya/8727076/How-the-special-forces-helped-bring-Gaddafi-to-his-knees.html.

intelligence from surveillance aircraft and drones. The fighting continued through the week and the city was finally overrun.

The downfall of Gadhafi certainly was a success, but this was not a declared objective of the operation. One author argued that "NATO successfully achieved all of its stated military objectives. It maintained and arms embargo, facilitated humanitarian relief, created and sustained a no-fly zone, and helped protect Libya's civilian population."[21] American NATO Ambassador Ivo Daalder and NATO's Supreme Allied Commander James Stravridis also declared victory.[22] The operation cannot be considered a success if one takes into account that during the seven months of the operation, the political objectives of protecting the civilians failed. First, estimates about the number of casualties were wrong. Human Rights Watch has documented in February 2011 only 223 deaths across all of Libya at the time when NATO started to discuss the intervention.[23] Second, there were no reports about the indiscriminate killing of civilians. Alan J. Kuperman wrote in *International Security* that "Gadhafi's regime never threatened or perpetrated killings against civilians in areas that it recaptured from the rebels".[24] Finally, Kuperman assessed that "approximately 1,100 Libyans – including government forces, rebels, and noncombatats – likely would have died without NATO intervention".[25] *The Guardian* observed that "If the Libyan war was about saving lives, it was a catastrophic failure."[26] Exact figures are not available, but according to the opposition, the National Transition Council, some 25,000 Gadhafi troops, protesters and civilians were killed and 3,000 missed.[27] Early 2013 the Libyan government's high end estimate was 11,500 killed. After the war the country fell victim to lawlessness and corruption. The killing on September 11, 2012 of the US Ambassador to Libya, Christopher Stevens, made clear that the country was far from safe and stable. After the

21 Christopher S. Chivvis, "Libya and the future of Liberal interventions", *Survival*, December-January 2012-2013, p. 78.

22 Ivo Daalder and James Stravridis, "NATO's victory in Libya: the Right Way to Run an Intervention", *Foreign Affairs*, March-April 2012, pp. 2-7.

23 Human Rights Watch, "Libya: Governments Should Demand End to Unlawful Killings: Death Toll Up to at Least 233 Over Four Days", February 20, 2011. http://www.hrw.org/news/2011/02/20/libya-governments-should-demand-end-unlawful-killings.

24 Alan J. Kuperman, "A Model Humanitarian Intervention? Reassessing NATO's Libya Campaign", *International Security*, vol. 38, no.1 (Summer 2013), p. 112.

25 Kuperman, "A Model Humanitarian Intervention?" p. 118.

26 http://www.guardian.co.uk/commentisfree/2011/oct/26/libya-war-saving-lives-catastrophic-failure.

27 http://news.smh.com.au/breaking-news-world/residents-flee-gaddafi-hometown-20111003-1l49x.html.

end of formal hostilities radical Islamists took control over large parts of the countries. Extremists intimidated the local population by destroying ancient tombs. Other militia groups imposed protection schemes and took over lucrative cross-border trafficking of goods. In addition, the new government took too few steps towards ensuring reconciliation and justice.

New doctrines

The operations discussed in this chapter did not require large-scale, mechanized maneuver forces. If the adversary disperses, Western armies must disperse themselves. This will result in a swarming type of warfare with increased mobility of small units. Special Operations Forces and specialized forces, such as air-maneuverable forces, are key elements. Units are connected by advanced communications, including uplinks and downlinks with manned and unmanned aircraft, and satellites to enable quick response strikes against high-value targets.

This has led to two maxims. The first is that a tactical engagement fought for too high a price for too little return will itself determine the outcome of coercion. Somalia underscored this maxim. The second is that as the opponent disperses in order to avoid destruction by air power, he makes his force increasingly vulnerable to defeat by maneuver. A dispersed force cannot mass quickly, nor can it hold terrain from static positions. Thus, the intervener will be able to occupy the uncovered and unprotected terrain in its midst by air maneuverable forces. This was demonstrated during the Gulf War and Operation Allied Force.

Insurgents, terrorists, and criminal organizations already use network forms of organization attuned to the information age. They use the Internet, not only to promote their cause, but also for command and control purposes. Al-Qaeda is a typical network organization. It is not a single hub originally designed around its leader, but a network with multiple centers and peripheries. The spreading of these virtual organizations makes them resilient and hard to defeat.

The concept of networks is also beginning to take root in military thinking.[28] This comes with effects-based operations (EBO) as a manifestation of the RMA (see chapter 4) with network-centric warfare (NCW) as the

28 J. Arquilla, D. Ronfeldt (eds.), *Networks and Netwars: the Future of Terror, Crime and Militancy* (Santa Monica, CA: RAND, MMR-1382, ODS, 2001); D.S. Alberts, J.J. Garska, F.P. Stein, *Network Centric Warfare: Developing and Leveraging Information Superiority* (Washington DC: CCRP

critical enabler. Technological, doctrinal, and organizational innovations revolutionized the way wars were fought. Precision and stealth are the two technological developments that spearhead this development. Novel command arrangements, such as the appointment of only one air component commander overseeing the planning and execution of air strikes, greatly enhanced the efficacy of air power. The air campaign could now be conducted in a more coherent way. Advanced Information and Communication Technology made centralized command and control – based on information dominance – possible. The fusing of data streams originating from different units, services, and non-military organizations such as the CIA, and new surveillance capabilities and sensors, offered greater situational awareness. In the latter part of the 1990s, NCW was proposed as an overarching concept. NCW is defined as an information superiority-enabled concept of operations that generates increased combat power by networking sensors, decision makers, and shooters to achieve shared awareness, increased speed of command, higher tempo of operations, greater lethality, increased survivability, and a higher degree of self-synchronization. NCW translates information superiority into combat power. NCW derives its power from networking a geographically dispersed force. Information technology will be used to achieve decisive military advantage by networking forces, giving them unprecedented operational awareness, and enabling them to react better than was traditionally possible under fluid conditions. Thus, NCW allows the force to achieve an asymmetric information advantage. The idea is an attempt to achieve full spectrum dominance and thus elaborate ideas first envisioned in the US Joint Vision 2020 and Joint Publication 3.0.

The key question is whether these doctrinal innovations hold the promise that conventional and unconventional operations can be conducted simultaneously. NCW allows conventional armed forces to conduct nonlinear operations, that is, operations without clearly defined lines of operations. Thus, potentially NCW could indeed be the solution for the centuries-old problem that conventional forces are incapable of conducting unconventional operations against irregular forces. The nonlinear nature of NCW is usually associated with chaos and complexity theory, where events do not happen in an orderly and predictable fashion. The relatively small force may exploit that chaos. This is a radical departure from the tradition of "sequencing" military operations. Parallel warfare was the first manifestation of this, but most future engagements will take the form of a series of

Publication Series, 1999); E.J. Dahl, "Network Centric Warfare and the Death of Operational Art", *Defence Studies*, vol. 2, no. I (Spring 2002), pp. 1-24.

small-scale battles fought in parallel with small, extremely flexible, mobile, and versatile forces, supported by air power.

To understand NCW, one has to focus simultaneously on three domains of warfare and the interactions between them. In a report to Congress, the US Department of Defense summarized these domains as follows:

1 The *physical domain* is the domain of strike, protect, and maneuver. Combat power has traditionally been measured in this domain.
2 The *information domain* is where information is created, manipulated, and shared. It facilitates the communication of information among the war fighters. Sensors observe the real world and produce data.
3 The *cognitive domain* exists in the minds of the participants. It is the place where perceptions, awareness, understanding, beliefs, and values reside and where, as a result of sense-making, decisions are made. Battles are lost or won in this domain.

NCW focuses on linking together or networking all three domains to achieve synergistic effects. They require very advanced Command, Control, Communications, Computers, Intelligence, Surveillance, Target Acquisition, and Reconnaissance (C4ISTAR). Satellites, and manned and unmanned reconnaissance planes transfer data to shooters, such as aircraft or individual soldiers. The result should be unprecedented battlefield awareness that could even lift the fog of war. A future military network consists of battle space entities or nodes, such as shooters and platforms, and the links among them. Information is both an input to decisions and – in the form of decisions themselves – is passed over links from one node to another. Linking these nodes will greatly increase effectiveness because it enables getting more out of the battles' space entities.

Thus a fundamental shift took place, one from linear platform-centric warfare to nonlinear network-centric warfare, applicable across the mission spectrum. First, NCW could make traditional command and control processes outdated. Thus, former US Air Force Colonel John Boyd's famous "observation, orientation, decision, action"(OODA) loop will be replaced by a much more integrated and parallel command and control cycle, based on superior battle space awareness and knowledge. Second, NCW will affect the fundamentals of war. Mass will be challenged, because the attacker fights in a dispersed manner and any kind of mass will become a target. Simplicity, another fundamental, will lose its meaning because the nonlinearity of NCW is based on the principles of chaos and complexity. Centers of gravity, the focus of conventional warfare, will become less important because NCW is aimed at destroying the system itself. Consequently, the culminating point of victory, the fourth principle of war, is difficult to define. Third, as armed forces operate in a network, the traditional hierarchical structure of armies will be affected. This requires a different mind-set because, unlike traditional formations, it has less hierarchy and less emphasis on combined arms operations. Relatively small units (companies rather than brigades or divisions) will be core elements of that network. Consequently, junior commanders will take decisions having strategic implications. Fourth, the levels of war will be redefined. The strategic level will define rules of engagement and other preconditions, and have the overall supervision; the operational level has the overall operational responsibility for the conduct of all operations and the allocation of scarce assets within the theater of operation; at the tactical level, dispersed units will conduct different types of operations based on mission order for relatively autonomous junior commanders.

During the end of the 1990s, a debate about targeting also emerged. As demonstrated in chapter 3, successful coercion could require decapitation, incapacitation, punishment, or denial. One school of thought advocated massive and overwhelming force, whilst others pleaded in favor of gradually increasing intensification to provide room for political maneuver. As has been argued, this is the distinction between military coercion and coercive diplomacy. Eventually, these schools of thought were conceptually tied into an overarching concept called EBO. In 2001, this concept became part of the US joint targeting doctrine. EBO aims to produce distinctive and desired effects through the application of appropriate movement, supply, attack, defense, and maneuvers. EBO focuses on functional systemic and psychological effects well beyond immediate physical results and could take nonmilitary means to coerce an opponent into account as well. As has been seen, a combination of military and economic pressure and political isolation is most likely to produce the desired results. This requires detailed knowledge of the opponent as a "system." Consequently, the ability to plan and conduct EBO is predicated on a task force operating along the principles of NCW.

Although much remains uncertain, innovative concepts like EBO are likely to dominate future wars. They come with the restoration of the offensive as the dominant form of war, with speed and movement as key elements. Speed will allow forces to shift quickly about the battlefield to check, block, and strike almost contiguously. The objective is not to kill as many of the opposing forces as possible, but to paralyze them, wear them down, and eventually break their will. The ability to see the battlefield and to know the enemy will thus change the dynamics of fire and maneuver fundamentally.

During Operation Enduring Freedom, the Americans applied EBO and NCW with considerable tactical success. Situational awareness, provided by vastly improved command, control, communications, intelligence and strategic reconnaissance, contributed to synchronism, simultaneity, and speed of the combined and joint operations. Land power reinforced air power and vice versa. Everything that could be seen on the battlefield was destroyed almost instantaneously and with great precision and focus. The targeting focused more on emerging and mobile targets. For example, Navy F-14s or Special Operations Forces acquired emerging targets, determined the coordinates and passed the information to B-52s by way of AWACS aircraft. Also A-10 "tank killers" were used in an anti-personnel role.

The targeting process was not hampered by bad weather or nighttime. But increased emphasis on emerging targets precluded aircrews from taking their time in deriving and inputting GPS coordinates or laser designating a target. As a consequence, accuracy was traded for time. With a 15,000-foot altitude imposed, at times it was impossible for pilots to see what their colleagues were observing on the ground. Some would then fly near the targets, using their binoculars, or talk with Special Operations Forces on the ground. Others refused to drop bombs if they were not convinced of the target. In fact, many targets did not look like military targets and it was sometimes impossible to distinguish combatants from non-combatants. This is a typical characteristic of unconventional warfare.

The time lag between sensor and shooter was sharply reduced. Information technology linked sensors to military capabilities, from the most advanced such as the B-2 bomber, to aging systems such as the 40-year-old B-52, to soldiers on horseback. Junior commanders called in air strikes. American forces worked with local Afghan forces.

Special Operations Forces used ground-target laser designators and laptops to locate enemy forces. They signaled information to aircraft that attacked with precision-guided munitions. When 400 Taliban rebelled in a fort near Mazar-e-Sharif, a sergeant pinpointed positions and radioed for air support by F/A-18s, carrying 2,000-pound bombs. It took just 15 minutes to respond. Almost 90% of the targets were not pre-planned, but identified by manned and unmanned systems such as Global Hawk and Predator UAVs, U-2, and P-3 reconnaissance planes, satellites, Special Operations Forces and HUMINT. Interestingly, most of the ordnance dropped was precision guided. During Operation Desert Storm, some 7 to 8% of all ordnance was precision-guided; during Operation Allied Force some 40%; and, during Operation Enduring Freedom, some 60%. The key to the success was the Joint Direct Attack Munitions (JDAM). In fact, the JDAM is a GPS device attached to a conventional "dumb" bomb to steer it to any target, day and night and under all weather conditions with pinpoint accuracy.

As has been argued before, Operation Enduring Freedom was fought by proxy with US Special Operations Forces, specialized forces, and air power as force multipliers. Proxy wars, however, cannot be fought all around the world. Consequently, the US and its allies may have no other option but to do the fighting themselves. But Operation Anaconda demonstrated that fighting unconventional wars with regular forces is still a fundamental weakness of Western armed forces.

EBO and NCW are typically American approaches, with a technology-driven doctrine, but whether these new concepts are applicable under all circumstances is unclear so far. As has been argued before, during the stabilization phases following Operation Enduring Freedom and Operation Iraqi Freedom, US forces had great difficulties in winning the peace. They were unable to win the hearts and minds of large portions of the local populace. On the contrary, the Americans were widely considered to be an occupying force. This suggests that technology cannot compensate for the lack of political progress. Moreover, despite technological superiority and doctrinal innovations, US forces found dealing with lightly armed insurgents extremely difficult, both in the mountainous regions of Afghanistan and the cities of Iraq. In April 2004, American forces fought their first big classic urban battle in the streets of Karma, east of Baghdad. This was not high-tech war. They fought house to house with machine guns and mortars. As the area was densely populated, the ground forces were refused air power.

Table 6.1 Simplified connection between EBO and NCW

Level of war	Example of desired effect	Guidance
Political strategic level	Weakening the regime	Overall or grand strategy
Military strategic level	Paralyzing the regime	Military strategy
Operational level	Denial of military options	Operational doctrine for network-centric, joint and combined campaigns
Tactical level	Denial of success on the battlefield	Tactical doctrine for network centric engagements

Nevertheless, EBO and NCW are truly revolutionary: new technologies produce new operational concepts, which in turn, enhance the efficacy of military operations in such a way that quick victories with few friendly casualties can be achieved. European armies have only modest capabilities for this revolutionary way of waging war. This not only undermines transatlantic interoperability, but cooperability as well. As a result, NATO embarked on a project called the NATO Response Force (NRF) – a rapidly deployable force, trained and equipped for this new type of warfare. It became a European test bed for EBO and NCW, intended to spearhead force transformation in Europe. As most EU-NATO countries will contribute the same units to the NRF and the Union's Rapid Reaction Force, this development will undoubtedly have an important impact on the force transformation of European armies. If Europe wants to join US-led combat operations, it must take this development into account. This requires substantial investment in interoperable C4ISTAR to plug into the network, and precision-guided munitions to achieve desired effects on the battlefield. A separate but related trend is that towards light logistics, enabling small forces to operate autonomously and to be transported rapidly over large distances.

Operation Iraqi Freedom

Compared to Afghanistan, Iraq provided an even better testing ground for the new concepts. US Commander General Tommy Franks said that a number of important lessons learned during Operation Enduring Freedom were carried over into Operation Iraqi Freedom.[29] First, the cooperation between the Pentagon and the CIA worked well in Afghanistan. CIA Special Operations Forces were important for intelligence-gathering, forward air control, and search-and-destroy missions. Second, the mission determined the coalition rather than the coalition determining the mission, as was the case during Operation Allied Force. Unity in command was a prerequisite to conduct a complicated mission with ground, air, and naval forces, together with Special Operations Forces. Combined and joint training and operations were a key factor in Afghanistan.

The planning for Operation Iraqi Freedom was dominated by a clash between new and old thinking. Defense Secretary Rumsfeld was presented with various versions of Operations Plan 1003 Victor. Especially the Army presented options with big, mechanized divisions. The majority of the force packages presented to him were rejected as being "too big." The Secretary placed his trust in net-centric operations, with precision bombing, a small,

29 Statement of General Franks before the Senate Armed Services Committee, July 9, 2003.

fast-moving attack force, and heavy reliance on Special Operations Forces. Initially, the Pentagon's premier war-planning document, the time-phased forces-deployment list (TPFDL) called for the advanced deployment of tanks and other heavy equipment for three or four divisions.[30] Instead, Rumsfeld decided to rely on the equipment for one division that was already in Kuwait. Consequently, the 3rd Infantry Division, which was to play a key role during Operation Iraqi Freedom, arrived without organic equipment. According to his critics, the Defense Secretary ignored the possibility of protracted warfare, because he put units in the field with few reserves and insufficient amounts of heavy equipment. Moreover, the 500- kilometer supply line from Kuwait to Baghdad could easily become overextended, so that troops would run out of fuel, water, food, and ammunition.

Finally, Rumsfeld was accused of relying too much on "shock and awe." This brute force concept was named after a book by Harlan Ullman and James Wade, entitled: *Shock & Awe: Achieving Rapid Dominance.* The authors argued that rapid dominance envisions a wide application of force across a broad spectrum of leverage points to impose shock and awe: "This breadth should lead to a more comprehensive and integrated interaction among the specific components and units that produce aggregate military capability..."[31] In fact, the idea was clearly in line with the concept of achieving rapid full-spectrum dominance. The debate in the Pentagon demonstrated that large segments of the Army had not really embraced the new thinking, and relied on heavy options to carry out the old and proven concept of massive and overwhelming force.

The final plan called for the unleashing of 3,000 precision-guided munitions and missiles during the first 48 hours of the conflict, to be followed quickly by ground operations from the north and the south. The 4th infantry brigade, equipped for network enabled operations, would spearhead the attack from Turkey; the 3rd Infantry Division and the 101st Airborne Division, together with US Marines and British forces, would attack from Kuwait. The battle plan called for the 4th Infantry Division to sweep from the north to fight the Republican Guard in the oil-rich region around Mosul and Kirkuk, and then head south to Tikrit, Saddam Hussein's home base. However, the bulk of the forces would come from the south. British troops would take Basra and the oil fields in the south. Marines would also seize oil

30 S.M. Hersh, "The Battle Between Donald Rumsfeld and the Pentagon", *The New Yorker,* April 7, 2003.

31 H. Ullman, J. Wade, *Shock & Awe: Achieving Rapid Dominance,* National Defense University, Washington, 1996, p. 49.

installations and would head northwest in the direction of Kut, east of the Euphrates, and then head for Baghdad. The 3rd Infantry Division together with the 101st Airborne Division would take cities west of the Euphrates and then head north to Baghdad. The helicopter units of the 101st would leap ahead of armored units to seize bases for their armored helicopters. This plan could only be carried out partially, because the Americans were refused bases in Turkey, so that they had to rely on troops stationed in Kuwait and onshore in the Gulf and Mediterranean. On March 19, the war started with merely a third of the size of the force that had liberated Kuwait 12 years before. US Special Operations Forces were already in Iraq, some of them operating from Jordan. They hunted for weapons sites and Scud launchers, established a communication network and sought potential defectors.

During the early days of the intervention, Rumsfeld listed the eight objectives that the Bush administration sought to achieve: regime change; seizure of biological and chemical weapons; driving out of terrorists who found a safe haven in Iraq; collection of intelligence about terrorist networks in Iraq and beyond; collection of intelligence about the global network of illicit weapons of mass destruction activity; the ending of sanctions and the delivery of humanitarian relief, food, and medicine; securing Iraq's oil fields; and finally, creating conditions for a rapid transition to representative self-government.

The war started on March 19, when US warplanes and cruise missiles bombed a bunker in southern Baghdad in which Saddam Hussein and his aides were thought to be staying.[32] In the days that followed, more intensive bombings took place, but there was no shock and awe to cause the almost-immediate collapse or surrender of the regime. The plans changed with the attempt to kill Saddam Hussein and his aides the night before. Because of this opportunity target, the operation plan was put in motion 24 hours earlier.

In fact, Operation Iraqi Freedom consisted of different types of operations within one theater. First, there were traditional conventional maneuver warfare operations against regular forces. The 3rd Infantry Division, supported by the specialized 101st Airborne Division, raced north, bypassing southeastern cities. This clarified that the objective was not to conquer Iraq and control the entire country. During the first days of the war, it was unclear whether the Americans would be able to adequately protect

32 Early analyses of Operation Iraqi Freedom include: A.H. Cordesman, *The Lessons of the Iraq War* Washington, D.C.: CSIS) 2003; *Jane's Intelligence Review,* Iraqi Analyses, July 2003, pp. 6-48.

their flanks, and whether the logistical support would be able to keep pace with the fast-moving 3rd Infantry Division. The critical crossroads city of Nasiriyah had become a shooting gallery for American convoys. Time and again, Americans were ambushed on an overextended supply line. Mostly irregular fighters attacked the supply line relentlessly with rocket-propelled grenades and small arms. On March 27, 36 soldiers and Marines were killed, while Apache helicopters were beaten back by small-arms fire that downed one helicopter and riddled 33 others with bullets. But the supply line held. This probably was the turning point of the war.

Then a heavy sandstorm grounded all helicopters and brought the entire land operation to a halt. Things looked bad and critics said that the Rumsfeld strategy was not working. Nevertheless, by March 28, the Republican Guard, deployed around Baghdad, was the prime target. Planners divided Iraq into 30-mile by 30-mile kill boxes. Within these boxes they focused on Republican Guard units. The operation was known as "kill box interdiction close air support" (KICAS).

On April 2, a message was intercepted that seemed to indicate that a gas attack was imminent. It was expected that Saddam Hussein would use gas when American troops crossed a "red line" of the last defenses near the capital. Wind patterns were in favor of such an attack, but the gas attack did not materialize. Instead, the Iraqi defenses disintegrated and the commanders no longer had operational control over their troops. Their command and control did not function any longer and when it did, at the tactical level, it revealed positions so that units were destroyed within minutes. Iraqi forces were simply not capable of keeping pace with the tempo of US forces. The next day, the Americans took Saddam International Airport, just 15 kilometers from Baghdad. General Franks suspected that Iraqi forces had not fallen back into the city to wage an urban warfare campaign, but had melted back into the countryside. During the previous weeks, most Republican Guard units had abandoned their weaponry and fled.

Attacking a capital city with 5 million inhabitants was a worrisome prospect. The plan was to cordon the city and then send in probing attacks to find out how much resistance could be expected. On Saturday, April 5, Franks ordered a unit of tanks and armored personnel carriers to make a swing through the center of the city and then back to the airfield. The unit met disorganized but well-equipped formations of Iraqi fighters who were no match for the Americans. Approximately 2,000 to 3,000 Iraqis were killed during the three-hour tour. Many fighters attacked the column equipped just with light arms. They were killed immediately, thus demonstrating either their incompetence or their desire for martyrdom. In the days that followed, other incursions were conducted; on April 9, Baghdad fell.

Second, unconventional warfare operations involving urban operations against militias were carried out in the south where US Marines and British troops had to take the border town of Umm Qasr first, before marching to the peninsula of Al Faw and the major oil terminal of Basra. Seizing these cities was expected to be easy. Twelve years previously, the Shiite population had risen against Saddam Hussein, but this did not happen now. During the 1991 Gulf War, the Americans had encouraged the Shiites to rise up against Saddam Hussein, but when they did so, they received no allied support. The result was Shiite mistrust. In addition, the Iraqi leadership managed to insert the militia of the Fedayeen Saddam in the cities mentioned. Their aim was to prevent the population from rising up and to fight coalition forces in the cities. The end result was heavy urban warfare in the south. It took almost a month to get the region under control; Umm Qasr fell on March 25, Basra on April 7. For the coalition, the paramilitary Fedayeen Saddam mentioned earlier was the big, unpleasant surprise of the war. Led by Saddam's eldest son, Uday, they turned out to be the most loyal and best-motivated fighters of the regime. They could be found in most cities throughout the country, where they stayed in private homes and fought in civilian clothes. After the formal declaration of the end of the war, urban combat escalated against American forces, especially in Baghdad. Here, Fedayeen Saddam applied traditional guerrilla tactics. They used high-rise buildings and busy streets as avenues for surprise attacks. At first, they attacked only at night, but after a few weeks they attacked in the daytime as well. The attacks on US troops frustrated the peace-building effort because bombs and exchanges of fire not only killed an increasing number of Americans, but Iraqis, too.

The third type of operation carried out in Iraq were special and specialized forces operations carrying out missions from Jordan, where the population was kept ignorant of the things that were happening in the border region. The aim was to seize airfields in order to mount an offensive from the east, to seize complexes linked to weapons of mass destruction activities, and to hunt down Scuds which could reach Israel.

Fourth, in the north, Special Operations Forces carried out attacks against terrorists who used the Kurdish territories as a safe haven. Moreover, they tried to secure the oil fields near Mosul.

Fifth, a hearts and minds campaign was conducted to gain the support of the population. Psychological operations involved EC-130C Command Solo aircraft broadcasting above Iraq. Tens of millions of leaflets were dropped to persuade troops to surrender and to inform the population about the objectives of the intervention.

Finally, the US fought a proxy war by helping Kurdish fighters in their struggle against Republican Guard Forces. A related operation took place in the east. Here a search-and-destroy operation was carried out against Iranian pro-Saddam forces, the Mujahedeed Khalq.

Most observers were surprised by the speed of the intervention. The first analyses all pointed in the same direction. First, the Iraqi military had defended their country incompetently. Guidance emphasized commanders and troops to prepare for defensive operations that did not take into account air and missile attacks. Moreover, the guidance called for jihad and martyrdom instead of effective resistance. Instructions to units of the 51st Republican Guard division near Basra emphasized tactics like climbing up palm trees for reconnaissance purposes and other methods totally unrelated to modern warfare. Moreover, Saddam made a major mistake by keeping his best and most loyal troops out of Baghdad and other major cities, perhaps out of fear that they would turn on him. By doing so, he exposed the Republican Guards to the relentless precision strikes of American air forces. At the same time he was not able to organize the much-feared resistance in urban areas. The Fedayeen Saddam took over the defense of the cities, but were neither trained nor equipped to engage American forces effectively. Had Saddam Hussein defended his country more intelligently, he still would have lost because the performance of the coalition forces was so overwhelmingly superior that the war would have been won even without a good operations plan:

- Air superiority was a prerequisite for success. Whoever controls the air, controls the fight on the ground. Gaining air superiority was not really a problem, because ten years of Northern and Southern Watch had degraded Iraqi air defenses and its air force. In the months preceding the actual war, US and British forces bombed 80 air defense sites. By March 25, Secretary Rumsfeld claimed air superiority.
- EBO and NWC were experimented on a large scale. The networking of sensors, intelligence, and shooters was unprecedented. The backbone of the operation was advanced C4ISTAR. A combination of satellites, U-2 spy planes, Joint STARS, AWACS, and UAVs were used. During the heavy sandstorms, both the target acquisition process and the targeting continued. The United States possessed information dominance and cleverly exploited this advantage. Enemy forces using electronic means of communication were destroyed immediately.
- More than 70% of all ordnance was precision. Due to superior intelligence, it took approximately 12 minutes to destroy a confirmed target; in some

cases it was 5 minutes after detection. For the first time, precision-guided munitions were used for close air support, thus greatly enhancing the relationship between Army and Air Force. During the 1991 Gulf War, only 15% of strike aircraft were capable of dropping precision-guided munitions, now all aircraft were.

- Tempo was crucial. Air strikes continued day and night, and small, fast-moving forces defeated larger forces. There were only 125,000 coalition forces in Iraq, whilst Iraqi forces numbered 400,000 including some 100,000 well-trained and well-equipped Republican Guard troops. In a single week, the coalition destroyed 1,000 tanks and reduced the Republican Guard by 50%. The war had all the hallmarks of EBO: speed, precision, and effectiveness.
- Defense Secretary Rumsfeld demanded “jointness”. Arthur Cebrowski, a retired vice admiral and director of the Pentagon’s Office of Force Transformation, observed tighter integration between land and air operations. Indeed, Operation Iraqi Freedom was a joint operation, with air power and land operations integrated. For the first time, forces were integrated, rather than de-conflicted. However, the integration of the land components – Marines, US Army and British forces – was far from satisfactory. Moreover, British forces lacked the logistics to go further north, and the interoperability to join the Americans on the battlefield.
- Lift was one of the factors contributing to success. The Americans conducted some 3,500 in-theater airlift sorties. They moved some 3,600 tons of cargo and 5,500 passengers. During the night of March 26, 15 long-range C-17s delivered 1,000 paratroopers and 40 vehicles in northern Iraq. This demonstrated that the Americans could do without the northern front.
- Special Operations Forces and Specialized Forces, as many as 10,000, played a vital role in the overall success. Their tasks varied from covert missions for intelligence-gathering on Iraqi troop deployments, the whereabouts of the leadership, the position on Scud launchers and the hunt for weapons of mass destruction, and forward air control and severing of enemy lines of communication, to overt missions such as seizing air fields to use them as operational bases for covert operations or staging areas.

Despite technical and doctrinal innovations, unconventional urban warfare remained the biggest challenge. It underscored the conclusion that Western armed forces still encounter great difficulties dealing with this threat. Doctrine and technology matter, but were not decisive during urban combat. One explanation is that EBO and NCW were still being applied in a rudimentary form. There was no "system of systems." Many systems remained service-centric. Command and control was improvised around each new contingency. The US Army, the US Marines, and the British forces had different levels of digitalization. The US Army was most advanced, but the only truly digitalized force – the 4th Division – was not deployed. Nevertheless, the regime change phase was a success. Without too many difficulties, Saddam Hussein was removed from power. The real challenge was the subsequent stabilization phase.

Stabilization operations: reinventing population-centric COIN

The stabilization phases following the regime change phases in Iraq and Afghanistan proved to be more difficult. The limited objectives of regime change were relatively easy to achieve with a combination of massive firepower and superior maneuver forces which were no match for the adversaries. When the adversaries recognized that they had little chance against the superior opponent, a wait-and-see approach turned out to be the best tactic. In Iraq, a portion of Saddam Hussein's forces just evaporated. They simply took off their uniforms and went home. In Afghanistan, Taliban forces blended into the population. In both cases the insurgency developed during the subsequent stabilization phases. During the first years of the stabilization operations, hard lessons were learned. First, an insurgent-centric COIN approach was counterproductive. In Iraq, urban warfare turned out to be the main challenge during the stabilization phase. British forces, with their vast experience in Northern Ireland, got the situation under control in Basra, but American troops faced enormous difficulties when dealing with insurgents in what was called the "Sunni Triangle" in the center of the country. The battle for Fallujah demonstrated what could go wrong. Operation Vigilant Resolve was an unsuccessful attempt by the US military to capture the city of Fallujah in April 2004. The situation in the city deteriorated when 700 members of the 82nd Airborne Division and 150 members of Charlie Company entered the city in April 2003. The troops occupied a primary school. On April 28, 2004, the citizens of Fallujah demanded that the Americans vacate the building and allow the school to re-open. The protests escalated when US forces were attacked and US forces returned fire, killing 17 people and wounding more than 70. The conflict escalated further when four Blackwater USA private military contractors and five American soldiers were killed in nearby al-Habbaniyah. Subsequently, an additional 1,500 troops entered the city to help quell the growing resistance. On the night of April 4, 2004, American forces launched a major attack to "reestablish security in Fallujah."[33] In the opening days of the siege approximately a third of the population fled the city. Hospitals had to close and fighting broke out in large parts of central Iraq.

On April 9, 2004, the US announced a cease-fire and called for negotiations between the Iraqi Governing Council, insurgents, and city spokespersons. For the American troops, the siege was a disaster because the use of "brute force" backfired. It was estimated that approximately 600 Iraqis were killed, at least half of whom were non-combatants. American forces only managed to gain a foothold in the industrial district to the south of the city, and on May 1, 2004, American troops withdrew from the city. Lieutenant General James Conway agreed to unilaterally leave any remaining operations to the newly formed Fallujah Brigade under the command of former Baathist Army General Jasim Mohammed Saleh.

Saleh, however, had been involved in military actions against Shiites under Saddam Hussein. The group dissolved and turned over the US weaponry to the insurgency. This prompted the second battle of Fallujah in November, code named Operation Al-Fajr. The battle involved the heaviest urban fight since the Battle of Huế City in Vietnam in 1968. The second battle was much better prepared than the previous one. Some 13,500 US, Iraqi, and British troops were deployed outside the city. The city was defended by 3,000-4,000 insurgents who prepared spider holes, dug tunnels and trenches, built a large number of IED and booby-trapped buildings and vehicles. Early in the morning of November 8, 2004, coalition forces attacked the city. To prepare the battlefield, the operations started with artillery barrages and air attacks. Within a few days, the coalition carried out a search and destroy operation to clear the city from insurgents. By November 13, most of the fighting had ended, but sporadic fighting against pockets of resistance continued until December 23.

Operation Al-Fajr demonstrated that military success in conquering a city is possible with brute force and search-and-destroy operations. The battle was the bloodiest of the Iraq War and the bloodiest since the Vietnam War. Approximately a fifth of all the buildings were destroyed and two-thirds of the remaining buildings were badly damaged. Approximately 60 of the 200 mosques were destroyed. Many had been used by Islamist forces as weapons storages and sanctuaries. Still remembering the battle of Grozny, the world

33 http://edition.cnn.com/2004/WORLD/meast/04/05/iraq.main/.

was shocked by the damage done. Consequently, the battle for Fallujah contributed to the shift from insurgent-centric to population-centric COIN.

The second lesson learned was that, after the regime change, indigenous security forces and leaders could still play a crucial role. Under pressure by Shiite and Kurdish leaders, the Americans decided to abolish Iraqi armed forces and started a program of "de-Baathification." As the entire security apparatus and bureaucracy were dismantled, the responsibility for Iraq's security was left entirely to the coalition forces. Sunni Arabs, however, believed that these measures were attempts to impose domination on them. This was a powerful incentive to start the insurgency.

The third lesson learned was that early planning for conflict termination by the stabilization and reconstruction of Iraq was a prerequisite for success.[34] In Iraq the decision not to plan for a stabilization and reconstruction phase was based on the wrong idea that Iraq could pay for the reconstruction through oil revenue. During the counterinsurgency, stabilization and reconstruction can be used to win the support of the people. But the Americans did not anticipate an insurgency when they invaded Iraq. Consequently, deployed forces were unprepared for the full-fledged insurgency that followed the regime change phase. They lacked both the experience and the doctrine. The poor execution of Operation Iraqi Freedom left the US no other choice but to develop a new counterinsurgency doctrine, which famously became known as the "Petraeus Manual."

A fourth lesson learned was that Western templates of state building did not take the dynamics of the local conflict into account. In Iraq, the Americans tried to create a stable, secure, democratic, and functioning state. This attempt failed completely. As too few troops were deployed, the stabilization operations failed. Reconstruction was difficult if not impossible because of the dissolving of the old security forces and the old bureaucracy. The decision to finish the old leadership and its supporting structures seemed like the right thing to do, but the exclusion of the former ruling elite from the political process contributed to the later Sunny insurgency. Moreover, the absence of alternative structures resulted in chaos. But the biggest mistake was to back Nouri al-Maliki for the post of prime minister over Ayad Allawi in 2010, because a Shiite Islamist was believed to be more credible than his secular rival. As a result, Maliki had no incentive to compromise with Allawi on a power-sharing agreement. When they reached such an agreement, the

34 Anthony Cordesman, *Iraq: Too Uncertain to Call* (Washington, D.C.: CSIS, November 14, 2003), p. 2.

Americans did not actively support it. As a result, rifts within the society became deeper so that the political process was stalled.

Only after a number of military setbacks, the President decided to send more troops. Since 2003, the war in Iraq gradually shifted from a war on terror to counterinsurgency. As has been explained above, a successful COIN operation requires both kinetic operations and non-kinetic operations aimed at winning the hearts and minds of local populations. Too much focus on kinetic operations undermines the willingness of the population to cooperate with the coalition. In addition, too few troops increases the number of insurgent attacks. Precisely for these reasons the commanding officer in Iraq, General David Petraeus, argued in favor of a troop surge. In his testimony before Congress in 2007, Petraeus argued that, "due to the surge, the number of incidents declined to 8 over the past 12 weeks, with the number of incidents in the last two weeks at the lowest levels since June 2006." But this observation did not say much about the prospects of achieving the political and military objectives set.

Field Manual 3-24

These lessons learned provided a context for major doctrinal innovations. In conjunction with a US Marine Corps team, General Petraeus and his staff produced Field Manual (FM) 3-24 on counterinsurgency operations, otherwise known as "COIN." The new manual drew heavily on the work of classical thinkers including Sir Robert Thomson and the French military officer and theorist David Galula. Galula's famous book *Counterinsurgency Warfare: Theory and Practice* (1964) built on Mao Tse-tung's observation that "revolutionary war is 80% political action and only 20% military." Contemporary thinkers such as John A. Nagl and David Kilcullen were influential as well. [35] Army Lieutenant Colonel Nagl co-authored the new counterinsurgency manual as part of a team overseen by Petraeus and led by his old West Point classmate, Conrad Crane. Kilcullen was the Chief Strategist in the Office of the Coordinator for Counterterrorism at the US State Department and later became a counterinsurgency advisor to General David Petraeus.

35 John A. Nagl, *Learning to Eat Soup with a Knife* (The University of Chicago Press: Chicago and London, 2002); David J. Kilcullen, *The Accidental Guerrilla: Fighting Small Wars in the Midst of a Big One* (Oxford University Press, New York, 2009) and *Counterinsurgency* (Oxford University Press, New York: 2010).

The new manual was built around two European ideas which were drawn from the doctrines of European colonial warfare.[36] First, that protecting the population is the key to success in any counterinsurgency campaign. At the same time, insurgents will try to deprive the population from any sense of security. Second, that to succeed in counterinsurgency, armed forces have to learn and adapt more rapidly than the enemy. America's new counterinsurgency doctrine dramatically increased the performance of its troops in Iraq. A new clear, hold, and build approach was showing some results before Petraeus came to Iraq, but as a new commander he decided to apply it throughout the Sunni regions. Petraeus called this approach "the Sons of Iraq," which consisted of recruiting, equipping, and paying former militiamen for the fight against the local franchise of al-Qaeda. The Sons of Iraq approach spread the "awakening" to other Sunni areas where the Americans and local leaders shared the same interests, that is, the fight against al-Qaeda.

The new manual demanded a different mind-set and counterintuitive action. The manual observed that "the admonition 'Sometimes, the More Force Used, the Less Effective It Is' does not apply when the enemy is 'coming over the barricades'; however, that thought is applicable when increased security is achieved in an area. In short, these paradoxes should not be reduced to a checklist; rather, they should be used with considerable thought."[37] Other examples are "sometimes, the more you protect your force, the less secure you may be" and "the more successful the counterinsurgency is, the less force can be used and the more risk must be accepted."

The manual contained a list of successful and unsuccessful practices which are useful to quote in length (table 6.2). Stability and reconstruction operations could go hand in hand with COIN operations. Another doctrine publication of the US Army stated that stability "ultimately aims to create a condition so the local populace regards the situation as legitimate, acceptable and predictable. These conditions consists of the level of violence; the functioning of governmental, economic and societal institutions; and the general adherence to local laws, rules, and norms of behavior."[38] Thus, stabilization and reconstruction are part of a population-centric approach; COIN operations can be necessary to maintain or enforce peace. The centerpiece of the Afghan reconstruction efforts were the Provincial Reconstruction

36 John A. Nagle, "Constructing the Legacy of Field Manual 3-24", *Joint Forces Quarterly*, issue 58, 3rd quarter 2010, p. 118.

37 FM 3-24, *Insurgency and Counterinsurgency* (Washington, D.C.: Headquarters, Department of the Army, December 15, 2006) pp. 1-26.

38 FM 3-24, pp. 1-29.

Teams (PRTs) first fielded in 2003. They consisted of 50 to hundreds of troops, diplomats, and representatives from development agencies.

Table 6.2 Successful and unsuccessful COIN practices according to FM 3-24[39]

Successful practices	Unsuccessful practices
- Emphasize intelligence - Focus on the population, its needs, and its security - Establish and expand secure areas - Isolate insurgents from the populace - Conduct effective, pervasive, and continuous information operations - Provide amnesty and rehabilitation for those willing to support the new government - Place host-nation police in the lead with military support as soon as the security situation permits - Expand and diversify the host-nation police force - Train military forces to conduct counterinsurgency operations - Emned quality advisors and special forces with host-nation forces. - Deny sanctuary to insurgents - Encourage strong political and military cooperation and information sharing - Secure host nation borders - Protect key infrastructure	- Overemphasize killing and capturing the enemy rather than securing and engaging the populace - Conduct large-scale operations as the norm - Concentrate military forces in large bases for protection - Focus special forces primarily on raiding - Place low priority on assigning quality advisors to host-nation forces - Build and train host-nation security forces in the US military's image - Ignore peacetime government processes, including legal procedures - Allow open borders, airspace and coastlines

NATO Doctrine

The Petraeus manual inspired subsequent publications including the Army's fundamental operational doctrine Field Manual 3-0 *Operations* (2008), Field Manual 3-07 *Stability Operations* (2008), Joint Publication 3-24 *Counterinsurgency* (2009) the Army Capstone Concept *Operational Adaptability* (2009), the British Army Field Manual *Countering Insurgency* (2009), and NATO's *Allied Joint Doctrine for Counterinsurgency* of February 2011. The

39 ADP 3-07, *Stability* (Washington, D.C.: Headquarters, Department of the Army, August 31, 2012), p. 1.

NATO publication introduced the new thinking on counterinsurgency to America's allies. The doctrine emphasized the political nature of the counterinsurgency as well, by defining counterinsurgency as "the set of political, economic, social, military, law enforcement, civil and psychological activities with the aim to defeat insurgency and address any core grievances."[40] This aim can only be achieved by a comprehensive approach to crisis management that focuses on three levels, which must function in a complementary manner to achieve success:

- At the political and strategic level, NATO concentrates on building confidence and mutual understanding between international actors.
- At the theater level, NATO force commanders must be empowered to conduct effective cooperation and coordination with indigenous local authorities and other international actors in the execution of operations.
- At the operational level, the priority is to cooperate with other international actors in the overall planning for complex operations in which a large degree of civil-military interaction will be required.[41]

The manual conceptualized the nature of the insurgency, as shown in figure 6.1, and concluded that the nature of insurgency required defense, development, and diplomacy (3D) as shown in figure 6.2. In other words, "long-term efforts should aim to be more developmental and political than military until the presence of NATO forces is no longer required."[42] Subsequently, the manual linked this to an operational approach, as shown in table 6.2. The manual argued that an effective clear, hold, and build approach depends on the ability to carry out the following:

- physically and psychologically separate insurgents from the population;
- provide the conditions for economic, political, and social reforms;
- safeguard the population and key infrastructure;
- provide training and opportunities for host-nation's security forces to improve and take the lead in taking and maintaining control;
- provide opportunities for the host-nation's police and other governmental institutions to establish and maintain the rule of law;
- provide essential services and address the core grievances of the insurgency;

40 AJP-3.4.4, Allied Joint Doctrine for Counterinsurgency, February 2011, pp. 3-18.

41 AJP-3.4.4, pp. 1-4.

42 AJP-3.4.4, pp. 4-7,8.

- assist with resettling displaced persons and refugees to their homes (this task is done by UNHCR, and only in extreme circumstances will the military be asked for assistance);
- use and train local workers and materials to rebuild and provide a sustainable economic and social system;
- deny the enemy active and passive support; and
- gain the support of the populace.[43]

Figure 6.1 The nature of the counterinsurgency, according to NATO doctrine[44]

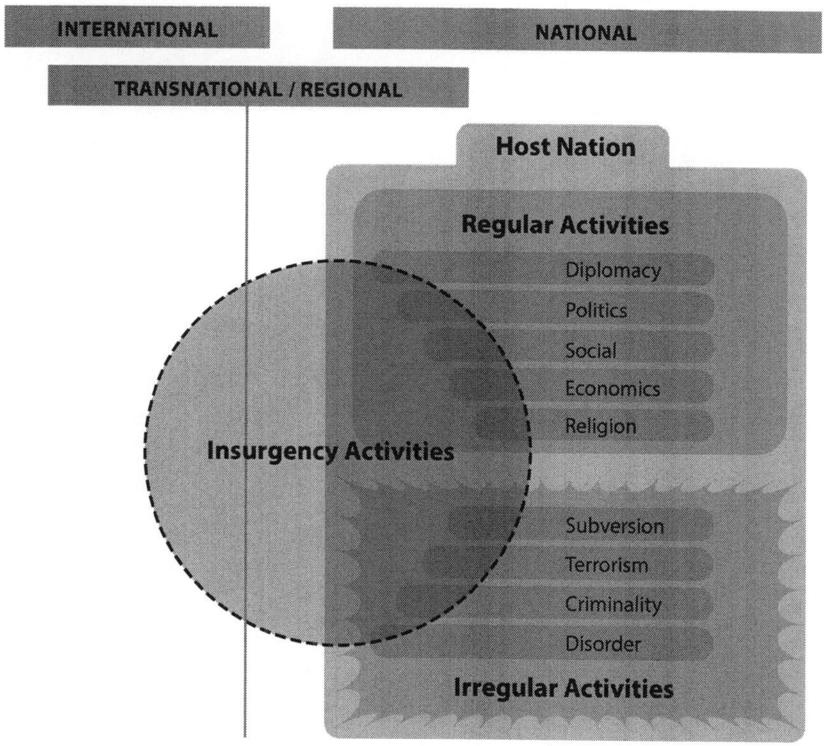

Other doctrinal innovations included the Comprehensive Approach and the Whole of Government approach.[45] The latter "integrates the collaborative efforts of the departments and agencies (...) to achieve unity in effort

43 AJP-3.4.4, pp. 5-14, 15.
44 AJP-3-07, pp. 3-4.
45 Fred Kaplan, "The End of the Age of Petraeus", *Foreign Affairs*, January/February 2013, p. 89.

towards a shared goal." The former integrates those efforts with partners and NGO and private sector activities. Both approaches are consistent with population-centric operations which require the harmonized use of economic, diplomatic, political, and military instruments.

Figure 6.2 Counterinsurgency Range of Options NATO doctrine[46]

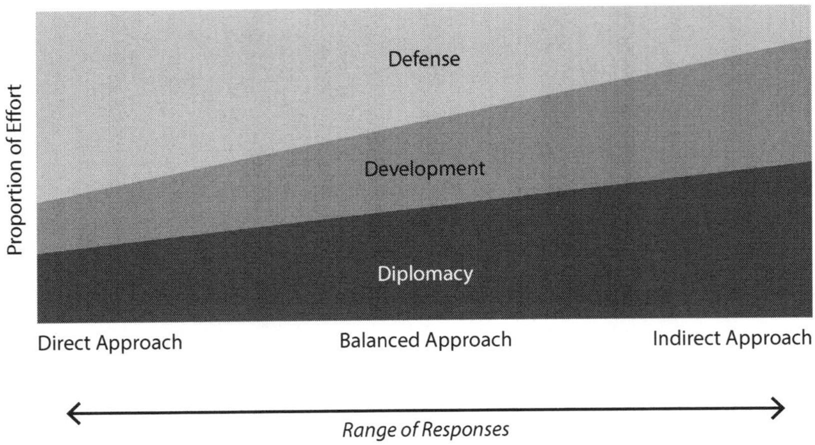

A fundamental doctrinal principle has always been that only through the physical control of an area or the isolation of the opponent can one's political and military objectives be met. SOF and specialized forces, such as air maneuver units, were key elements. As the insurgents were unlikely to possess aircraft, air superiority was not considered a big worry. Nevertheless, as has been argued before, MANPADS (man-portable air-defense systems) stolen after the collapse of the Soviet Union from Russian warehouses and after the collapse of the Gadhafi regime from Libyan warehouses caused some nervousness during the conflicts in Afghanistan, Syria, and Mali. But the actual role of the air force in COIN remained limited to close air support and interdiction. The use of drones, SOF, advanced intelligence techniques, and network-centric operational concepts turned out to be an effective way to disrupt terrorist organizations with limited risks for friendly forces. A key issue, however, was collateral damage. For that reason, a debate emerged within NATO on the legality of armed unmanned aerial vehicles. In February 2013, the UN launched an investigation unit to examine the legality

46 AJP-3.4.4, p. 3.2.

of drone attacks in cases where civilians are killed in so-called "targeted" counterterrorism operations.

Unfortunately, the new doctrines were no guarantee for success. As the Afghan insurgency turned out to be more complex than the insurgency witnessed in Iraq, the American COIN doctrine developed for Iraq could not be easily transferred to the Afghan theatre. A number of factors explains the failure of COIN in Afghanistan. First, al-Qaeda and the Taliban were intertwined adversaries. Second, compared to Afghanistan the sectarian and tribal divides were more complex. Because of this, local and allied leaders shared few common interests. Consequently, as Fred Kaplan observed: "the problem (...) was that Afghanistan was not susceptible to COIN."[47]

Figure 6.3 Clear, hold, and build – interconnected and evolving activities, according to NATO doctrine[48]

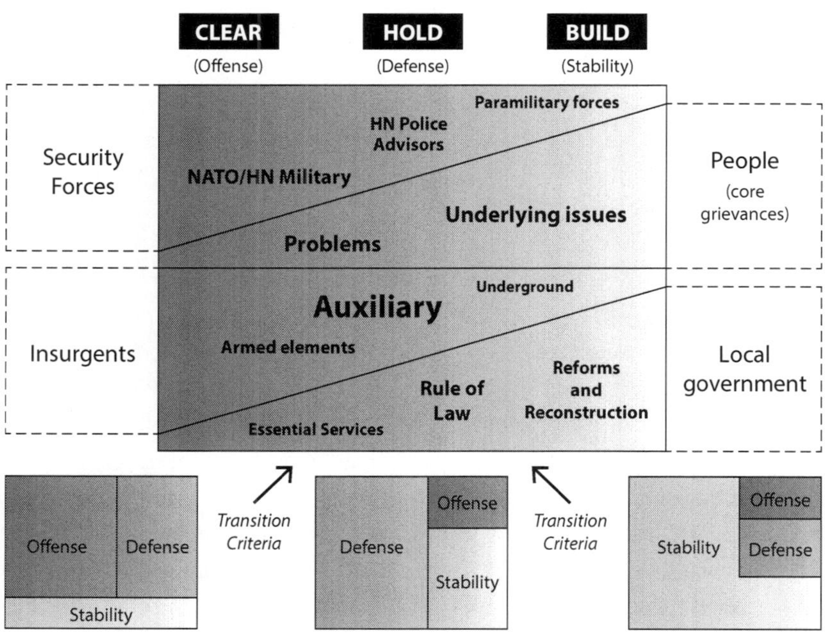

47 AJP-3.4.4, pp. 4-7.
48 AJP-3.4.4, pp. 5-14.

Measuring success in Iraq, Libya, and Afghanistan

Early in 2012, Ned Parker observed in *Foreign Affairs* that, "Nine years after US troops toppled Saddam Hussein and just a few months after the last US soldier left Iraq, the country has become close to something as a failed state." The key issue was a failing political process: "Prime Minister Nouri al-Maliki presides over a system rife with corruption and brutality, in which leaders use security forces an militias to repress enemies and intimidate the general population."[49]

The conclusion was similar to the conclusions drawn after the interventions in Afghanistan and Libya. In all cases, the insurgency gained strength after the regime change. David C. Gompert and John Gordon IV argued that empirically, the likelihood of success is 50% when insurgencies gain full strength.[50] They also observed that the strongest statistical predictors of successful insurgency existed in the Muslim world:

- populations excluded from politics and estranged from the state;
- authoritarian, unresponsive, inept, and corrupt government;
- insurgents committed to destroying such a government;
- significant popular sympathy for the insurgents.

In the cases of Afghanistan, Iraq, and Libya the major achievement was the removal of a hated regime. But in all, regime change contributed to state failure. Stabilization and reconstruction brought neither security nor stability. In both countries, the population was worse off after the regime change and after the end of the stabilization missions. Due to ongoing political battles for power, the absence of a functioning security apparatus, and an ineffective bureaucracy, the general population had to cope with a worsening security situation and decreasing political stability after foreign troops had left. States were not able to provide basic services, including sanitation, drinking water, electricity, and health care. This made the population easy recruits for militias and criminal gangs. State building is extremely difficult when, as was the case in the above-mentioned cases, indigenous security forces, bureaucracies, and the historic leadership evaporate. As those countries were run by dictators, alternative structures for providing security and stability were not in place. Consequently, taking the high number of

49 Ned Parker, "The Iraq we left behind: Welcome to the World's Next Failed State", *Foreign Affairs*, March-April 2012, p. 94.

50 David C. Gompert and John Gordon IV, *War by Other Means* (Santa Monica, CA: RAND Corporation), 2008, p. xxv.

casualties into account as well, one can conclude that the stabilization and reconstruction efforts were not successful. Stabilization and reconstruction efforts are the result of a moral or legal obligation towards the target country. In contrast to the insurgent, during the stabilization phase no vital interests are at stake for the intervening powers. As explained in Coercive Mechanism 3, better motivated insurgents applying asymmetrical tactics are very difficult to counter. This explains why, despite the successful *tactical* application of innovations, including EBO, NCW, the comprehensive approach, the whole of government approach, and new COIN concepts, stabilization and reconstruction were a *strategic* failure. In addition, due to the shortage of troops, there was a classical mismatch between political ends and military means.

Lessons learned in Afghanistan and Iraq explain why the intervention in Libya was not followed by a stabilization operation, and why the peacekeeping operation following the French intervention in Mali in 2013 was carried out by indigenous and regional forces. Other factors were mission fatigue and the financial crisis, which affected the defense budgets of all European countries.

Postmodern warfare

Operation Enduring Freedom and Operation Iraqi Freedom offer a glimpse of what postmodern land warfare looks like. The colossal maneuvers of the traditional battlefields are no longer applicable. Technology allows dramatic reductions in the numbers of friendly casualties and collateral damage. In this respect, the first Gulf War was a watershed. Postmodern warfare is therefore more "humane" both for the soldiers who fight it and the adversaries.[51] This constitutes a break in the trend. Until the end of the 1980s, the costs, risks, and problems that are related to the deployment of military force were expected to continuously increase, while the benefits would decrease.[52] The assumption was that through this development, military force would become a useless option in international relations. This assumption is no longer valid. During the 1990s and the early 21st century,

51 For example: C. Coker, *Humane Warfare* (London: Routledge, 2001).

52 For example: K. Knorr, *The Power of Nations* (New York: Basic Books, 1975); J. Mueller, *Retreat from Doomsday: The Obsolescence of Major War* (New York: Basic Books, 1989); R. Ullman, *Securing Europe* (Princeton: Princeton University Press, 1991); R. Rosecrance, *The Rise of the Trading State: Commerce and Conquest in the Modern World* (New York: Basic Books, 1986); F. Fukuyama, *The End of History and the Last Man* (New York: Avon, 1992).

regime changes and other interventions with limited objective were carried out within a short time frame and with astonishingly low levels of friendly losses, and acceptable levels of collateral damage.

Not only technology has contributed to postmodern warfare. The people no longer accept the cruelties of war. One explanation is the impact of television. The management of television images is now part of war management. Moreover, societies in industrialized liberal democracies put humanity first and have become risk averse. Politics is about the control of risks.

After 9/11, the differences between the US and the Europeans have become very clear. Most Europeans emphasize conflict prevention and peace building, while rejecting the use of force. If force must be used, it should be in a multilateral context and based on a UN resolution. But EU member states cannot fight wars the way it suits their political culture best. The EU developed into a postmodern Kantian pacific union, with a distinct political and strategic culture. Its armed forces however, remained "modern," while the US transformed its armed forces into "postmodern" ones. This has resulted in a serious mismatch between US and European armed forces. Europe has very limited capabilities for advanced expeditionary warfare, that is, capabilities to conduct high-tempo, large-scale conventional and unconventional combat operations in distant parts of the world with minimal risk for friendly forces and acceptable levels of collateral damage. Force transformation, based on new technologies and innovative doctrines, could turn Europe's armed forces into more usable instruments of foreign policy.

Following the American example could make Europeans less reluctant to use force if necessary. Operation Iraqi Freedom made many Europeans aware of the ever-increasing gap, not only in military technology, but in doctrine as well. Interoperability between European and American forces is jeopardized; joint and combined operations are no longer possible.

Postmodern warfare, however, creates an antithesis in the form of asymmetric responses, which mainly take the form of unconventional warfare and terrorism. In other words, creating postmodern armed forces will not solve the problem of asymmetry and political struggle.

Conclusion

The context in which the armed forces of the West are deployed is changing rapidly. First, the lessons learned from Operations Enduring Freedom, Iraqi Freedom, and the ISAF stabilization mission confirms the thesis that the

West's military might scarcely matters if the opponent applies asymmetrical tactics and the heart and minds of the populace cannot be won. Until recently, the military believed that they existed to fight large-scale wars. Unconventional warfare was not considered "real war." Due to this mind-set, the military neglected the fact that most wars were fought in an unconventional manner. Historically, Western armed forces have been ill prepared for this kind of warfare as numerous disastrous experiences have demonstrated. However, in the 2000s, the missions in Afghanistan and Iraq had a powerful impact on force restructuring and doctrine development. Battles were now seen as a series of small-scale, tactical engagements. A swarming type of warfare was developed with increased mobility of small units, with great firepower. If the adversary disperses, Western armies must themselves disperse. Cordon operations and search-and-destroy operations, together with offensive operations to seize critical terrain and nodes, such as airfields, industrial complexes, and power plants, were now crucial. Special Operations Forces and specialized forces became the key elements of ground forces. Armed drones were seen as a relatively effective and low-cost option. Innovative concepts such as EBO, NCW, and the reinvention of population-centric COIN operations became attempts to get to grips with the new challenges. The application of new concepts holds the promise that unconventional and conventional wars can be fought with a single set of forces. The US is on track with the development of those forces; most European allies are reluctant to get involved in force transformation. Together with advances in technology, both the US and some allies including Australia, France, the Netherlands, and the United Kingdom, have created postmodern armed forces that can gain quick tactical successes, with limited numbers of friendly losses and acceptable levels of collateral damage. However, as long as the enemy remains opposed to what they considered as occupation forces, and the hearts and minds of the populace cannot be won, a strategic victory is impossible. When the foreign troops left, a stable peace in Afghanistan and Iraq was not won.

Second, the rise of China and other emerging economies restricts the West's room to maneuver in international politics. It is harder to obtain mandates in the UN Security Council for interventions. In addition, emerging powers use their economic wealth to increase their military and consequently their political power. Countries like China develop anti-access/area denial capabilities to prevent American forces from defending their interests in a particular region. In response, the US developed the AirSea Battle concept, indicating that geopolitics had become once more a powerful driver for force restructuring and doctrine development.

7 The Art of Military Coercion

A good strategy is a prerequisite for successful coercion. But tactical challenges increasingly jeopardize success at the strategic level, while preconditions at the strategic level jeopardize execution of operations at the tactical level. The close link between the technical, tactical, and strategic levels of war is characteristic of contemporary coercion. The explanation is that unconventional warfare and asymmetry are the most likely options for the adversary. As Western military power is unmatched, opponents find that unconventional warfare and asymmetry are the great equalizers. Unconventional warfare is a series of small-scale, sometimes isolated tactical engagements to achieve strategic objectives. Hit-and-run tactics and terrorism are useful strategies of countercoercion. These attacks create insurmountable problems for the coercer. As unconventional warfare is primarily a political undertaking, military victories are difficult to achieve. Winning the hearts and minds of the population is crucial. The opponent's tactics are aimed at undermining the credibility and legitimacy of the coercer, and time is on their side. As politicians in liberal democracies focus on the next elections, their time horizon, by definition, is short.

Experience with Operation Enduring Freedom and Operation Iraqi Freedom shows that for the adversary, the rational choice is to apply these strategies during the stabilization phase. Thus, the coercer's success during the coercive phase could be nullified. Three other observations reinforce this conclusion. First, liberal democracies have become increasingly risk-averse. Too many friendly casualties are unacceptable. Second, coercion is about achieving limited political and military objectives, which require the constrained use of force. High levels of collateral damage will not be tolerated. Third, the media play an increasingly important role. Journalists within the theater of operations tend to focus on tactical, rather than strategic issues, and will blow up relatively minor issues. For these reasons, military commanders must be more sensitive to the strategic implications of tactical mistakes, while decision makers should be aware of the consequences of interference in military operations. Domestic pressure created by the media is the most likely cause of too much political interference in the actual conduct of operations.

As the principles of military operations are the bedrock of doctrine, the military commander will base planning of military action on it. Understanding how these principles could be jeopardized by unrealistic political preconditions and other forms of interference is therefore crucial. This concluding chapter deals with the friction between political decision making and military principles. But first it summarizes some of the main findings.

The first conclusion is that the end of the Cold War required rethinking the use of armed forces as a coercive instrument. Defense planners always try to find ways to adapt their forces to the new circumstances. But as the mind-set of many Western soldiers and politicians has been shaped by the threat of global war between NATO and the Warsaw Pact, this was not easy. It is now generally accepted that expeditionary forces are required, capable of fighting conventional and unconventional wars in distant places. Fighting unconventional wars is especially demanding. Traditionally, Western armed forces are not trained and equipped for wars against irregular forces. New concepts such as EBO with NCW as its critical enabler hold the promise of quick victories with few friendly losses and acceptable levels of collateral damage. Moreover, innovative concepts could transform armed forces into more usable, postmodern instruments of power which can be used against both regular and irregular opponents.

Military coercion is not about occupying territories. Rather, it is about influencing the strategic choices of an actor. Compellence strategies of incapacitation, decapitation, control, and denial are the most likely choices. Limited objectives require limited means. The most attractive coercive instrument is air power, but if air power alone cannot coerce the adversary, ground forces must be used. When adversaries apply asymmetric tactics Special Operations Forces and specialized forces together with naval and air forces should do the trick. Specialized forces could then create hubs or bridgeheads from where Special Operations Forces could conduct covert and overt operations. At all times, a hearts and minds campaign is of crucial importance. As coercion is about achieving limited objectives, the hearts and minds campaign should make it clear to the populace that the war is not against them, but against their leaders. During the stabilization phase, winning the hearts and minds is essential to drive a wedge between the insurgents and the populace, so that the peace can be won.

The second conclusion is that the end of the Cold War has laid bare the differences in political and strategic culture between the US and most of its European allies. Here, the modern and the postmodern world clash. The Americans put emphasis on the defense of interests, while most Europeans emphasize the promotion of values and the strengthening of the international rule of law. After the end of the Cold War, many European political leaders believed that, in the new world order armed forces would only be used in the context of risk-free peacekeeping and humanitarian operations under the umbrella of the UN. Due to the disappearance of a large-scale threat to Europe, most Western nations decided to cut back their armed forces, lower their defense budgets and collect the "peace dividend." They kept armed forces both as an insurance against a radical change in the international security situation and for peace support operations. This would require lightly equipped forces for peacekeeping operations and a back-up of heavy, largely mobilizable forces for waging war. This approach proved to be wrong. Although global and major wars had become obsolete, local wars and terrorism would also have major consequences for international security. Relatively small crises could result in threats to interests. Refugees could destabilize entire regions and violate human rights on a massive scale. Preventing terrorism at home could require the destruction of terrorist organizations abroad. This could demand interventions in failed and weak states, especially ungoverned territories used by terrorists as sanctuaries. These challenges required expeditionary forces, capable of waging war in distant places. As most armed forces in Europe were not restructured, only very few countries could join the Americans in Operation Enduring Freedom and Operation Iraqi Freedom.

The third conclusion is that, despite the West's military superiority and new military concepts, military coercion still involves considerable risks. This is especially true for America's European allies, who lag behind in the force transformation process. As a matter of fact, the EU is a postmodern system with a collection of national, mainly modern forces. Paradoxically, the US still is a modern state, whilst its armed forces are increasingly postmodern.

On the one hand, interventions have become less risky because there is no longer the threat of escalation of a major clash between the two military superpowers, and Western superiority cannot be matched by the military power of any actor. Moreover, new methods of warfare reduce the risks associated with interventions. On the other hand, hostile states and terrorist groups are in a position to equalize the military balance with weapons of mass destruction and asymmetrical means of warfare, including attacks on troop-contributing countries. As the 1997 American Quadrennial Defense Review put it: "US dominance in the conventional military area may encourage adversaries to use such asymmetric means to attack our forces and interests overseas and at home."[1] Asymmetrical means will not undermine intervention capabilities of Western liberal democracies. They will, however, undermine the capability to control a hostile environ-

1 US Department of Defense, *Report of the Quadrennial Defense Review,* Report to Congress, May 1, 1997.

ment. This very prospect could deter interventions by liberal modern and postmodern democracies.

The fourth conclusion is that new threats have important legal implications with possibly adverse effects on the relations between the West and the rest of the world. Due to the threat of religious anti-systemic terrorism and geopolitical shifts, the cornerstones of international law, sovereignty, and non-interference are under revision. Combatting terrorism could demand interventions in rogue and failed states. Interventions require UN mandates. But emerging powers such as China are increasingly hesitant to support Western "adventurism" in the UN Security Council. If mandates cannot be obtained, liberal democracies are likely to put aside these cornerstones. In addition, the laws of war apply to interstate wars. A basic principle is that the use of force should only be directed against the opponent's military forces. However, the new opponent is usually not a traditional military force. Rather, it is most likely a collection of civilian fighters organized as irregular forces, using the population either as a shield or for logistical purposes. Consequently, during military operations, the distinction between combatants and noncombatants is difficult to make. As a result, the concept of the "prisoner of war" must also be redefined. During Operation Enduring Freedom, the status of the captured al-Qaeda fighters was unclear. They were consequently moved to Guantanamo Bay in Cuba, far away from TV cameras and civil rights groups. Finally, non-observance of the laws of war is likely to be an asymmetrical tactic. A weak enemy is unlikely to have much regard for internationally agreed rules of restraint, while the coercer has no other choice but to observe them.

The final conclusion is that only limited interventions with well defined, achievable political objectives are likely to be successful. Only then a balance between political objectives and military means can be achieved. This explains the success of the interventions in Haiti (1994), Bosnia (1995), East Timor (1999), Kosovo (1999), Sierra Leone (2000), the regime change phases of the interventions in Afghanistan (2001) and Iraq (2003) and Mali (2013). Complex operations in hostile territories such as the Chechen wars (1994-2009), the stabilization missions in Bosnia, Afghanistan, and Iraq and most Israeli interventions in the Palestinian territories failed. In those cases, the proper balance between means and objectives could not be achieved. Moreover, a key lesson learned is that initial successes could be nullified when the adversary regroups and adapts to fight an unconventional asymmetrical war whilst the coalition is confronted with a hostile or indifferent population whose hearts and minds cannot be won. Successful regime change operations could thus turn into failures. This has led to a rethinking of interventions. The intervention in Libya (2011) was not followed by a stabilization mission.

The successful application of force

Regarding the successful application of power, three conclusions are important. First, the intervener must focus on the strategies of the target. Only after 9/11 did interest in unconventional wars and asymmetrical reactions increase. But the key to *any* intervention strategy is to alter the calculations by which the antagonists arrive at particular outcomes. In the case of a military conflict, this supposes that the intervener designs a strategy that makes it unattractive for the parties to continue fighting. This can be done by either making the military costs too high, or by making the benefits of not fighting attractive. The protection of national interests requires an intervention emphasizing the military costs for the adversary. The "mind-set" of politicians and military planners is shaped by conventional strategies to protect interests. Neglecting the strategies of the target is a recipe for disaster.

Second, a strategy must be based on clear and achievable objectives. Objectives can only be achieved if there is a sound military plan underlying the strategy. In this book, I have argued that military coercion can only be effective if Western powers are willing to apply military force aimed at denying the adversary the ability to use his military potential (denial) and/or occupy key territories and nodes (control). Coercive diplomacy requires a carrot and stick approach. In this case, military power should be used in a limited way, to punish the adversary or by denying him the use of his military potential. Coercive efforts start with defining a strategy, which should be based on:

- the interests at stake;
- knowledge of the adversary;
- attainable objectives;
- the dynamics of the interaction between the intervening power and the target;
- a balance between political objectives and military means; and
- proportionality in response to the situation and the objectives to be achieved.

Third, success of any strategy ultimately depends on the use of force in a decisive manner. If the intervener is not willing to take risks, and consequently accept casualties, the operation is doomed to fail. A clear link exists between the issues at stake and the way force is used. Force will only be applied on a massive scale if vital interests are at stake.

Grand purposes are clearly linked to the survival of the state or ideology. Historically, wars fought for grand purposes implied a willingness to accept casualties in large numbers. Edward Luttwak wrote that war fought for grand purposes is a product of the French and American revolutions.[2] It implies the decisive employment of large forces in large operations. In 18th-century Europe, demonstrative maneuvers were intended to induce enemy withdrawals without firing a shot. They were called off if serious fighting ensued. Prolonged sieges were preferred, and even superior forces avoided battle if there was a risk of heavy casualties. Edward Luttwak argued that Napoleon triumphed over such cautious military practices with bold strategic offenses powered by the massive momentum of rapidly concentrated forces. This was also the kind of warfare that Clausewitz advocated. The era of modern warfare had begun.

Wars for grand purposes are still being fought. During the Cold War, East and West were willing to defend the Communist and capitalist systems with all possible means. Operation Enduring Freedom and Operation Iraqi Freedom again demonstrated that liberal democracies are willing to accept casualties when their vital interests are at stake. However, liberal democracies find it increasingly difficult to fight wars, especially postmodern societies.

Van Creveld wrote that in any war, the readiness to suffer and die, as well as to kill, represents the single and most important factor: "take it away, and even the most numerous, best organized, best trained, best equipped army in the world will turn out to be a brittle instrument."[3] Luttwak argued that tolerance for accepting casualties is changing. A certain tolerance "was congruent with the demography of pre-industrial and early industrial societies, whereby families had many children and losing some to disease was entirely normal. The loss of a youngster in combat, however tragic, was therefore fundamentally less unacceptable than for today's families, with their one, two, or at most three children."[4]

Avoiding risks clearly undermines the effectiveness of the military and says much about a nation's political and strategic culture. Indeed, there is a clear link between risk-taking and the success of an intervention. As has

2 E.N. Luttwak, "Toward Post-Heroic Warfare", *Foreign Affairs,* May-June 1995, p. 113.
3 Van Creveld, *The Transformation of War*, p. 160.
4 Luttwak, "Post-Heroic Warfare", p. 115.

been argued in chapter 3, only in the case of a violation of vital interests can politicians of liberal democracies quickly reach consensus to intervene and use force decisively. Without exception, states agree that the violation of their territorial integrity leaves them with no other choice but to act. A clear consensus existed for the United Kingdom to defend the Falklands against Argentine aggression. In most West European states, support for the liberation of Kuwait emerged when people realized that Saddam Hussein could gain access to a large portion of the world's oil reserves.

There is an important distinction between modern and postmodern countries, as well as between big and small liberal democracies. Especially in the smaller postmodern democracies, moral and ethical considerations play an important role in the decision-making process. In the case of humanitarian contingencies, especially among the smaller liberal democracies, there is an urgent need "to do something." Unfortunately, fundamental questions regarding political and military objectives and the required military means are being neglected. Lord Owen has argued that this approach contributed to the tragedy of Srebrenica in July 1995: "The consequence of the failure of the members of the Security Council to match rhetoric with realities was that Dutch troops were placed in such an ignominious position at the Serb massacre. The Dutch government and a number of Dutch Members of Parliament had been among the loudest in laying claim to the moral high ground throughout the wars in the former Yugoslavia." Due to the fall of Srebrenica, "the Dutch were cruelly caught out and the terrible hollowness of their 'principled course' was exposed."[5] The bigger liberal democracies are more reluctant about moral and ethical considerations for interventions. They are likely to put more emphasis on defending vital interests and are less interested in using military force for humanitarian purposes and peacekeeping.

The principles of military operations

A coercive strategy could be put at risk if decision makers ignore the principles of military operations. These principles are defined as regulations of a fundamental nature for the application of military means. If military commanders cannot conduct an operation properly, they are unlikely to be successful, so that political objectives cannot be achieved either. Decision

5 D. Owen, "An effective CFSP for the Future", in Owen et. al, *How Can Europe Prevent Future Conflicts* (Brussels: The Philip Morris Institute, November 1997), p. 34.

makers should know how their preconditions could affect these principles, without being military experts themselves.

The general principles for military operations are:

- concentration: the establishment of the main effort at the right time and the right place;
- credibility: the nature of one's forces in the context of the goals to be reached;
- flexibility: the ability to adapt a plan to a changing operational environment;
- initiative: the means to achieve and maintain freedom of action;
- legitimacy: the legal and social context for military operations. Legal legitimacy refers to the rules of national and international law; social legitimacy refers to public and political support;
- objective: the military goal that has to be reached;
- security or force protection: the precondition for maintaining freedom of action;
- simplicity: the requirement for operational planning to deal with chaos, stress, friction, and confusion;
- unity in effort: the synchronization of all means and all efforts to reach an objective.

A number of principles apply specifically to combat operations:

- mobility: the method to carry out a surprise attack at an unexpected location;
- offensive actions: the method for acting effectively and decisively in order to achieve the objective;
- surprise: the method of attacking at an unexpected location or in an unexpected way.

Decision makers can easily jeopardize these principles and, as a result, doom a coercive strategy to failure. The remainder of this chapter explains how political decision making can jeopardize the principles of military operations.

The timing of an intervention

Political decision makers tend to see force as a last resort, after diplomatic initiatives and sanctions have failed. But waiting until other policies have failed could be counterproductive and preclude the effective use of force.

Slow and cumbersome multinational decision making and bad timing could undermine two fundamental principles; gaining the initiative and unity in effort. Intervening too late can be costly because the adversary could take countermeasures, for example by consolidating his gains. In 1990, just after the Iraq's intervention in Kuwait, President George Bush Sr. concluded that, after a few months, there would no longer be a Kuwait to save. For that reason he decided to act swiftly.

Waiting too long can also result in intervening in the wrong phase of the conflict. This is an underestimated aspect of interventions. A conflict generally has three phases: dispute, conflict, and hostilities. A dispute is a quarrel about something. If the quarrel is not solved, the dispute might escalate into a conflict. In this phase, the use of force becomes plausible. Parties start to arm themselves, mobilize, and conduct provocative military "exercises," and use threatening language. Infighting breaks out, a conflict moves into the hostilities phase, or armed conflict. The fourth phase, the cessation of hostilities, can emerge if one of two conditions have been met. The first condition is a stalemate when the conflicting parties no longer consider the use of force a viable option. The second condition is a clear victory and capitulation of the adversary. The final phase is entered into when the conflict peters out and the parties resolve their quarrel. Successful interventions are only possible when a dispute has not turned into armed conflict.

Especially in the case of third-party interventions, the coercer should take these thresholds into account. Early intervention can prevent crossing the threshold from the first to the second phase or from the second to the third phase. Unfortunately, the coercer usually intervenes too late. There is always hope that further escalation will be avoided because the conflicting parties themselves do not want to cross the threshold. But if a threshold is crossed, organizing an intervention will take some time. Preparation for a full-scale intervention is a lengthy process and could require steps such as:

- international diplomatic efforts for a concerted response to the crisis;
- negotiations in the UN Security Council on a mandate;
- diplomatic enquiries (*demarches*) by a lead nation or the UN to find out whether countries are willing to contribute;
- national decision making on the contribution to an international coalition;
- negotiations on command and control arrangements and rules of engagement;
- preparation of national contributions;
- development of a strategy and operational plans;

- force generation;
- movement of units to the theater of operations;
- composing and training of coalition forces;
- actual deployment of the coalition force.

During the decision-making process, many things can go wrong. Interventions require a mandate issued by the UN Security Council. Mandates usually take a long time to negotiate, because many interests are at stake. As pointed out, Russia and China frequently opposed interventions in the past, because they were against interference in internal affairs. Also, much disagreement exists among liberal democracies about the course to be steered. After the nuclear tests of India and Pakistan in May 1998, the US was the only country to immediately impose economic sanctions. Other major powers, such as France and the United Kingdom, refrained from sanctions. In the case of agreement on a mandate, countries should be approached to contribute to a coalition of the willing and able. National decision making must take place about the possible contribution to the coalition. In some countries, parliamentary agreement is required, so that the whole process could be stopped. National units will prepare for deployment. They may need additional training and assets before they are sent to the crisis area, or force elements may not be available due to commitments elsewhere. Finally, national units must be plugged into a multinational coalition. Lack of interoperability could severely undermine the effectiveness of the coalition.

The whole process of putting together an armed force can require months, depending on the size of the operation, the geographic location of the area of operations, and the speed of the decision-making process. The latter will depend on the interests at stake. Due to the slow speed of the process, the crisis might have become uncontrollable.

Unclear mandates and rules of engagement can also endanger the operation. The mandate should be clear in order for the force commander to understand what he is expected to accomplish. Rules of engagement (ROE) define the actual use of force and will be derived from the mandate. But strict ROE can restrict the actions commanders deem necessary. Once set, they are difficult to change. Unclear mandates will jeopardize three important principles of military operations: objective, credibility and legitimacy; strict ROE could undermine flexibility. For example, UNPROFOR suffered from unclear and contradictory mandates. The UN Security Council authorized a transition operation under Chapter VII to maintain safe areas. The integrity of the safe areas, however, was to be maintained by deterring any action against it. Rules of engagement were strict; military commanders were not allowed to return fire or to receive close air support unless actually engaged. Thus "deterrence" was a hollow concept and, as a result, defending the safe areas was impossible.

Unfortunately, the Security Council can usually only reach consensus on unclear mandates. More precision would imply a willingness to impose a pre-determined outcome. This could have resulted in accusations about interference in internal affairs and consequently a veto of some members of the Security Council.

In summary, as reaching an agreement is difficult, and taking the initiative is a prerequisite for success, a government or a coalition will have a limited amount of patience with the proposition that it must receive an authorization to carry out an intervention.

Coalition warfare

After the end of the Cold War, most interventions were carried out by coalitions. A coalition is defined as a collection of actors cooperating to achieve a common objective. Coalitions are fine as long as they are united. This will be the case if common vital interests are at stake. Otherwise frictions within the coalition are likely to occur. Coalition warfare will undermine one of the key principles of military operations, unity of effort, in two ways. The first is a lack of interoperability; the second is a lack of unity in command.

Regarding the latter, UNOSOM II is an interesting example. After the militias of warlord Aideed had killed Pakistani peacekeepers, the US tried to capture him. To achieve their objectives, the US used gunships to attack his headquarters. Italy protested against this aggressive approach, which could undermine the UN objectives, that is, negotiations and humanitarian relief. Italy threatened to withdraw its 2,400 peacekeepers, thus putting the coalition at risk. Ultimately, Italy was asked to remove the commander of its contingent, because he and other Italian officers had not obeyed orders from the UN force commander in Somalia and had unilaterally negotiated with Aideed, while the UN and the US were trying to isolate him.

Unity in effort will be jeopardized if a coalition lacks technical, doctrinal, and organizational interoperability. Technical interoperability refers to critical items such as command, control, communications, and intelligence (C3I), and the caliber of ammunition and logistics. One of the most important functions of NATO is to improve interoperability through its Standardization Agency, which produces Standardization Agreements

(STANAGS). The same holds true for regulations and procedures, which are elements of organizational interoperability. NATO is also developing Allied Joint Doctrines that describe the organization and principles of operations. Once ratified by NATO members, this will become the framework for the development of national doctrines. Due to differences in procurement schemes, national industrial policies, and national doctrinal preferences, only a certain level of interoperability can be achieved.

In 1994, in an attempt to improve interoperability, NATO introduced the *Combined Joint Task Force* (CJTF) concept. Such a military ad hoc coalition was to be multinational (combined) and multi-service (joint). CJTFs can be configured for a NATO – or an EU – led intervention. Without sufficient interoperability, the CJTF concept is meaningless.

Joint and combined war fighting operations require combined arms operations and, consequently, a high degree of doctrinal, organizational, and technical interoperability. During Operation Allied Force, new NATO members Hungary, the Czech Republic, and Poland were not able to contribute to the regular military operations of other NATO members because they did not use similar procedures and doctrines. Moreover, most of their aircraft were not equipped with NATO-compatible "friend or foe" systems, so that there was a considerable risk that their NATO colleagues would identify them as the enemy.

NCW has increased the problems associated with interoperability. American forces are so advanced that it is unlikely that other countries' armed forces could achieve full interoperability. Even the United Kingdom, the world's second military power, lacked interoperability, as was demonstrated during Operation Iraqi Freedom.

Unconventional warfare and peace support operations do not require combined arms operations. Instead, small units, such as battalions, companies, and even groups can conduct operations. In unconventional warfare and peace support operations, dividing the theater of operations into sectors or national areas of responsibility is possible. In the Balkans, the contributors to IFOR and SFOR were responsible for maintaining peace and stability in their sectors. During Operation Enduring Freedom, British Special Forces got their own sector due to differences in Special Operations Forces doctrine and technical capabilities. According to British doctrine, small teams are clandestinely integrated into the theater of operations, where they will stay for days or weeks to conduct operations. US doctrine requires larger teams to conduct hit-and-run style tactics, with infiltration and exfiltration within a very limited time frame. Thus, lack of interoperability will dictate the way coalition operations will be conducted.

Even if sufficient interoperability exists, coalition warfare is likely to undermine unity of effort because it will be at the expense of unity of command. Operation Allied Force serves as an example. NATO Supreme Commander General Clark suggested in his memoirs on the Kosovo war that the battle was prolonged because he was not able to achieve a military victory with air power alone.[6] He continuously argued with his superiors in Washington to introduce ground troops, yet this was refused on the basis of the great risks involved. The war was eventually brought to an end through a diplomatic offensive, where the Russians played a key role. Operation Allied Force started as a typical case of military coercion, but ended up as a typical case of coercive diplomacy.

According to Clark, a military victory was not possible because all the founding principles of modern-day warfare were neglected. There was no unity of effort because there was no singular command, the operational plans were not simple, concentrating the combat force into central points proved impossible, the economic use of means was not in order, and the decision could not be forced through offensive action and maneuvers. For all these reasons, the Americans chose to act alone during Operation Enduring Freedom. The British joined the operation, but were not fully integrated into the US effort.

Political micromanagement and confusing command arrangements can undermine flexibility and unity in effort. Again, UNPROFOR serves as an example. During UNPROFOR, there was considerable political interference in all aspects of execution of the operation. The Special Representative of the UN Secretary-General, Yasushi Akashi, and the troop contributors all tried to influence the force commander and his subordinates. Moreover, the operation suffered from unclear command procedures. Actually, the command structure centered on the Special Representative and a NATO commander. Air support and air strikes could only be delivered once the military was given the green light from the Special Representative. This "dual key" procedure was very lengthy and ineffective. In particular, the UN command structure was burdensome, leading to frequent delays. Air support usually came too late, if there was any air support at all. By the time air support had been authorized, the Serbs already had achieved their objectives.

6 Two useful books by Clark on modern warfare: Wesley K. Clark, *Waging Modern War: Bosnia, Kosovo, and the Future of Combat* (New York: Public Affairs, 2001) and *Winning Modern Wars: Iraq, Terrorism, and the American Empire* (New York: Public Affairs, 2003).

For political reasons, there is no other choice but to form coalitions. However, coalitions could enhance two principles of military operations: credibility and legitimacy. Coalitions shore up the coercer's domestic and international support. If a UN Security Council mandate is lacking, coalitions could thus make interventions legitimate. This happened during the 1999 war for Kosovo. On the one hand, NATO could not obtain a mandate for the intervention. NATO knew that from a legal perspective an intervention in Kosovo would be illegal. On the other hand, NATO argued that an intervention would be legitimate because of the humanitarian disasters taking place in Kosovo. In addition, NATO maintained that international peace and security was jeopardized because the conflict could undermine regional stability. Gaining support from other countries is important for communicating the objective of the intervention. States intervening unilaterally will be accused of waging a war of conquest, trying to get control over land or scarce resources. The "just cause" of an intervention will be more credible if many countries support it. This was a major problem during Operation Iraqi Freedom. As most members of the UN Security Council opposed the intervention, the coalition was very thin. The largest contingent was provided by the United Kingdom, while limited numbers of Australian Special Operations Forces also contributed to the operation. In an effort to broaden the coalition, during one of his press conferences, Iraqi Freedom commander General Franks asked officers to join him. The Danish and the Dutch officers accompanying the general caused considerable political problems at home, because neither country participated in Iraqi Freedom. The officers were liaisons for Operation Enduring Freedom, the war on terrorism, which was also directed by Franks.

In summary, the problem of coalition warfare is that, due to the lack of interoperability and unity in command, the synchronization of all means and all efforts to reach an objective is unlikely. For that reason, the Americans argued that the mission should define the coalition. As their vital interests were at stake, they took the lead during Operation Enduring Freedom and Operation Iraqi Freedom. Coalition partners were welcome, but only in a supportive role.

Political preconditions

At the beginning of the war for Kosovo, NATO Supreme Allied Commander General Wesley Clark mentioned three political preconditions: no body bags, no collateral damage, and keep the alliance unified. Political preconditions clearly reflect how democracies fight wars. These preconditions could undermine the principles of military operations if they are too strict. Leaders must be well aware of this and must constantly balance preconditions against the need to allow military commanders to apply the principles of military operations. Thus it could be necessary to accept higher levels of collateral damage in order to achieve a higher degree of military effectiveness. This could require tough and unpopular decisions, which are hard to explain to the general public, especially in those states with political cultures that reject the use of force. Only strong, visionary leaders will be able to explain why military force must be used.

The problem, however, is that preconditions could undermine credibility, slow down the operation and leave the initiative to the opponent. This is what happened during Operation Allied Force. The "no body bags" requirement prevented pilots from dropping bombs from low altitudes. Below 15,000 feet they would be vulnerable to air defenses such as surface-to-air-missiles. This severely limited the tempo of the operation, so that the adversary was able to take the initiative on the ground. In addition, NATO refused to plan for the "ground option."

Reducing collateral damage required the extensive use of precision-guided munitions and a prohibition on dropping dumb bombs near cities and villages. Moreover, pilots were not allowed to drop bombs through clouds. As a result, under bad weather conditions they could not drop bombs at all. Reducing collateral damage not only reduced the tempo of the air campaign, it also allowed Serb troops to conduct asymmetrical tactics. First, they tried to provoke collateral damage by storing heavy weapons near schools and hospitals. Second, due to the limited intensity of the air war, they were able to step up operations against the Albanians.

In general, precision strikes did not impress the population. Indeed, Operation Allied Force was probably the first war where families took their deckchairs to watch bombardments. The use of precision-guided munitions primarily reduced the number of sorties, thus limiting the risks for aircrews.

Limiting collateral damage may not always be possible, and is sometimes undesirable. First, in unconventional conflicts the distinction between combatants and non-combatants is very difficult. Thus, the intervener may have no other choice but to inflict "unacceptable" levels of collateral damage in achieving his objectives. Second, for military reasons, limiting collateral damage could be counterproductive because it might decrease the tempo of the operation, thereby leaving the initiative to the adversary. Third, limiting collateral damage could preclude a limited strategy of attrition. Industrialized countries are in a weak position to resist the systematic bombing of their industrial base. When NATO stepped up the Kosovo air campaign, the deputy mayor of Belgrade argued that he could not see his town surviving months or years under these conditions, thus indicating that the destruction of Yugoslavia's critical infrastructure could contribute to ending the war. International humanitarian law however, prescribes that force may only be used in proportion to the situation and if it is a military requirement.

To maintain popular support, political leaders try to limit risks, both for their troops and for the population of the adversary. But caveats can put mission effectiveness at jeopardy. ISAF commander General David McKiernan expressed his frustration in a February 2009 briefing at the Pentagon: "we have advantage with our military capabilities, with speed, with mobility, with intelligence, with firepower, with logistics. When we place caveats on our military contributions, we tend to reduce those advantages.'[7]

In Europe, the political left especially has had a long-term flirtation with pacifism and antimilitarism. During the Kosovo war, the political left in Germany and Italy threatened to withdraw support for the war effort if too much collateral damage was inflicted. One of the reasons for the change in strategy, by the end of May 1999, was the fear that because of losing popular support, some countries might step out of the coalition. As a consequence, the Serb leadership could have sensed that there might be limits to the extent of NATO's bombing. Thus, increasing collateral damage by storing heavy weapon systems in densely populated areas became part of their asymmetrical tactics.

Public support

Richard Sobel has concluded that "the inconsistent and limited survey in this area makes it extremely difficult to analyze what the public actually thinks during flare-ups in foreign affairs."[8] This may be true, but politicians usually have a good instinct for public opinion. They will not act if this would upset a large part of the population. But the effect of the media on the decision to intervene is equally unclear. The media's lack of attention to the situation in Somalia in the early 1990s is well known.

7 US Department of Defense, "Briefing with General McKiernan from the Pentagon", February 18, 2009.

8 R. Sobel, "Polling on Foreign Policy Crises: Creating a Standard Set of Questions", *The Public Perspective,* February-March 1996, pp. 13-16.

Only after President Bush's decision to send troops did media attention explode. Indeed, the media and pressure groups did not seem to play a significant role in the decision to go to war. However, the media will be decisive during the operation itself. The media undoubtedly played a crucial role in the decision to withdraw forces from UNOSOM II. Both President Bush's and Prime Minister Blair's positions were undermined when, months after Operation Iraqi Freedom, no weapons of mass destruction, the main reason for the intervention, could be found, while at the same time the number or American casualties during the peace-building effort rose dramatically.

Lack of public – and hence political – support will undermine legitimacy. If the population no longer supports the cause, the intervention will lose legitimacy. Operation Iraqi Freedom was not supported by the majority of the European populations, nor by most governments. As a result, the coalition was denied a mandate. In the eyes of most Europeans, the war was not justified. Europeans did consider Iraq a rogue state. They recognized that Saddam Hussein terrorized both the region and his own population, and that he was willing and capable of producing and using weapons of mass destruction. The Europeans, however, differed regarding the method for dealing with Iraq's leaders. They argued that the containment policies of the 1990s had worked quite well.

If an operation is seen as illegitimate, the morale of soldiers will decrease. They will no longer believe in the cause they are fighting for. Consequently, they will become risk averse, so that their performance is likely to decrease. This happened during the Vietnam War. Initially, soldiers thought they would combat the spread of Communism. In Vietnam, many asked themselves why they were fighting against an enemy they could not see. Moreover, the local population not only looked or spoke different, but it was unclear whether they supported the Americans or the Communists. Finally, many other countries, most notably European allies, opposed the war. Without a cause to fight for, soldiers will merely fight for their own survival. Only strong, visionary political leadership can avoid this happening. A clear political vision and rhetorical talents are prerequisites to keep public support, especially when the intervention loses tempo. As pointed out in chapter 3, there is a strong correlation between the interests at stake and the willingness to bear the costs of a risky intervention. Consequently, if the public perception of what is at stake is low, politicians are unlikely able to count on public support for a lengthy period.

Concept of operations

An unrealistic concept of operations and the wrong means will undermine credibility. Gradualism is politically tempting. The logic of gradual escalation is to use force politically and militarily, both to avoid an unwanted response and to leave room for diplomacy.

Gradual escalation could be part of a strategy of coercive diplomacy, where an armed force is primarily used to demonstrate resolve. As no military objectives should be reached, tempo is unimportant.

For military coercion, gradual escalation or incrementalism makes little military sense. The slow tempo will leave the initiative with the opponent. He will be able to adjust and adapt, politically and militarily. To gain the initiative for quick and decisive victories, massive and overwhelming force has to be applied. Grenada, Panama, the Gulf War, Operation Enduring Freedom and Operation Iraqi Freedom are successful examples of forceful interventions. Except for the Gulf War, all interventions were carried out unilaterally by the US, while the US unmistakably led the Gulf War. Due to a strategy of gradual escalation, the initiative was lost during Operation Allied Force. Politically speaking, gradual escalation was the preferred strategy. First, a strategy of gradualism was deemed necessary to gain support at home. Second, a strategy of gradualism would serve as a signal that large-scale destruction could still be avoided if the Serb leadership would give in and resume the negotiations of Rambouillet. This was, however, a bad strategy. Operation Allied Force consisted of a phased air campaign to increase pressure on the Serbs. This did not work.

What makes most sense militarily will also make most sense politically. As gradualism is unlikely to lead to military victory, acting with maximum effect will be necessary to gain public support. Too much force is usually better than too little. Coercion may not work if the coercer tries to achieve his objectives with the commitment of as few military resources possible. There is nothing wrong with massive and overwhelming force if this leads to a quick and decisive victory with little friendly losses and costs. Overwhelming force can also reduce friction or the difference between real war and war on paper.

In summary, this approach can be less risky and was used to good effect in Grenada, Panama, and Operation Desert Storm, Operation Enduring Freedom, and Operation Iraqi Freedom. Too little force was used in Somalia, Haiti, and Bosnia. In the latter cases, no interests were at stake and a coalition dominated the course of action. In the former cases, the United States took the initiative and carried out the intervention on its own terms.

Balancing means and ends

Disappointing results of stabilization operations led to new debates about the right balance between military means and political objectives. As has been argued in the previous chapter, during the second half of the first decade of the 21st century, population-centric COIN was reinvented. But, despite tactical successes during the stabilization and reconstruction phases, a stable and security environment could not be achieved in Iraq and Afghanistan.

The conceptual difficulty of stabilization and reconstruction was that the operation tried to reconcile two opposing objectives. On the one hand, stabilization is coercive action to fight insurgents and spoilers. As has been argued throughout this book, the use of force is likely to have a negative effect on the relationship between coercer and target. On the other hand, reconstruction involves activities to win the support of the populace. New approaches, such as the Comprehensive Approach, the Whole of Government approach and the defense, diplomacy and development (3D) approach aimed at reconciling the opposing objectives of combating insurgents and winning the support of the population.

Despite the new concepts and approaches, stabilization and reconstruction turned out to be more risky than interventions with limited political objectives. Regime changes could take place with few friendly casualties, while stabilization operations turned out to be high-risk undertakings with dubious results. Moreover, post-regime change operations in Iraq and Afghanistan have demonstrated that the lack of success of stabilization and reconstruction could nullify the results of successful interventions and weaken public support for long-term involvements. This notion has again led to rethinking COIN.

Unsurprisingly, the cases studies of this book have revealed that the right balance between military means and political objectives can be achieved easily when coercers carry out short interventions with limited, clearly defined political goals. This is nothing new, because classical thinkers including Sun Tzu and Von Clausewitz already stressed the importance of balancing means and ends. Large-scale, complex operations are likely to fail because of budgetary constraints, political caveats, unrealistic objectives, ignorance of the local dynamics and the asymmetrical tactics of the insurgents.

The disappointing results of the stabilization and reconstruction missions in Iraq and Afghanistan have undoubtedly contributed to the decision to refrain from a similar mission after the removal from power of the Libyan leader Gadhafi in 2011. The principal political objective during the coercive phase was to enforce compliance with UN Resolutions. But the involvement of the international community after the fall of Gadhafi was limited to economic and humanitarian aid and advice to the new rulers. The coercer did not interfere in the post conflict dynamics to the population and local population. Reconciliation and the reconstruction of the country were left to the local authorities. The theoretical advantage was that Libya would not be turned into an "aid economy" with a deadlocked political process. This happened to the Balkans. Decades after the end of major hostilities, countries like Bosnia and Herzegovina still cannot function without foreign assistance. An interesting comparison can be made with the genocide that took place during the mid-1990s in Rwanda and Burundi. No foreign intervention took place in these two countries. Local authorities, supported by civil society initiatives, managed to start a process of reconciliation which led to political stability and security relatively quickly. This process of reconciliation laid the basis for economic development. The absence of such a dynamic process in Bosnia and Herzegovina prolonged the peace process considerably.

A better balance between means and ends suggests that the following limited coercive efforts can be carried out with a high chance of success:
- decapitation (the killing of Bin Laden, 2011);
- preemption and prevention (Regime change Iraq, 2003);
- compliance (Libya: enforcing UN Resolutions, 2011);
- protection (Somalia: anti-piracy, 2006-...);
- threat mitigation or containment (Pakistan, Yemen, Somalia: cruise missile attacks and SOF deployments against terrorists);
- "regime change only" (Libya, 2011).

Threat mitigation or containment is probably the most promising one. It takes shape in a number of countries and regions. In west Pakistan, Yemen, and Somalia, a SOF and drones approach was used to keep the threat of terrorism local. The application of this approach would imply a shift from an expensive COIN operation with tens of thousands of troops to protect the population to a small force that strikes insurgent leaders, bases and training camps. Unlike population-centric COIN, this approach is not meant to facilitate the political process. Instead, the SOF and drone approach is meant to keep threats at a manageable level. The objective of the SOF and drone approach is to turn global terrorist threats into local challenges. This approach, however, is rather controversial if strikes are carried out without approval of the leadership of the target state. Such strikes raise many political and legal questions. Politicians must weigh mission effectiveness and reduced global threats against those legal and political issues.

When the vital interests of the coercer are not at stake or budgetary realities and mission fatigue preclude long-term involvements, stabilization and reconstruction could be left to regional or indigenous forces. Involvement of Western forces could then take the form of limited military aid.

Military aid

A subset of limited operations is *military aid* to assist a country, multinational organizations such as the UN, or even insurgents in their defense efforts or attempts to maintain control over territory. Military aid could involve offensive operations to shape the battlefield, that is, to eliminate the enemy's capability to fight in a coherent manner before committing forces to decisive operations by regional or indigenous forces. Military aid in its most basic form was provided by US special forces supported by US air power and intelligence in support of the Northern Alliance during the regime change phase in Afghanistan in 2001. Another example is the French *Operation Serval* which began on 11 January 2013 after Tuareg tribesmen and extremists took over the north of Mali. Within a matter of weeks the French drove the insurgents from the northern part of the country. When MINUSMA, the UN stabilization mission in Mali, started later that year the UN Security Council uniquely authorized "French troops, within the limits of their capacities and areas of deployment, to use all necessary means, from the commencement of the activities of MINUSMA (...) to intervene in support of elements of MINUSMA when under imminent and serious threat (...)".[9] By providing a critical enabling force to MINUSMA without getting involved in actual combat operations, other European powers provided military aid as well. The Dutch intelligence contribution to MINUSMA of special forces, armed helicopters and an intelligence fusion cell falls in this category.

Conclusion

Efforts to coerce others have so often had disappointing results for three main reasons. First, coercion is conceptually difficult. Successful coercion

9 Resolution 2100 (2013), adopted by the Security Council at its 6952nd meeting, on 25 April 2013. Para. 18.

is the outcome of a dynamic process based on creativity and an understanding of coercive mechanisms. This is extremely demanding for political decision makers. They often lack basic knowledge about the use of power instruments in foreign policy. Crucially, most decision makers lack basic knowledge of military doctrine as well. Political preconditions can conflict with military principles and thus jeopardize the entire coercive effort.

Second, asymmetrical reactions of a weaker opponent could easily offset Western military superiority, and consequently undermine the coercive efforts. During the stabilization phase, the opponent could destroy most of what has been achieved during the preceding coercive phase.

Third, the West has not only become risk averse, but there are also divergent views on the use of force. Transatlantic differences in political and strategic culture that became visible after the end of the Cold War explain the different approaches to coercion in the US and Europe.

For these reasons, Western political leaders should not exaggerate assumptions about what can be achieved with the use of force if they do not want to use force decisively. Indeed, the West's military superiority scarcely matters if decision makers do not know how to use military might best or have a completely different understanding regarding whether force should be used at all.

Appendix

Date	Case	Opponent	Declared Objectives	Overall strategy of intervention	Elements of control?	Interests at stake for the coercer*	Interests at stake for the opponent*	Strategy of countercoercion	Balance between the coercers' use of force and declared objectives**	Expected theoretical outcome***	Real outcome
1986	USA-Libya, *El Dorado Canyon*	M. Gadhafi	End support for terrorism	Military coercion	no	Medium	High	Terrorism	no	failure	failure
1989	USA-Panama, *Operation Just Cause*	M. Noriega	Regime change	Military coercion	yes	Medium	High	None	yes	success	success, but pre-strike pressure did not coerce

January-March 1991	UN, USA/Iraq, *Operations Desert Shield and Desert Storm*	Regime of Saddam Hussein	Restore international peace and security	Coercive diplomacy leading to military coercion	yes	High	High	Horizontal escalation, partial passivity, hostages, scorched earth tactics	yes	success	Desert shield was a failure; Desert Storm was a success
End of 1991-early 2003	USA, UK/Iraq *Operations Northern Watch* and *Southern Watch*	Regime of Saddam Hussein	Enforce UN resolutions, enforce no-fly zones	Coercive diplomacy	no	Medium	Medium	Continuation of behavior, increase of population suffering	no	failure	failure
1991-1995	UN, NATO/ former Yugoslavia *Operations Deny Flight* and *Sharp Guard*	Serb leadership	Enforcing UN resolutions during UNPROFOR Contain conflict	Coercive diplomacy	no (despite UNPROFOR)	Medium	Medium	Human shields, continuation of behavior, hostages	no	failure	failure, incomplete compliance
End of 1992-beginning of 1993	USA/Somalia *Operation Continued Hope*	Militia leader Farrah Aideed	Stop interference with humanitarian aid	Coercive diplomacy	yes	Low	High	Terrorism and guerrilla tactics	no	failure	failure, withdrawal of US forces

June 1994	France / Rwanda, *Operation Turquoise*	Local warlords	Humanitarian intervention	Military coercion	yes	Low	High	Guerrilla tactics	no	failure	failure, with-drawal of French forces
Septem-ber 1994	USA/Haiti; *Op-eration Uphold Democracy*	Regime of Raoul Cedras	Regime change	Coercive diplomacy	yes	Me-dium	High	None	yes	success	success
1994-1995	Russia/ Chechnya 1st Chechen War	Chechen rebels	Defeat Chechen separatist movement	Military coercion	yes	High	High	Guerrilla tactics, terror-ism	yes	success	failure
August 1995	NATO/Bosnia; *Operation Deliberate Force*	Serb leadership	Coerce Serbs to cease-fire and accept negotiations	Coercive diplomacy	yes (UN-PRO-FOR)	Me-dium	Me-dium	hostages, partial pas-sivity	yes	success	success
April 1996	Israel/Leba-non; *Operation Grapes of Wrath*	Hezbollah	End shelling of Northern Israel	Military coercion	yes	High	High	Continuation of behavior	yes	success	failure

December 1998	USA and UK/ Iraq; *Operation Desert Fox*	Regime of Saddam Hussein	Punishment for non-compliance with UN resolutions	Coercive diplo-macy and military coercion	no	Me-dium	Me-dium	Continuation of behavior	no	failure	failure
August 1998	USA/ Afghanistan and Sudan; *Operation Infinite Reach*	Retaliation for the bombings of American embassies in Kenya and; deter further attacks	counterterror, destroy al-Qaeda network	Military coercion	no	Low/ Me-dium	Me-dium	Terrorism	no	failure	failure
March-June 1999	NATO/former Yugoslavia; *Operation Allied Force*	Regime of Milosevic	Stop to all military action and the *immediate* ending of violence	Coercive diplomacy leading to military coercion	no	Medi-um-High	High	Partial passiv-ity, increase population's suffering	yes	failure	failure
Sep-tember 1999-Feb-ruary 2000	Australia led INTERFED operation in East Timor; *Operation Warden*	anti-inde-pendence, pro-Indonesia militia	Restore peace and security, protect and support UNAMET, facilitate humanitarian assistance	Military coercion	yes	Me-dium	High	Sporadic hit-and-run tactics	yes	success	success

1999-2008	Russia/ Chechnya, 2nd Chechen War	Chechen rebels	Defeat Chechen separatist movement	Military coercion	yes	High	High	Guer-rilla tactics, terrorism, horizontal escalation	yes	success	failure
May 2000-September 2001	UK / Sierra Leone; *Operation Paliser*	Rebels of the Revolution-ary United Front	Evacuation of foreign citizens and besieged peacekeepers	Military coercion	yes	Me-dium	High	Guerrilla tactics	yes	success	success
Septem-ber 2001	NATO/ Macedonia, *Operation Amber Fox*	Albanian insurgents	protection of international monitors; Enhance stability of Macedonia and region	Coercive diplomacy leading to Military coercion	yes	Me-dium	Me-dium	Violence and terror	yes	success	success
October 2001-2014	USA/ Afghanistan, *Operation Enduring Freedom*	Taliban, al-Qaeda incl. Osama bin Laden	Regime change. counterterror	Coercive diplomacy leading to military coercion	yes	High	High	Terrorism	no	success	success
2002	USA, Philip-pines/ Abu Sayyaf	Abbu Sayyaf Group	counterterror	Military coercion	yes	High	High	Guerrilla and terror	yes	success	success

2002-2014	NATO/Taliban; *ISAF*	Taliban, warlords, al-Qaeda	Create secure conditions to enable reconstruction	Military coercion	yes	Medium	High	Guerrilla terrorism, increase population's suffering	no	failure	failure
2003	USA, UK, Australia; *Iraqi Freedom*	Regime of Saddam Hussein	Regime change	Coercive diplomacy leading to military coercion	yes	High	High	Partial passivity, scorched earth, guerrilla	yes	success	success
2003-2012	USA/Iraq stabilization mission	Insurgents	Create stability and democracy	Military coercion	yes	Medium-High	High	Guerrilla tactics, terrorism	no	failure	failure
2006	2nd Lebanon War	Hezbollah Insurgents	Remove missile threat to Israeli territory	Military coercion	yes	High	High	Guerrilla, terrorism	yes	success	success
December 2008-January 2009	Israel / Gaza; *Operation Cast Lead*	Hamas	Remove missile threat	Military coercion	yes	High	High	Guerrilla, missile attack	yes	success	failure
November 2012	Israel / Gaza; *Operation Pillar of Defense*	Hamas	Remove missile threat	Military coercion	yes	high	high	Guerrilla, missile attack	yes	success	Partial success

March-October 2011	Libya / NATO, led by France and the UK. Initial coalition of Belgium, Canada, Denmark, France, Italy, Norway, Qatar, Spain, UK and US. The operation expanded to 19 coalition partners	Gadhafi	Protection of civilians (regime change became an undeclared objective)	Military coercion	no	Medium	High	Step up operations against the populace	yes	failure	failure (regime change was a success)
January 2013	France / rebels in Mali *Operation Serval*	Insurgents and Muslim extremists	Military Aid to the Milanese government; counterterror, prepare the deployment of UN forces	Military coercion	yes	Medium	Medium	Guerrilla, kidnaps, terrorism	yes	success	success

* Low: no interests at stake; medium: important economic or humanitarian interests at stake; high: the survival of the regime or the state is at stake.

** No means no or too few troops on the ground.

*** Coercive mechanisms suggest that, regardless the interests at stake, a militarily superior coercer will prevail if the balance between military means and political objectives is right and control with ground forces is not ruled out.

About the author

Rob de Wijk is the Director of the Hague Centre for Strategic Studies (HCSS) and Professor of International Relations and Security at the Campus the Hague of Leiden University. He studied Contemporary History and International Relations in Groningen, and wrote his PhD dissertation on NATO's "Flexibility in Response" strategy at the Political Science Department of Leiden University. Rob de Wijk started his career in 1977 as a freelance journalist and later became lecturer in International Relations at Leiden University's Political Science Department. He also worked at the Ministry of Defense, where he was instrumental in the restructuring of the Dutch armed forces in the early 1990s. Other positions he held, include Professor in the field of International Relations at the Royal Netherlands Military Academy.